DIPLOMACY OF CONSCIENCE

DIPLOMACY OF CONSCIENCE

AMNESTY INTERNATIONAL AND
CHANGING HUMAN RIGHTS NORMS

ANN MARIE CLARK

PRINCETON UNIVERSITY PRESS

PRINCETON AND OXFORD

Copyright © 2001 by Princeton University Press

Published by Princeton University Press, 41 William Street,

Princeton, New Jersey 08540

In the United Kingdom: Princeton University Press,

3 Market Place, Woodstock, Oxfordshire OX20 1SY

Library of Congress Cataloging-in-Publication Data

Clark, Ann Marie

Diplomacy of Conscience: Amnesty International and
Changing Human Rights Norms / Ann Marie Clark

p. cm.

Includes bibliographical references and index.

ISBN 0-691-05742-7 (cloth : alk. paper) — ISBN 0-691-05743-5 (pbk. : alk. paper)

1. Amnesty International. 2. Human rights. I. Title

JC571.C613 2001

323'06'01— dc21

00-056509

This book has been composed in Baskerville

www.pup.princeton.edu

Printed in the United States of America

10 9 8 7 6 5 4 3 2 1

10 9 8 7 6 5 4 3 2 1

(pbk)

For JAM and my parents

The chances of factual truth surviving the onslaught of
power are very slim indeed; it is always in danger of being
maneuvered out of the world not only for a time but,
potentially, forever.
(Hannah Arendt, *Between Past and Future*, 231)

CONTENTS

ABBREVIATIONS

AI	Amnesty International
AIUSA	Amnesty International–United States of America (U.S. section of AI)
CAT	Campaign for the Abolition of Torture
CELS	Centro de Estudios Legales y Sociales (Center for Legal and Social Studies, Buenos Aires)
COPACHI	Comité de Cooperación para la Paz en Chile (Committee of Cooperation for Peace in Chile)
ECOSOC	Economic and Social Council
EJE	Extrajudicial execution
IACHR	Inter-American Commission on Human Rights
IAPL	International Association of Penal Law
ICCPR	International Covenant on Civil and Political Rights
ICJ	International Commission of Jurists
ICRC	International Committee of the Red Cross
IEC	International Executive Committee (of Amnesty International)
IGO	International governmental organization
NGO	Nongovernmental organization
OAS	Organization of American States
SCAT	Swiss Committee Against Torture
UA	Urgent Action
UDHR	Universal Declaration of Human Rights
UN	United Nations
WGEID	Working Group on Enforced or Involuntary Disappearances
WHO	World Health Organization

ACKNOWLEDGMENTS

M ANY PEOPLE have helped and encouraged me in this research. I especially thank Kathryn Sikkink for encouraging my interest in human rights as a subject for study when I entered the University of Minnesota's graduate program in political science, for her professional example, and her generous mentoring. I thank David Weissbrodt of the University of Minnesota Law School for helpful guidance in the early stages of the research, and for access to primary documents. Access to research materials was also provided by the University of Minnesota Human Rights Library, the Documentation Centre of Amnesty International's International Secretariat, London, and the Human Rights Archive of the University of Colorado at Boulder. Kathryn Sikkink permitted use of selected research interviews conducted in 1992 and 1993.

Research in Argentina, Chile, and Guatemala in 1992 was assisted by an International Predissertation Fellowship from the Social Science Research Council and the American Council of Learned Societies with funds provided by the Ford Foundation. In addition to supporting initial research, the grant enabled me to study Spanish, and I thank my language teachers, particularly those who taught at the Proyecto Lingüístico Francisco Marroquín in Antigua, Guatemala, in the early months of 1992. A Small Grant for Research from the Conflict Resolution Consortium of the University of Colorado—Boulder in 1988, with James A. McCann, helped plant seeds for this project. The research was also assisted by a 1996 Purdue Research Foundation Summer Faculty Grant.

While the book was in the making, I received helpful comments on various parts and versions from Michael Barnett, Peter R. Baehr, Louis René Beres, David P. Forsythe, John R. Freeman, Roger Haydon, Lawrence LeBlanc, Silvo Lenart, James A. McCann, W. Ofuatey-Kodjoe, Kathryn Sikkink, Jackie Smith, Frances Spivy-Weber, Howard B. Tolley, Jr., Daniel Warner, David Weissbrodt, Frank L. Wilson, and members of the 1996 Summer Workshop on International Organization Studies sponsored by the Academic Council on the United Nations System and the American Society of International Law. I am grateful for other forms of advice, aid, inspiration, or encouragement from Malcolm Campbell, Chris Catton, Kathryn Askham Elliott, René Epelbaum, Marketa Freund, Elisabeth J. Friedman, Mark Gibney, Scott Harrison, Kathryn Hochstetler, Henriette Horenovsky, Allan Leadbeater, Eve Leadbeater, Ellen

Moore, Mary Ann Morgan, Aletta Norval, Ronald B. Rapoport, William Shaffer, Michael Stohl, Walter J. Stone, Kristina Thalhammer, Claude Welch, and Emmy, George, Elizabeth, and Will. Doug Dion read the whole manuscript as it neared completion and offered much-appreciated collegiality and support. Marybeth Lorbiecki shared her intelligent, invaluable reader's eye, editing suggestions, and most of all, friendship.

To my husband, Jay, I offer special appreciation for his abiding encouragement and his own enjoyment of the hard work of research. Finally, I thank my parents, George V. and Marion W. Clark, for their love, support, and constant openness to the curiosity and adventures of their children.

DIPLOMACY OF CONSCIENCE

Chapter One

AMNESTY INTERNATIONAL

IN INTERNATIONAL POLITICS

A SMALL COLLECTION of individuals founded Amnesty International (AI) in 1961 to translate human rights principles into practical action. They invited others to join them in calling for the release of people in many countries who were in prison for expressing their beliefs. Amnesty International became intimately acquainted with the suffering of individual people killed, tortured, or imprisoned for political reasons, and gradually began to work for better general human rights protection through laws and public pressure at the international level.

Governments have jealously guarded their sovereignty. As Amnesty International started its work for better human rights law, it acted as an outsider lacking the status and resources of the states it was trying to influence. It was unimaginably ambitious for a third party like AI to undertake advocacy that entailed basic changes in international norms, the standards of behavior expected of states and articulated in international institutions.

The community of nations exhibited almost no willingness to hold individual states accountable for human rights violations when Amnesty International started its public campaigning. The United Nations (UN) set down core human rights principles in 1948 in the form of the Universal Declaration of Human Rights (UDHR), but even as it drafted the declaration, the governmental representatives who made up the UN Commission on Human Rights ruled that it had no power to act on specific human rights complaints.[1] States did not permit the UN to pry into their internal affairs, especially not potentially embarrassing human rights violations. Negotiations over multilateral treaties supposed to give international legal force to the principles of the Universal Declaration bogged down during the Cold War. Practical measures to give life to human rights principles began to lag far behind the rhetoric.

Yet, since 1961, the entire context for international human rights discussions has changed. In contrast to the weak human rights norms of the 1960s, it is now possible to point to the fruits of Amnesty's efforts to build norms and elicit behavior more consistent with human rights principles. Numerous treaties and monitoring mechanisms are in place. Every year, UN bodies receive reports from states and nongovernmental organizations on human rights conditions in scores of states. Special UN rapporteurs, individuals responsible for monitoring and investigating allegations of human rights violations for the UN, may be assigned to troubled countries, and other special rapporteurs are empowered to investigate worldwide reports of certain categories of severe human rights violations such as torture. Human rights standards are now built into peacekeeping agreements and many types of multilateral treaties. Although there is no doubt that many governments still resist practical observation of the principles they have officially endorsed, the legal force of human rights claims in the international context has grown significantly stronger over recent decades. Given what we know about state sensitivity to international interference, in the vivid words of Nigel Rodley, former legal adviser of Amnesty International and current UN Special Rapporteur on Torture, "Why do states give us these whips to flagellate them with?"[2]

Indeed, the emergence of norms based on moral principles is not as well understood as it should be, although scholars and practitioners recognize that advocacy groups are on the international scene to stay. A thorough understanding of how international norms have been constructed on the basis of human rights principles requires devoting both empirical and theoretical attention to the human rights organizations that have advocated such changes.

We also need to understand more about the nature of these actors, and the international context, to explain the emergence of norms. Amnesty International was a pioneer of the establishment of international standards, or norms, of human rights. Through its reporting on human rights violations, the organization was exceptionally placed to recognize and identify the need for stronger human rights guarantees. When Amnesty was founded, an international "human rights" regime, or complex of rules, as we now know it did not exist—and there was no good reason to expect one.

On the whole, governments do not seem to have changed their stripes; yet we have witnessed more international constraints on government behavior. In spite of governments' lack of respect for human rights principles, Amnesty International and some other nongovernmental organizations (NGOs) pressed for deeper and more binding guarantees. Amnesty International forged techniques that publicized the gap between international human rights principles and practices. No one had framed the task before as such an urgent—and public—undertaking.

The norms that we recognize today as part of human rights law have for the most part been created through a process in which Amnesty International and a few other nongovernmental organizations have been key participants. The norms include core treaties, intergovernmental monitoring and inquiry mechanisms, official guidelines for implementation of human rights, and, perhaps most importantly, an altered consensus on how much the principle of sovereign noninterference entitles states to ignore international criticism. While an identifying feature of mature international norms is that they serve as behavioral standards, the emergence of norms is a cumulative process. As they emerge, norms are contested in different ways by different kinds of actors with varying motivations. This book is a study of how such norms dealing with torture, disappearances, and political killings have emerged, and of the unique historical and theoretical place of Amnesty International, and by extension other NGOs, in their emergence.

AMNESTY INTERNATIONAL'S BEGINNINGS

Amnesty International was founded on a big idea and minimal material resources. In May 1961, Peter Benenson, a London lawyer, published an impassioned newspaper editorial describing six "forgotten prisoners" in countries of varying political stripes, all nonviolent and all jailed because of their political or religious beliefs.[3] Despite Benenson's legal background, he placed little faith in international legal remedies for human rights violations. He hoped, instead, that international condemnation of the injustice suffered by the prisoners because of their nonviolently held beliefs would pressure their governments to release them. Benenson therefore decided to appeal straight to the public.

Benenson's editorial highlighted the contrast between the ringing words of the United Nations' Universal Declaration of Human Rights and the plight of someone "imprisoned, tortured, or executed because his opinions or religion are unacceptable to his government."[4] But he did not stop at publicizing the situation of the prisoners. Instead, he invited readers to contact his office, to learn more, and to write letters to urge the release of the "prisoners of conscience" named in the article. Benenson had organized the newspaper appeal with the help of Louis Blom-Cooper, a well-known attorney who also wrote a legal column for the London *Observer*, and Eric Baker, a Quaker academic who was then serving as secretary of the National Peace Council in Britain.[5]

With their help, and the help of other volunteers, the initial campaign was broadened to other countries and extended for work on behalf of more prisoners. Benenson's article was published in Paris, Geneva,

Bonn, New York, and "hundreds of other newspapers" worldwide in the first few weeks of the campaign.[6] After one year, Amnesty International had registered as a charity in Britain, published its first annual report, and tallied seventy prisoner adoption groups meeting in local communities in six countries, with a total of 210 active Prisoner of Conscience cases. Most of the first adoption groups were based in Britain, with others in Australia, Ireland, Norway, Switzerland, and Sweden.[7] By 1963 and 1964, Amnesty's work seemed to bear fruit, with releases of prisoners in Ireland, East Germany, and other countries.[8]

Staff and volunteers in Amnesty's central office at first gleaned information about political arrests from newspapers. They would assign verified prisoner of conscience cases to adoption groups. Group members met regularly to write letters to authorities, seeking humane conditions and release for the prisoner. On the basis of information provided by AI headquarters, groups also undertook other steps to generate publicity and raise money in aid of their adopted prisoners. Often, they established contact with prisoners' families, offering moral and sometimes material support. When it would not put the prisoner or the prisoner's family at risk, they also wrote directly to the adopted prisoner. In its first annual report, Amnesty defended the unique practice of "writing openly to prisoners": "Even if the letter is confiscated and never reaches [the prisoner], it will be opened by the government or prison authorities. Realization that the man or woman concerned is not forgotten has often resulted in the prisoner receiving better treatment and an improvement in his conditions."[9]

Idealistic but pragmatic, Amnesty's creators strived for loyalty to the principles of human rights, for political impartiality, and for knowledge of the facts of individual cases. Amnesty was an outsider to international affairs, lacking the resources and diplomatic standing of states, as well as the size and authority, however limited, of an intergovernmental organization like the United Nations. Still, confident determination permeated the organization's approach.

Despite good reasons for skepticism about what could be accomplished at the United Nations at the height of the Cold War, the fledgling Amnesty International sought and received NGO consultative status in 1964 in the United Nations Economic and Social Council (ECOSOC). Consultative status gave NGOs observer privileges and access to UN documents and diplomatic offices, but NGOs then had almost no independent voice in UN proceedings. Benenson himself was skeptical about the UN as a forum for the enhancement of human rights. He played down the importance of the UN to Amnesty's earliest work, joking that, if nothing else, UN consultative status added official weight to the tiny organization's letterhead.[10]

For its first decade or so, Amnesty approached the United Nations mainly through volunteers. One of its earliest volunteers was no ordinary lay person, however. At the seat of the UN Commission on Human Rights in Geneva, the Irish diplomat and jurist Sean MacBride acted as a liaison and an inside "ear" for Amnesty in the early days of its consultative status. In a voluntary capacity, MacBride was an active member of Amnesty International's main executive body, the International Executive Committee (IEC), composed of eight elected AI members and one elected AI staff member, from 1963 to 1974. Professionally, MacBride was secretary-general of the International Commission of Jurists (ICJ) from 1963 to 1970. His contacts within the ICJ and the International Committee of the Red Cross (ICRC), also based in Geneva, facilitated information exchange between the small, essentially activist organization and established consultative NGOs at the UN. MacBride spearheaded the creation of a coalition of human rights NGOs in anticipation of the UN's 1968 International Conference on Human Rights in Tehran, where he also represented Amnesty.[11] The coalition of human rights NGOs became a permanent subcommittee of the Conference of Nongovernmental Organizations in Consultative Status at the UN (CONGO).[12]

Amnesty's early representation in New York—at ECOSOC and the UN General Assembly—was tenuous at first. For the first year after AI attained UN consultative status, a member of the Danish AI section was listed as its representative.[13] At that stage, AI requested little from UN delegations, and the UN wanted little from NGOs. Amnesty International's advocacy activities focused squarely on individual prisoner-of-conscience cases and relied mainly on correspondence between AI members and government authorities who could release prisoners. At that time, the International Committee for the Red Cross actively consulted with governments on political imprisonment issues, while Amnesty saw itself as a more independent "movement." For these reasons, Amnesty International had little reason to view the UN as crucial to its work for prisoners of conscience. In the mid-1960s, the United States section of Amnesty International established a national office in New York, and ordinary monitoring and liaison work from the mid-1960s devolved for a time to the one-person office staff of the U.S. section and volunteer appointees, with occasional visits from London staffers. The makeshift arrangement continued until the mid-1970s, when AI professionalized its representation at the UN. Amnesty's decision to address the problem of torture, described in chapter 3, prompted the organization to begin working more intensively at the UN on general human rights problems as well as on aid to individual prisoners. The expanded focus entailed an expansion of Amnesty's mission and organizational structure. To pursue better human rights standards internationally, the organization set up a legal department within the International Secretariat and hired its first legal adviser, Nigel Rodley, an international lawyer, in 1973.

In New York, Andrew Blane, then a professor of Russian history at Hunter College, was assigned the voluntary job of New York UN liaison as part of his portfolio upon his election in 1974 as a member of Amnesty's International Executive Committee. The IEC was then working closely with the International Secretariat to follow up on the goals Amnesty had set as part of its work on torture. Blane quickly realized that he would need help, and in 1975 he persuaded Margo Picken, a young Britisher who had just finished master's level graduate study in international relations and Russian, to come to work for him part time on his academic research and part time on the UN liaison assignment. Blane recounts that Picken's "gift" for the work was such that, while still paying her salary, he soon ceded his private claims on her time to the human rights cause.[14] Picken set up shop in the cellar of Blane's Greenwich Village townhouse, on a picturesque street blocks southwest of the steel-and-glass UN complex. Blane, who still lives in the house, characterizes the cramped space as AI's first "UN office." Although Picken had in fact been working at the job for some time, she was formally hired by Amnesty's International Secretariat in 1977 as its first professional UN liaison at the United Nations, and she remained in the position for another decade.

This background illustrates the fact that neither the UN agenda nor Amnesty's own mission was intensively directed at the establishment of general international standards for human rights when Amnesty International formed. When AI did begin to press the UN, as I will show in the chapters to follow, the pressure was rarely welcome. Unlike the U.S. Congress, for example, where interest groups regularly lobby Congress members and offer testimony, the UN was not set up to process public demands. Most government diplomats "didn't want to talk" to Amnesty when Margo Picken arrived at the UN, although they had begun to listen more closely by the end of her tenure in the mid-1980s.[15]

NGOs IN INTERNATIONAL POLITICS

Amnesty forged many of the techniques that are now the common stock of international NGOs. Its research and monitoring activities and its public membership legitimated its efforts to influence the creation of norms through the UN. These activities began in the early 1970s, when NGO involvement in the process of articulating formal standards was unusual. Whether to preserve its access or to maintain its distance from governments, Amnesty rarely publicized its participation in norm-drafting activities and never claimed authorship of specific drafting language. But the different perspectives of NGOs and governments, and the frequently diverging purposes inherent in their decisions to collaborate, are now taken for granted. In a casual conversation in 1996, a ten-year staff member of the UN Centre for Human Rights observed that "nongovernmental organizations participate in UN drafting exercises all the time," listing the Convention on the Rights of the Child, which had recently been opened for signing, as well as a series of other human rights initiatives as examples of efforts in which NGOs participated with governmental representatives. However, neither the creation of new legal norms nor the participation of NGOs were routine until decades after the UN's founding. The fact that both are implicitly accepted by professionals in an area as sensitive as human rights marks significant change.

Amnesty, in essence, developed and "field tested" direct letter-writing networks and other tactics of transnational protest campaigns, tactics many other transnational activists now use against governments and businesses on behalf of the environment, labor practices, and other causes. Like Amnesty, other NGOs now combine such tactics with efforts to develop new international legal norms on humanitarian issues. The speed with which the International Campaign to Ban Landmines recently moved from accounts of the damage done by mines to the drafting of a viable international treaty and its signing in Ottawa in 1997 can be viewed as a progression of "campaign" activity. This campaign, in which Amnesty did not participate, depended on the now tried-and-true tactics that Amnesty has helped to develop on a global scale: publicity, marshaling citizen support from around the world, musical concerts, and celebrity appearances, all directed toward changing official government policies and international law. The campaign's founder, Jody Williams, explained that "a thousand NGOs in 60 countries," many involved in victim assistance, campaigned against mines before the political campaign for a treaty; "however, the campaign fundamentally believed that we had to establish a new norm. . . . We wanted to stop use and we want to see the 100 million mines in arsenals destroyed. . . . [T]he political ban was the linchpin." Now that the treaty has been achieved, Williams noted, the next stage of the campaign will be to work for wider adoption and implementation of the new norm.[16] Collectively, NGOs have acquired broad experience using transnational pressure from citizens to affect norms of government practice in varying issue areas. Scholars have observed that the now-frequent use of such techniques indicates a qualitative change in transnational social activity.

Indeed, the number of human rights groups has expanded greatly since Amnesty was founded, but Amnesty's combination of a public international membership and transnational activism is unique among nongovernmental organizations concerned with human rights. Among NGOs with a grassroots membership, only Anti-Slavery International (formerly the Anti-Slavery Society) is older.[17] Among nongrassroots groups founded before Amnesty, the International Committee of the Red Cross, which since 1864 has monitored prison conditions under the Geneva Conventions, has no public membership, and, with some exceptions, "does not normally release to the public the details of what its delegates have witnessed."[18] The International Commission of Jurists, founded in 1952, works with a professional membership and concentrates mainly on legal issues related to the international rule of law, although its mandate now incorporates a strong, nonpartisan, human rights orientation. Human Rights Watch, now a prominent member of the cohort of international human rights groups, was founded much later in the United States as a group of regional "Watch Committees," beginning with Helsinki Watch in 1978. Human Rights Watch did not open a UN office until 1994, after deciding to devote more programmatic attention to international norms than it had before.

Early Amnesty International leaders learned from and worked with both the ICRC and the ICJ, but their focuses and methods were different. Amnesty now cooperates in many of its projects with the ICJ and other newer NGOs, such as the New York–based Human Rights Watch, and most NGOs see the differences as positive and complementary. Only Amnesty International, however, has steadfastly maintained a policy of completely public and nonpartisan advocacy of human rights concerns over the period that has given rise to the new complex of human rights norms now extant internationally.

NGOs AND THE EMERGENCE OF NORMS

While NGOs are dogged promoters of norms using some of the now-popular techniques outlined above, sheer effort does not guarantee success. Although "new" norms are emerging in many sensitive international subject areas, we do not have an established theory of norm emergence. The thesis that norms matter in international relations has spawned much research, but the question of where international norms come from and how they emerge has not been thoroughly explored, as this study will do in the chapters to follow.

The idea of human rights challenges state sovereignty by imposing international standards of protection for individual citizens from cruel or arbitrary treatment by governments. If we assume that states are power-seeking actors with regard to other states, then why have governments acknowledged and begun to protect human rights at the international level? The human rights issue presents a challenging and potentially fruitful case for the study of norm emergence.

Human rights norms are social expectations that have been codified to some degree in formal international legal instruments. Within this study I use the phrase "principled norms" to refer to norms that are based on beliefs of right and wrong, such as norms of human rights.[19] Human rights norms are social and legal standards that specify how moral beliefs rooted in the Western liberal conception of universal human dignity, as articulated in the UN's 1948 Universal Declaration of Human Rights, should direct behavior. Norms are discussed in more detail in the next chapter.

In the case studies to follow on the development of international legal norms on torture, disappearances, and extrajudicial execution, Amnesty International plays a critical role. Its ability to influence human rights norms rests on three unique attributes: it bases its actions on loyalty to the moral principles of human rights; it cultivates a position as a disinterested and autonomous "third party" actor in the international system; and it deploys expertise and large amounts of specific information in the service of general assertions about the need for norms. I argue that these particular attributes have lent legitimacy to Amnesty International in the international system and have enabled it to serve as a model for other NGOs. Each attribute serves a practical function as NGOs seek to influence international politics on behalf of moral principles to which more self-interested actors may pay only lip service.

KEY ATTRIBUTES OF THE PRINCIPLED NGO

Before NGOs became active at the United Nations, Amnesty International improvised its own role as a global actor by challenging states' long-sheltered freedom from international supervision on human rights. The attributes of loyalty to principles, political impartiality, and attention to facts were part of Peter Benenson's vision for Amnesty, but they took on an extended life when the member-governed organization sought ways to bolster procedural, institutional protection for human rights victims. Below I describe how those three attributes developed and formed a basis for the NGO's ability to contribute to the emergence of principled international norms. This evolution was particularly evident in the first dozen years after Amnesty's inception.

Loyalty to Principle

Benenson's original "Appeal for Amnesty" sought participants who were willing to "condemn persecution regardless of where it occurs, who is responsible or what are the ideas suppressed."[20] His appeal to the public rested on human rights principles present in core UN documents. While Benenson and his fellows no doubt considered moral principles their own reward, such loyalty to principle had its practical effects. Most important for efforts to influence the emergence of human rights norms, Amnesty's loyalty to principle enhanced the clarity of the organization's public message, making it difficult for states to ignore, and inspiring the loyalty and respect of onlookers.[21]

Amnesty International established its loyalty to principles early, with a focus on the "prisoner of conscience," the term Amnesty's founders coined to refer to "any person who is physically restrained (by imprisonment or otherwise) from expressing (in any form of words or symbols) any opinion which he honestly holds and which does not advocate or condone personal violence."[22] From the first, Amnesty defined whom it would adopt in universal, principled terms.

The principles of freedom of speech and conscience were enshrined in the Universal Declaration of Human Rights, a document accepted by all UN member states.[23] Amnesty's reliance on internationally endorsed principles was significant: at that time, human rights was far from a household word. One of Benenson's first employees, Stefanie Grant, said that the phrase, human rights, "wasn't really used" when she joined the Amnesty staff in 1966. Grant, who helped to shape AI's international research program and eventually became Head of Research in her ten years of work at AI headquarters, was a recent university graduate when Benenson hired her to write reports on prison conditions in southern Africa and Romania. People thought of Amnesty International as "an adoption organization" then. That was "a very, very long time ago," she observed in 1996, "and there really wasn't such a thing as 'human rights work' at that time."[24]

Unassailable human rights principles provided a kind of shield for Amnesty International, enabling it to pursue independent action regardless of political alignments. To honor human dignity without regard to a prisoner's religion, gender, race, age, or political beliefs was paramount for Benenson.[25] That principle became the central tenet for Amnesty in its later efforts to develop and reinforce international human rights norms within the United Nations.

Independence and Impartiality

A second important attribute of the organization has been its conscious effort to remain politically impartial by, first, taking no stand on political questions and, second, working for the rights of individuals living under any type of government. Inevitably, Amnesty's impartial advocacy of human rights principles led it to criticize governments publicly, at the same time that it wished to gain the ear of authorities regarding individual cases of abuse. While the approach would not be recommended if the organization were seeking to maximize its own power, it has been a significant component of Amnesty International's leverage among states.

Public criticism of governments' human rights records was not accepted diplomatic practice for states or NGOs at Amnesty's inception. At the United Nations, for example, protocol dictated that governments not criticize one another by name in the proceedings of the Commission on Human Rights. Consultative NGOs were limited even further by explicit rules and unspoken expectations.

The experience of the Anti-Slavery Society illustrates the pitfalls of the traditional limitations on NGO autonomy at the UN. In accordance with traditional NGO techniques in support of human rights, the Anti-Slavery Society from 1946 to 1966 operated on the principle that it would not publicize slavery "in the hope of securing governmental and international co-operation" to end it.[26] Frustrated by lagging government compliance in spite of its efforts at discretion, the Anti-Slavery Society eventually declared an end to its self-imposed confidentiality, noting that its public support had also suffered as a result of the policy. In its 1968 report to the UN, the Society remarked that it was "bitterly disappointed" and saw publication of reports as its only option.[27] In contrast, Amnesty International's publicly critical approach showed a break, from the beginning, with post–World War II standards for the behavior of consultative nongovernmental organizations at the UN.

Although the first consultative NGOs were not as global in their activism as some of the leading human rights, women's, or environmental organizations of today, most of the NGOs associated with the UN since its inception expressed similar loyalties to the democratic, universalist ideals upon which the UN had been founded. Thus, it was predictable that a rhetorical and incremental approach to the achievement of human rights would disappoint and frustrate nongovernmental advocates. Amnesty's break from protocol was motivated by faithfulness to human rights ideals, flying in the face of states' affirmations that states themselves should control how and when human rights promises should be fulfilled.

Benenson and his associates emphasized a self-disciplined political balance in the group's prisoner adoption efforts. In fact, members were not permitted to work on behalf of fellow citizens: they had to engage in transnational correspondence. The rule against working for prisoners in one's own country was thought to protect both AI members and those whose cases they pleaded while enhancing the capacity to be impartial.

Further, according to Amnesty's own rule of "Threes," each adoption group was assigned one prisoner from each of three regions of the world corresponding to the range of political ideologies: the East, the West, and the Third World. In later years, as the number of adoption groups grew, political imprisonment gave way to or was accompanied by other forms of human rights violations in many countries. As Amnesty International responded to such changes, the "Threes" rule could not be implemented in the same way. The organization continued to strive to be what it called "apolitical," that is, to analyze all situations and regions impartially according to a carefully defined human rights mandate, its statement of purpose.[28]

In the broader political context of the highly charged Cold War milieu of the 1960s, such impartiality was especially germane. AI defined its goal as working to express politically impartial support for those imprisoned for their beliefs, a goal which was tested and clarified by events early in Amnesty's life as an organization.

In 1964, a conflict over whether to sponsor Nelson Mandela, leader of the African National Congress, as a prisoner of conscience, tested both Amnesty's impartiality and loyalty to the principle of nonviolence. Because Mandela maintained that violence was a justifiable last resort against apartheid, Amnesty decided it could not adopt the prominent anti-apartheid activist, despite "worldwide popular sympathy."[29] The policy of refusing prisoner of conscience status to those who had used or advocated violence preserved a universal standard for selecting prisoners of conscience, in the process preserving a level of neutrality on ideological issues that kept the organization open to a widespread membership. "Although most members would probably consider as individuals that there are some situations where violent action is the only solution, the membership would not agree on what those situations are," according to an AI statement.[30]

Amnesty's independence from governments, although marked and deliberate from the first, also was consolidated partly through tests of experience. Amnesty makes it clear today that it does not bargain with governments. However, an isolated comment in an early annual report suggests that Amnesty leaders discussed the possibility that selected confidential communication with governments might be beneficial to prisoners. At the organization's second annual meeting in 1963, Sean MacBride, referring to the practices of the International Committee of the Red Cross, stressed the importance of confidential negotiations with governments when circumstances warranted.[31] However, the organization soon cemented an unambiguous policy of refusal either to conduct private negotiations with governments or to take government funds, which worked itself out as AI and the ICJ responded to a series of troubling allegations in 1966 and 1967.[32]

First, there was an internal fight over a damning Amnesty International report on British use of torture in Aden (now Yemen), which had been a British colony. Benenson, at this time, had handed over the day-to-day operations of Amnesty. Under his hand-picked successor, Robert Swann, the report was embargoed. Benenson, who was also in poor health, suspected government infiltration of Amnesty and had the report published outside of Britain without AI's official approval. Second, Benenson himself was accused of mixing an AI mission to Rhodesia with British government business. Fact and innuendo in the two situations were never fully sorted out in public records, although Amnesty International carried out a detailed internal study whose records remain closed. Third, unrelated reports appeared in the U.S. press that the ICJ regularly received money from sources acting as fronts for the United States' Central Intelligence Agency. Political attacks broadened on NGOs in the UN under accusations of ideological bias, which prompted the reorganization of the NGO consultative status and a case-by-case review of consultative NGOs in ECOSOC beginning in 1967.[33] The independence of NGOs in general, as well as Amnesty's reputation and its organizational relationships with Benenson, MacBride, and the ICJ, seemed under siege.

Benenson resigned as Amnesty's president and ceased active leadership within the organization in 1967, although good relations were restored with time. Swann was asked to take an indefinite leave of absence, and Eric Baker, Amnesty's cofounder, stepped into the role of interim secretary-general. MacBride remained as chair of AI's International Executive Committee.[34] AI's commitment in principle to independence and impartiality thus seems to have been confirmed by the trials of experience. Benenson continued to maintain that Amnesty International's International Secretariat should be moved to a "neutral" country to avoid any appearance of political bias.[35] Amnesty pulled out of the troubles intact, but with new awareness of the importance of unimpeachable impartiality and professionalism in its pursuits.

Financial self-sufficiency bolsters Amnesty's political independence and impartiality. AI is funded entirely by membership support and voluntary donations, with strictures on the types and amounts that can be accepted from individuals, private groups, or governmental sources.[36] The organization accepts no monies from national governments, although intergovernmental funds have occasionally been accepted in particular circumstances. For example, in the past AI has received donations from the European Community earmarked for prisoner relief.[37]

Members and other private contributors fund their own national branches of Amnesty International, and Amnesty International's International Secretariat has come to rely for its operations on money contributed annually by the national sections. Other support may come from direct private donations and internationally organized fund raisers, such as concerts.[38]

Interpretive Capacity

The third attribute contributing to Amnesty's ability to play a role in the emergence of principled international norms is the ability to form new concepts about human rights based on collected facts. While the actual fact collecting is a valuable technique for the NGO, the *interpretation* of facts so that they elucidate normative concepts plays an important part in the emergence of norms. Norms become authoritative when there exists critical reflection upon behavior with reference to a common standard, according to the legal philosopher H.L.A. Hart. Such reflection may be displayed in "criticism . . . demands for conformity, and in acknowledgments that such criticism and demands are justified, all of which find their characteristic expression in the normative terminology of 'ought', 'must', and 'should', 'right' and 'wrong'."[39]

Comparing state behavior to a common standard requires accurate information about the behavior. Because human rights violations are so often hidden, detailed information about them is not available on demand. Neither is it easily acquired either within borders or across borders. Even when the political will exists, the details of human-rights-related performance are not cheap for states or intergovernmental agencies to collect. Thus, the major contribution of NGOs to basic fact finding has been emphasized in much that has been written about NGOs. In this vein, UN treaty bodies, committee chairs, and the General Assembly have all affirmed that none of the actors involved in official human rights monitoring could work well without NGOs.[40] Gathering facts is an important technique for nongovernmental organizations, which often have more expertise in their own subject areas than do states or intergovernmental organizations.

The deeper quality I wish to emphasize as central to NGOs' role in norm emergence is the mastery of the conceptual process necessary to collate facts and normative standards. It requires well-informed NGOs to reinforce normative standards by relating specific details to general concepts. Where facts are shockingly incongruous with known standards of behavior, as is often the case when "new" human rights violations are discovered, the interpretation of fact in a way that coheres with previous norms or precedents promotes the application of existing norms and the development of new standards.

Where few normative remedies exist for a violation, as was the case for disappearances in the 1970s, for example, Amnesty International's information and interpretation capacity helped to define the issue and elicit expectations of governmental accountability. Now that many intergovernmental reporting mechanisms already exist, NGOs contribute independent information and help to update state-sponsored reports that may have been written long before the reporting date. NGOs can immediately contest "inaccurate or misleading statements which may be made by government representatives."[41] Thus, not just the information itself but NGO responses to government statements based on independent investigation of the facts are critical.

Amnesty International developed this capacity as an outgrowth of its work for individual prisoners. While its earliest research was based in large part on secondary sources, by 1965 AI was receiving about half of its information about potential prisoner adoptions from independent contacts with international organizations, opposition groups, families and friends of prisoners, and sometimes prisoners themselves.[42]

This was especially significant since the fledgling organization was small, poor, and staffed mainly by volunteers. In 1966, 80 percent of Amnesty staff concerned with gathering information on new and continuing prisoners of conscience and advising groups were volunteers.[43] "It's hard to describe how tiny it was," said Stefanie Grant. When Grant and another staffer, Maureen Teitelbaum, were hired in Amnesty International's first general effort to investigate prison conditions, their endeavors marked a slight departure from Amnesty International's exclusive concentration on individual prisoner cases. Like prisoner adoptions, however, the early reports were also issued in trios according to government ideology. The first three reports analyzed prison conditions in Romania, South Africa, and Portugal: an Eastern bloc country, a Third World Country, and a Western country, respectively. All imposed harsh conditions on prisoners. "I remember [Peter Benenson's] pointing to me and saying, 'The important thing is that these should be absolutely impartial and as fact-based as possible,' " said Grant. "And that was how it began."[44]

What "began" with the country reports was Amnesty International's ability to assemble, interpret, and disseminate human rights information. Amnesty International's annual report wryly observed in 1966 that its first three country reports "attracted considerable attention," and noted that "many Governments quoted with approval from our reports where they criticized Governments of a different ideology but were remarkably silent about their 'allies.' "[45] Grant eventually helped to develop a full-fledged Research Department at the International Secretariat. The research staff maintained up-to-date information on prisoner cases and produced general reports on human rights conditions globally.

The origins of Amnesty International's independent reporting initiatives were modest and driven by the qualities of loyalty to principle and objectivity. Reaching for objectivity while remaining faithful to principles of truth, the nonviolent expression of political opinion, and most particularly to the well-being and release of individuals unjustly imprisoned, was Amnesty International's mainstay. As AI gathered knowledge of specific cases, it acquired a range of information on human rights conditions that few others could claim.

As patterns of human rights abuse became apparent, the central organization expanded its mandate beyond prisoner adoption, a move supported by its public membership.[46] AI's supervisory board, the International Executive Committee, approved an experimental campaign against torture in the early 1970s that resulted in the creation of both a Campaign Department and a Legal Department, which together coordinated public pressure informed by factual knowledge and supplemented with activities targeted at promoting legal norms through the United Nations.[47]

Grant likened grappling with the facts of human rights abuse to making a steady climb. When people first learn of a certain human rights violation, they tend to react with shock. When documentation shows that there are a lot of similar cases, the next observation is, "How extraordinary that it isn't illegal." Often, the realization hits that "it isn't illegal because we weren't aware that it was happening." Said Grant, "And so you have a moral principle which then finds that the practice it abhors is not illegal. . . . [I]t may be illegal if you extend the law, but it's not expressly illegal. And so then you move toward . . . creating new law, as a means of preventing. And then, you use that law as the basis of your work. And so, it's like . . . climbing the stairs of your house."[48] Amnesty International's commitment to human rights principles led to involvement not just in advocating existing principles, but in helping to advance international law on human rights.

CONCLUSION

Human rights principles present conflicting imperatives for states in the creation of new norms. States' paramount concern for security at the international level disadvantages moral principles. Indeed, new human rights norms are unlikely to arise without a great deal of contention over the principles important to states. How principled norms of right and wrong are worked out and accepted by supposedly self-interested actors, and why those actors will for moral reasons agree to limit their own ability to pursue their interests, is something that theorists continue to puzzle over.

The present study identifies a pattern of distinct phases in the emergence of principled international norms of human rights, and assesses the role of Amnesty International in constructing international human rights standards that govern the relations of states. Chapter 2 discusses theories about how international norms develop, situating Amnesty International according to how its qualities as an NGO have contributed to the development of international norms of human rights. It presents a theory of norm emergence that is applied in later chapters. Chapters 3, 4, and 5 present case studies of Amnesty International's role in the development of international norms to limit three kinds of political repression: torture, disappearances, and extrajudicial executions. The last chapter summarizes the findings and concludes by elaborating upon the role of NGOs at different phases in the emergence of international norms.

Amnesty International has been a key catalyst of change in the human rights arena. It began by focusing on the plight of individual prisoners and found that further international legal support for human rights was needed. In its effort to free prisoners of conscience, Amnesty International relied on the ethical and legal reference points found in the Universal Declaration of Human Rights. But only impartial application was likely to survive in a world where human rights discourse was purportedly universal but tinged with ideological overtones and the vicissitudes of power politics.

Amnesty International operated as an outsider to international affairs, without the resources of states and without the authority of an intergovernmental organization. While in 1948 a small group of states, calling themselves the United Nations, had declared loyalty to human rights principles, Amnesty International built up the authority of human rights declarations by invoking them in real cases. Its original purpose was to make a difference in the lives of individuals. In the process it began to make a difference in the general norms and practice of the international system.

The cases presented here highlight the importance of third-party advocacy for systemic change in international politics. The evidence shows that Amnesty International has had a surprising impact on the course of international human rights norms. As an independent actor on behalf of principle, Amnesty has refused to play politics even as it has used information and public pressure as instruments of influence. Rather than removing it from the debate, Amnesty's disinterestedness enhanced its influence. Thus, as a disinterested actor, Amnesty is an anomaly for traditional theories of international relations and a model for citizen involvement at the transnational level. Nongovernmental organizations' consistent advocacy, investigation, and reporting on principled issues has been a major factor in the emergence of international norms on women, children, the environment, and other topics in addition to the problems detailed in the case studies. Amnesty's growth from a tiny, mainly volunteer prisoner adoption group to a model for other citizen-based groups demonstrates the potential of nonstate actors to influence the morality of states. In the process, Amnesty's example provides the basis for understanding how principles and moral suasion influence international politics.

Chapter Two

HOW NORMS GROW

AMNESTY INTERNATIONAL challenged governments to change their behavior, against their sovereign prerogatives. It also has prodded the United Nations to back up idealistic statements of principle with legal norms specifying acceptable and unacceptable member behavior. Amnesty has been able to maintain its challenge to governments precisely because of its status as a bystander with few resources except its principles, objectivity, and information. Those qualities also make AI an interesting, and unusual, international actor. The previous chapter emphasized Amnesty International's origins and its historical role. The attributes that make it unusual also endow AI, and other NGOs that have followed in its path, with the power to shepherd the emergence of principled international norms.

Amnesty International's advocacy of principled norms is theoretically significant for the study of international relations in that it poses anomalies for realism, the prominent theory of international relations that sees states as the dominant actors in international politics and power as the primary determinant of action. Kenneth Waltz, a major proponent of realist theory, predicted even nonstate actors must possess the power attributes of states to be successful.[1] Amnesty's source of efficacy is clearly very different from that of states and yet, as the case studies will demonstrate, it has had significant effects on the actions of states and the rules by which they act. Second, realism looks to power and the lack of central coordination in the international system as key determinants of state action. Realists characterize the absence of centralized supranational rule as anarchy, which is said to be at the root of competition for power among sovereign states. By definition, anarchy is a condition of "no rule," in which governance is absent. In this view, all forms of authority are abstracted to expressions of power as "capability."[2] Yet Amnesty relies on a very different kind of authority, derived from principled ideas or beliefs about right and wrong.

Norms *are* limited when contradicted by power, but they are not extinguished. Norms based on principles of right and wrong suffer disadvantage when power is primary. If nation-states' security depends upon constant competition, norms of respect for persons and mutual accommodation more appropriate for a civil society are prevented from emerging. In theory, they would be unlikely to find proponents except, perhaps, among the weak. Thucydides' famous Melian dialogue is often cited as the exemplar of the triumph of power over principle. It is the overpowered representatives of Melos, about to be conquered by Athens, who advocate the preservation of comity between Melos and Athens. Responding to Athenian threats, the Melians argue, "As we think, it is expedient . . . that you should not destroy what is our common protection, the privilege of being allowed in danger to invoke what is fair and right."[3]

The Melians fight a losing battle in Thucydides' history, but a subtext of the history is its tragedy: Athenians' ability to sustain their acquired power degenerates in proportion to their disregard for the protective value of the shared culture of accountability that had woven together the fate of the city-states.[4] Contemporary international relations theory, too, has begun to attend to the kinds of social bonds that may arise in the international system. Recent theoretical and empirical studies have revised, to different degrees, the simple realist view of the meaning of anarchy. Although anarchy is commonly imagined as a world of amoral chaos, norms and principles of right action can and do exist in an anarchic world.

Scholars theorizing from varying epistemological perspectives point out that rule-following behavior is a fact of international life, since nation-states build historically specific relationships that, in turn, influence the structural environment. Robert Axelrod demonstrated in formal game-theoretic terms that norms of cooperation may evolve from simple but deliberate reciprocity even in an anarchic environment.[5] (Friedrich Kratochwil's critique of Axelrod suggests that minimal social norms may also be required.)[6] Structural anarchy does not have to produce an international system hostile to cooperation, according to Alexander Wendt.[7] In an empirical critique of the concept of anarchy, Lea Brilmayer concludes that moral principles are relevant to international behavior even if the norms cannot be enforced by a central authority.[8] Acutely aware of the strictures of anarchy and pessimistic about innovation in basic international arrangements like war, diplomacy, and balance of power, Hedley Bull also recognizes the social, and therefore potentially mutable, nature of such institutions in an international "anarchical society."[9] These authors give reasons to question the assumption of a normless anarchy. Recent theoretically motivated empirical studies reinforce their criticisms.[10]

HUMAN RIGHTS NORMS AS CHALLENGES TO SOVEREIGNTY

Principled norms pose significant challenges to other norms that have emerged as a result of key structuring principles of the international system. Since there is no centralized coordination or supranational governance in the global arena, both realists and neoliberal institutionalists characterize the relations as anarchic. By definition, anarchy is a condition of "no rule," and in this situation, it is to be expected that norms and international organizations will lack authority unless they are awarded power by coordinated agreement, either through force, codes, or custom. While anarchy is not necessarily a malign environment, altruism is not expected of states, since they are in theory expected to act based upon self-interest. The principle of sovereignty and the norm of noninterference are examples of practices said to emerge from and maintain a situation of international anarchy.

Because human rights norms call for international accountability as to how states treat their citizens, the norms potentially modify sovereign practices in important ways. Governments do not welcome external comment on, let alone external interference in, their internal governing practices. Indeed, the older, competing norm of noninterference accounts for the traditionally weak implementation of global human rights norms.[11] Nevertheless, although many governments still resist practical observation of human rights principles that they have officially endorsed, the legal force of human rights claims in the international context has grown significantly stronger over recent decades.[12]

An incisive realist could respond that perhaps even norms such as human rights, seemingly based on ideas of right and wrong, actually serve power interests in some way. Below I summarize the logic of such explanations, then show that they do not account for the actual emergence of human rights norms in the late twentieth century. The moral aspects of international norms cannot be completely subordinated to state purposes.

State-centric Explanations of Human Rights Norm Emergence

Human rights norms have commonly been portrayed as an international "regime" that formed as a more or less consensual reaction to the suffering of World War II. Regime theory in its classic form characterizes regimes as sets of shared international rules, adopted to coordinate state activity, usually in the service of mutual interest.[13] Regimes coordinate state activity on particular issues, also usually in the service of mutual interest. They reduce the costs and uncertainty that would normally be associated with collective action in an anarchic environment. Regimes become institutionalized by way of formal international agreements; thus, norms are fundamental building blocks of regimes. States may build regime participation into domestic law or create international arrangements to monitor compliance with regimes. Once regimes are institutionalized, in some cases they retain influence on states that can be demonstrated to counter states' narrowly construed self-interest. Thus, regime theory is one way for realism to account for the existence of shared rules. Regimes may be negotiated to accomplish mutually desired joint action; they are often promoted by a dominant state, or hegemon. In either case—whether regimes form due to states' mutual interest or the interest of one very strong state—regimes, and thus international norms, supposedly arise out of the power needs of states.

Regime theory as joint interest-based cooperation does not account for the increase in attention directed at human rights issues in more recent decades, however. The post–World War II surge in human rights concern was largely symbolic and heralded little action. Even the dominant regime analysis of human rights notes that "postwar frustration, guilt, or unease" prompted demand for norms that was more or less satisfied by the United Nations' 1948 adoption of the Universal Declaration of Human Rights and the Genocide Convention. National objectives did not stimulate further calls for human rights norms.[14] After a flurry of conventions in the 1950s, formal standard setting slowed dramatically, bogged down by the Cold War. One scholar doubted in 1964 whether the traditional process of creating international law by treaty would prove possible at all for human rights, lamenting that "the conclusion of international treaties has—temporarily, it is hoped—become unavailable."[15] As it turned out, the International Covenant on Civil and Political Rights and the International Covenant on Economic, Social, and Cultural Rights were concluded in 1966, almost twenty years after the adoption of the Universal Declaration. Even then, the fact that treaties did not gain enough signatures to come into effect until 1976 reminds us that human rights norms themselves once risked being left for dead by UN members.

A second possible explanation for the human rights regime is the interest of a hegemon that would help provide for and sustain such a regime. The United States, as Western hegemon, advocated the consideration of human rights at the San Francisco Conference to draft the UN Charter. Notably, the United States was prompted by NGOs consulting with the U.S. delegation.[16] Congress and the Carter Administration also gave human rights a central place in U.S. foreign policy in the 1970s, a fact that undeniably raised the international profile of human rights as a concept. But the United States has shown overt hostility to multilateral norms despite periods of foreign policy support for human rights at a bilateral level.[17] As its ambivalence toward the establishment of an International Criminal Court in the mid-1990s has illustrated, the United States has especially avoided adherence to UN standards that threaten to make national practices subject to international monitoring.[18] A proliferation of UN declaratory statements and related standard setting began in the late 1960s (see fig. 1), but was not driven by U.S. policy. If regimes

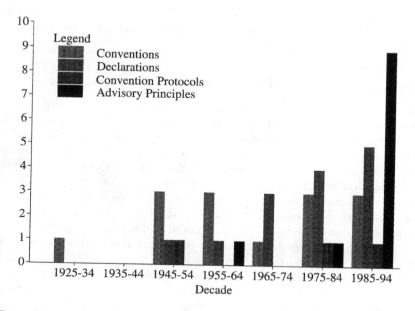

Figure 1. International human rights instruments. (Author's coding of information from "International Human Rights Instruments." University of Minnesota Human Rights Library, www1.umn.edu/humanrts/instree/ainstls1.htm. Research assistance for this figure provided by Margaret Hirschberg.)

are sets of shared principles, norms, rules, and procedures, the constellation of international human rights standards may be characterized as a regime. However, at its inception the regime did not comprise a self-sustaining set of standards. The Cold War lull in human rights shows that the international community's reaction to World War II did not determine a sustained trajectory for human rights norms.

Regime theory's modification of realism, therefore, does not provide a convincing explanation for the sustained development of human rights norms in the international system, given the hegemonic skepticism of multilateral norms and the challenge international human rights norms pose to state sovereignty. Although scholars increasingly accept that international norms matter, realism provides no adequate explanation for where principled norms come from and how they develop. In regime theory, state interests remain the key determinants of state action and the key to enforcement once a regime is established. The only way to see human rights norms as furthering state power is to redefine them as part of state self-interest, which would contradict other power-based norms such as sovereignty and noninterference. The "brute fact" of principled preferences that cannot be objectively imputed is an enduring difficulty for rationalist accounts of norms.[19]

International Institutions as Frameworks for Norm Formation

Recent emendations of regime theory incorporate processes of reflection, persuasion, criticism, and interpretation of behavior to account for the strengthening of behavioral standards over time.[20] Attention to the social and institutional aspects of regimes is compatible with an understanding of norms as communicative reference points in international society. Hedley Bull explains that states form a society in as far as they can recognize common interests and values and "conceive themselves to be bound by a common set of rules . . . and share in the workings of common institutions."[21] Others have noted that achieving agreement on moral norms requires procedures for adjudication of differences, which are enhanced by the formation of norms that permit "conversations" about differences. For that reason, shared procedures, but not necessarily shared goals, are a requirement for an international society, in Terry Nardin's view.[22] For Friedrich Kratochwil, international governance develops and is reinforced through social, communicative exchange at the international level in which grievances may be settled by referring to norms and common procedures.[23] On this view, if human rights norms are understood as common societal rules, one is led to ask whether new norms might be traced to the composition of international institutions or to changes in their structure.

The first question to answer is whether the United Nations' structure itself facilitated norm generation on human rights. Contemporary legal obligations with regard to human rights can be traced to the UN Charter, which held promotion of "universal respect for, and observance of, human rights" to be a purpose of the new organization.[24] Despite pervasive nods to state sovereignty, the UN's institutional purposes also included human rights and incorporated responsiveness to citizens' groups. UN consultative status vested NGOs whose purposes meshed with stated UN goals. Consultative status was created to allow for representation of public opinion and provide access to groups with special competence in areas of importance to the UN's Economic and Social Council.[25] However, early consultative NGOs had limited ability to act as independent promoters of human rights at the UN. They were expected to act as vehicles for the dissemination of UN humanitarian ideals rather than as critics of UN members' performance.[26] Neither did UN procedures pave the way for the construction of stronger norms on the foundation of early human rights rhetoric. Thus, while the UN constituted a frame for the possible creation of norms, it was only a frame.[27] The creation of an institutional climate supporting actual observance of human rights has been a much more contentious affair.

A second possible institutional source of change to examine is the historical change in the UN membership profile. Decolonization altered UN politics as newly independent states joined the organization during its first three decades. The new membership eventually constituted a majority in the UN, a majority that manifested the political will to condemn racial discrimination and apartheid in the southern African states. But while newly independent African states "almost all could agree" on support for racial equality in southern Africa,[28] support for criticism of southern Africa did not necessarily extend to support for wider international accountability on the full range of civil and political rights.

NGOs' Human Rights Advocacy in the UN

Thus, no state-centric explanation for norm emergence, even one that incorporates hegemonic or institutional leadership, accounts for why such challenges to sovereignty might gain a foothold in the society of states. At the same time, numerous studies document NGO involvement in the politics of human rights, either on their own or as part of a network of actors.[29] Henry Steiner and Philip Alston illustrate NGO-generated demand for stronger application of UN human rights mechanisms with the observation that the mid-1980s average of 25,000 human rights complaints per year submitted to the UN from all sources skyrocketed to a 1995 level of almost 300,000 complaints per year, but "many of these complaints [were] identical as a result of letter-writing campaigns by groups with a large and active membership."[30] Yet NGOs' prominence as a source of principled normative claims in international politics has not up to this point been fully analyzed with reference to normative challenges to sovereignty.

In many accounts of norms, both formal and informal institutions are framed as though they only exist in service of state interests. The possibility of their conditioning influence on state action is rarely considered.[31] Similarly, with overly state-centric assumptions about how international norms affect or are affected by states, a systematic role for nonstate actors in the development of international norms is simply assumed away. What is needed is a deeper understanding that accounts for how norms gain authority and how normative authority interacts with the motives of state and nonstate actors.

WHAT DO NORMS DO? THE TENSION BETWEEN
BEHAVIOR AND BELIEFS

If realist assumptions fairly represent the value states place on sovereign autonomy, realism is an overly restrictive framework for understanding how norms work. There is tension between the principled values many states endorse in their rhetoric and the power mandate dictated by adherence to the principle of sovereignty.

Norms are generally defined as rules or standards of behavior based on shared moral, causal, or factual beliefs. In his discussion of regimes, Stephen Krasner placed norms in a continuum of kinds of social rules, in which norms were "standards of behavior defined in terms of rights and obligations," based on principles, which are "beliefs of fact, causation, and rectitude."[32] While it might be criticized for too strict a separation among kinds of rules, and for limited acknowledgment of the socially constructed nature of such rules, Krasner's hierarchy is heuristically useful for two reasons. First, it attempts to be comprehensive. It leaves room for the many different kinds of regular behavior that may be observed in the international system. Second, it distinguishes between different kinds of norms, different kinds of beliefs, and implicitly, the different kinds of objectives that guide behavior. Krasner recognizes that regimes change when principles and norms that guide them change. However, the principles and norms are given in the regime model. It is only implicit in Krasner's definition that norms, being based on belief, are mutable.

To understand principled international norms more fully requires full recognition of norms as reference points for social action. Below, I discuss the increased attention that theorists have devoted to the socially negotiated character of norms. If norms are not simply given, but evolve, then the accumulated choices of international actors gradually impact how the rules of international life are interpreted and applied. Behavior is mediated through normative interpretation and application; therefore, normative standards fluctuate. In line with such a conception of the place of norms in social interaction, it is necessary to study intentions, behavior, and how intentions and behavior are expressed and interpreted in order to understand how international norms change.

When actors appeal to norms, they participate in a process of communication, which is evidenced through reflection, persuasion, criticism, and interpretation of behavior.[33] Friedrich Kratochwil and John Gerard Ruggie argued early that such an approach was lacking in regime theory's understanding of norms. They called for the incorporation of both communicative and behavioral analysis in the study of international institutions.[34] Kratochwil later described norms as prescriptions regarding proper behavior, to which actors refer when airing grievances.[35] Such an approach is pursued by Volker Rittberger et al., who draw explicitly from Jürgen Habermas's theory of communicative action, which understands actors to be advancing truth claims through discourse to arrive at common understandings undistorted by power relationships. Common understandings develop through appeals to principle, and the interpretation of such appeals.[36]

In a study of international norms and apartheid, Audie Klotz defines norms as "shared (thus social) understandings of standards of behavior."[37] I argue that norms go beyond shared understandings: the socially shared interpretation of behavior is a key first step in the development of norms, but shared understandings do not *make* norms. To become norms, shared understandings need some way to inform continuity and change in etiquette, traditions, mores, and, more deliberately, law. Shared understandings of observed behavior take on the power to shape future behavior. Thus, norms as shared standards for behavior have a basis in shared understandings and socially established rules. In a political system these standards may remain informal or be formally codified in law, but norms should be understood as regularly affecting action in a way that the mere existence of shared ideas or principles does not.

The above conception of norms reflects the concept long familiar to legal theorists that formal and informal rules of behavior derive their influence in large part from socially formed expectations. Principled norms of international human rights express obligations for states that reflect the rights due to human beings. In the present international system, the idea of human rights is rooted in the Western liberal conception of individual human dignity. This idea is the object of constant critique by those who would like to diminish it in some respect as well as by those who would like to expand it. For purposes of this study, in accordance with H.L.A. Hart's understanding of law,[38] I assume that legal standards of human rights can be understood as referents for the emergence of shared social understandings about human rights in international society. In the present international system, NGOs have worked to reinforce the social expectations that undergird and support human rights.

It is too often assumed in studies of international relations that spotty behavioral compliance with moral principles means that such principles are irrelevant. In the realist tradition, strategic priorities of states are expected to drive out morality when power and principle conflict. The persistent gap between moral standards and state actions is then interpreted as behavioral confirmation of the absence of authoritative norms. However, behavioral compliance and noncompliance are not fully transparent as measures of a norm's existence and authority. In describing the international system as an anarchical society, Hedley Bull noted that international norms and institutions hold sway for states because of a sense of obligation, even without a central enforcement mechanism: states form a society in as far as they "*conceive themselves to be bound* by a common set of rules."[39] Whether a specific action supports a norm depends in large part on how it is interpreted, justified, and criticized by actors and observers.

To summarize, human rights norms can be understood as standards of behavior defined in terms of rights and obligations, resting on beliefs. Human rights norms rest on beliefs of rectitude, or right and wrong. I have suggested that actors use norms as reference points in their communication and interaction. This communicative process serves as a primary means by which actors may arrive at new norms and reinforce existing principles by acknowledging one another's full or partial compliance with norms.

How Norms Grow

Instigating an interplay between facts and principles is a way that NGOs, even in a system dominated by states, both bolster rhetorical principles with meaning and create legitimacy for themselves. Amnesty International used the tension between human rights ideals and the facts of their incomplete realization as moral leverage in the intergovernmental system as it expanded its efforts to aid individuals by working to strengthen legal norms of human rights. The attributes that legitimated AI's intervention in the process of norm emergence rested on the principles that make principled norms themselves effective: invocation of right and wrong, independence, and conceptual generalization.

These attributes are qualities that governments can rarely afford in their relations with other states. Nation-states in the present international system are faced with contradictory expectations on the normative front. The norms of sovereignty buttress the expectations that states will be self-determining and independent of international accountability. Competing moral expectations based on the universal ideal of human rights demand that the government should protect the integrity of the person. Indeed, the demands are not completely contradictory since— in classic realist texts, at least—the purpose of sovereign power is to provide a buffer for a nation's subjects against the state of nature. If a government does not protect its citizens, to some extent it may yield its moral claim on sovereignty.[40]

The attributes of AI and other like-minded nongovernmental organizations following in its wake, then, appeal to principled norms rather than pressure states for material reasons. That means articulating beliefs of rectitude through loyalty to principle, invoking such beliefs in an impartial manner, and deepening the process by relating new facts to general concepts. The remainder of this chapter is devoted to elaborating a theory of how principled norms emerge, based on the history of Amnesty International's practical orientation to the sponsorship and invocation of norms in support of human rights.

The Creation of Legal Standards in the United Nations

The process of articulation and establishment of human rights principles as norms is complex. Much of the interaction takes place within the institutional context of the United Nations. Formal human rights standards are established through UN decisions, declarations, and treaties, which impose obligations of varying legal strength for governments with respect to human rights. A brief discussion of the types of formal standards that have developed in the UN is presented below.

Figure 1 above roughly compares the kinds of human rights standards that emerged from 1925 through 1994. Standard setting in the UN usually starts with a declaration concerning a specific topic, which is adopted by consensus. In theory, a declaration does not require a surrender of sovereignty, but since it is adopted by the UN General Assembly, it can be regarded as pertaining to all UN member states. Subsequent invocation of such statements with reference to concrete circumstances enhances their legitimacy. The level of obligation conferred through a declaration is not as well defined as that of a legally binding treaty, but because the efforts to conclude treaties became difficult during the East-West political conflict of the Cold War, declarations have been used to express international normative intentions on human rights since the founding of the UN.[41] Human rights treaty provisions (conventions and convention protocols), most of which are drafted through UN-affiliated working groups, mark a firmer set of obligations for states. A convention requires a definition of the phenomenon in question and legally binds the states that sign it.[42] A convention protocol is a separate attachment to a treaty that allows states to make binding commitments to stronger implementation measures on particular issues. Usually states that ratify a treaty must, at minimum, submit regular compliance reports to a central body.[43] UN members may also adopt further detailed recommendations, some technical, concerning how to conduct government activities in a manner consistent with broader human rights standards. While such guidelines may not be binding in and of themselves, they endorse behavioral standards of increasing specificity. Examples include UN recommendations for police conduct and detailed guidelines for using autopsy procedures to document evidence of suspected mistreatment by political authorities.[44] Insofar as the norms are reflected in international legal instruments, human rights norms are the outcome of an array of procedures that have been developed to generate statements that can then be understood as valid rules of international law. The legal norm-drafting process in the UN is therefore an empirical indicator of varying levels of normative understandings, although some norms do not have fixed authority.

Knowledge of how formal norms of human rights have developed in the UN is necessary as a prelude to a full understanding of how new human rights norms emerge and become part of the social context of international politics. Mature norms as shared standards of behavior represent the outcome of a process of socially mediated communication that draws from the articulation of tradition, interest, and moral principle, and places new knowledge in the context of those standards. Habermas notes that normative legal guarantees are grounded and defined through an inherently "unsteady" social process: "The institutions and legal guarantees of free and open opinion-formation rest on the unsteady ground of the political communication of actors who, in making use of them, at the same time interpret, defend, and radicalize their normative content."[45] In the human rights arena, interaction concerning potential legal norms of human rights began, historically, in the absence of strong institutional guarantees.

PHASES IN THE EMERGENCE OF HUMAN RIGHTS NORMS

From the case research presented in the chapters to follow, I have identified four phases in the emergence of human rights norms as a case of principled norm emergence. In the first phase, the groundwork for norm emergence is laid by the discovery and interpretation of facts. The publication and discussion of those facts comprises the second phase of building consensus among advocates of new norms and defenders of the status quo. The process may continue with the construction of discrete legal norms, which is the third phase. The application of newly created norms with regard to state behavior forms a fourth phase.

Phase I: Fact Finding

The first phase in norm emergence that I identify is the fact-finding phase. It forms a basis for all other steps in the emergence of new norms. In this phase, information about specific human rights violations is brought into the open.

When AI began collecting information on prisoners of conscience, there were no UN mechanisms for human rights monitoring. However, the situation is different now. The current institutional context is comprised of an array of monitoring mechanisms sponsored by the UN and regional organizations to publish and interpret information about human rights. NGOs are now widely recognized for their role in providing informational fodder for the operation of monitoring mechanisms. A less theorized but potentially more important function of NGOs is their role in independently interpreting and publishing information as a step in highlighting the gap between facts and normative expectations. To do so sets in motion the kind of reasoning and use of evidence that fosters deeper discussion and potential consensus about questions of right and wrong that must be worked out before formal legal norms can be constructed and ratified. In this phase, it is the NGOs' established history of accuracy, independence, and impartiality that will determine their credibility and authoritative power within international political and public arenas.

The case studies show that information about human rights abuses becomes a node around which clarification of existing normative standards can take place. The simple preservation and publication of facts about state-sponsored human rights abuses is a step toward the generation of norms about human rights behavior. Facts cannot be reconstructed in the absence of witnesses or physical evidence. To seek out and preserve the facts of state repression undermines the efforts of states to keep abuses secret.

The human rights problems in this book—torture, disappearances, and extrajudicial executions—represent secret ways that states evade accountability for quashing political protest. Without the facts of the cases, no judgment and no conscience is possible. For this reason, the moment Amnesty International began to collect facts about prisoners of conscience, the groundwork for principled norm emergence was laid. The ability of AI and other human rights advocates to maintain an uncompromisedly principled interpretation of the facts keeps the focus on the moral content of human rights claims.

Phase II: Consensus Building

It is a tragic reality that the impetus to generate stronger norms often comes after international outsiders realize their shocking failure or inability to aid victims of human rights abuses in individual countries. When facts become available, their interpretation by principled actors opens a state's internal affairs to scrutiny, analysis, and deliberation by members of the international community. In the United Nations, certainly, such deliberations are not the preserve of exclusively moral actors. Some states press their own political interests in the guise of moral claims. When interviewed for this study, more than one former Amnesty staff member has commented to the effect that, as Nigel Rodley put it, "the UN often does the right thing for the wrong reasons."[46] Principled motivations are many times congruent with the interests of certain actors. Whatever the motives behind such political deliberations, they provide an opening to the moral argument that states should bow to greater accountability in the face of human rights ideals.

New norms as formal legal rules cannot be engendered without some form of joint recognition of the need for stronger legal protection. To attain this, generalized patterns of abuse must be identified and publicized. The fact that, in a repressive society, those most aware of the need for protection—domestic human rights advocates and monitors, for example—are themselves likely to be targets of repression complicates the generalization process that is necessary for consensus about the need for human rights norms. State secrecy inhibits documentation of patterns of human rights abuses. The process of gathering and interpreting facts about human rights violations, as assisted by international nongovernmental organizations, enables the categorization and summary of state behavior with regard to human rights principles from outside the societies where abuses may be taking place.

NGOs' ability to present a full picture of human rights abuses raises public awareness of problems and encourages the public to demand action on human rights. Insofar as the ugly facts of repression elicit the response that systematic protection ought to be provided, collecting and publishing information advertises the need for norms. Using the expertise garnered through familiarity with the facts and sharing such information among elites, NGOs often can also help to form and direct demand for particular kinds of normative remedies. In sum, the second phase of norm emergence is one that problematizes facts by interpreting them with reference to the beliefs upon which norms rest, then builds a consensus about the need for norms that will serve as more specific guides for behavior.

Phase III: Principled Norm Construction

Developing legal standards that formally elaborate on principles of right and wrong is the third phase, principled norm construction. The primary activity in this phase for human rights involves the drafting of legal norms, but there is much political interaction throughout the process. Norm construction is performed by experts who define human rights problems in language that will accomplish the kind of normative limitations that are desired.

As a background to the norm construction process, states and NGOs compete over whose characterization of a given human rights "problem" will become the standard version. Negotiation also occurs over the level of obligation that will be imposed on states as norms are formalized. In addition, the norm construction phase requires argumentation in light of legal precedent, when precedent can be found. In this phase, publication of facts is still important, but the ability to participate competently in a norm-drafting process becomes important. Margo Picken, AI's former UN liaison, observed that, because they are not trained in human rights, "diplomats are usually less and less competent" as the details of human rights norms become more complex. At the same time, advocacy groups such as AI must remain wary of the ways in which human rights rhetoric may be manipulated for political purposes. To promote human rights principles, advocates "now need more expertise" than they used to.[47]

International norms, especially in legal terms, have almost always been articulated by states. Although it cannot participate in norm drafting at a level equal to that of states, which generally reserve formal negotiation status for themselves in such negotiations, Amnesty International has been an active participant in the norm-drafting process at the UN. It has regularly participated in debates and lobbying over what should be included, or excluded, over nuances of wording, and over the projected and actual implications of how new formal norms may be framed.

As the case studies will show, Amnesty International became a key actor and commentator in the construction of international norms on human rights. Despite the need for specialized knowledge in this phase, loyalty to principle and the ability to invoke a nonexpert public remains essential to NGOs desiring to influence norm construction. Interpretations that draw upon principle carry more weight when implicitly backed by public support, and such consensus enhances the ability to construct effective formal norms.

Phase IV: Norm Application

The fourth phase of norm emergence involves applying new norms to ongoing cases that challenge principles. Norm application, in some ways, represents a new point in a cycle or spiral of norm building, since to apply human rights norms does require information and building consensus as to how those norms apply.[48] However, the concept of a cycle also reflects the fact that norm emergence is a product of reference to earlier principles. The cycle leading to the application of norms becomes smoother as practice becomes more consistent with underlying principles.

CONCLUSION

To describe the norm generation process as a positive, step-by-step process risks implying that norm creation is a fait accompli as long as the principled actor remains steadfast. While I argue that the stewardship of human rights principles by NGO actors has been essential to the creation of human rights norms in the international system, in large part flowing from the fact that these actors have been disinterested yet constant promoters of human rights, I do not assume or wish to insinuate that norms automatically triumph given the right formula. Far from it. The process is a process of repeated trial and frequent error. NGOs and states are often at odds. Behind the description presented here is the assumption that discursive conflict over the content of human rights demands does not produce determinate outcomes, and we cannot assume that the outcomes will always be progressive. However, it is fair to assume that states generally want to minimize or place stringent conditions on multilateral accountability for human rights, while NGOs disregard state protests of sovereignty in favor of an emphasis on conformity with demands based on moral principles. Conceived in the terms of the potential influence of civil society on governance, NGOs may be successful in engendering norms if they are able to use their knowledge and influence to propagate their own interpretations of governmental decisions within the public sphere, thus catalyzing broader support and pressure for change. The degree to which NGOs are linked to principle rather than political interests enhances the legitimacy and moral force of their arguments.

The diversity of actors' attitudes and interests assures that working out international standards in rhetoric and behavior is a contentious process. Therefore, while the case studies I present in later chapters are all successful examples of norm emergence, they are characterized by conflict and backward steps as well. State resistance to constraints of transnational origin has been a relative constant. Among actors, including some states, who agree that stronger human rights standards are desirable, neither all NGOs nor all states have similar goals vis-à-vis human rights protection. Different NGOs balance their practical and symbolic goals in different ways. They sometimes disagree among themselves about normative priorities, and even about the degree to which they will associate themselves with states' established institutional processes.[49]

The theory I present outlines necessary ingredients for principled norm emergence, but it is not a foolproof recipe. Norms can be strengthened or weakened by the skill and knowledge of the actors and by the legitimacy of actors' appeals to principle. Many of the subtleties of the process are best discussed in the context of the case studies.

Chapter Three

TORURE

I N ITS FIRST FEW YEARS, Amnesty International sought relief and
release for prisoners of conscience on a case-by-case basis through its
volunteer adoption groups. However, for AI leaders and members,
familiarity with individual cases of political imprisonment drove home
the need for stronger, preventative international norms concerning prisoner treatment. The frequency of torture in such cases was particularly
troubling. AI recognized the need to try to shape state behavior at a
general level, through norms, as well as in specific cases. To that end,
the organization devised a series of practical actions to promote the
emergence of new norms to prohibit the use of torture by governments.

A study of those actions and events reveals a generalizable pattern in
the emergence of global norms against torture that can be used as a
template for understanding the development of norms on other human
rights themes. The development started with Amnesty International's
dissemination of contemporaneous reports on government use of torture. Those facts contrasted with official international principles of
human rights, and AI deliberately brought attention to the disjuncture
through public campaigning. AI helped to build a consensus about the
need for norms, both among the public and among elites. The moral
and political dissonance generated by the contrast between principles
and practice motivated the construction of norms in the United Nations,
where NGOs collaborated with and advised concerned governments who
had official standing to articulate statements on torture that implied
higher levels of obligation for states. The achievement of new norms
provided new official procedures which AI could use for continued mobilization in a cycle of further fact finding and application of existing standards in light of the newly constructed norms.

THE EARLY PRESCRIPTIVE STATUS OF THE
INTERNATIONAL PROHIBITION OF TORTURE

As a benchmark for assessing Amnesty International's role and impact,
it is important to describe the international legal status of prohibitions
against torture prior to Amnesty's activity. In fact, the international pro-

hibition against torture started out as a "paper" proscription with little force. Before Amnesty International became active on the issue, human rights concepts in general—let alone the prohibition on torture—were rarely applied internationally to persuade, criticize, or interpret states' behavior, which scholars have posited as a measure of the "prescriptive status" held by formal and informal rules in international relations.[1]

Between the UN's adoption of the Universal Declaration of Human Rights (UDHR) in 1948 and AI's founding in 1961, actual cases of torture did not come under international scrutiny. Article 5 of the UDHR prohibited torture, but there was no way to enforce the prohibition. The governments who adopted the declaration in 1948 did not consider it to be a binding document.[2] Rather, the declaration was seen as a symbolic articulation of principles that, if states pursued the question, might later form the basis for binding treaties. As mentioned in chapter 1, in 1947 the Commission on Human Rights of the UN's Economic and Social Council (ECOSOC) declared that it could take no action on specific human rights complaints, a decision that was reaffirmed in 1959.[3]

Although torture had never been defined in international law, on a moral level the concept of torture did not need to be "discovered" or clarified before making a case for its prohibition.[4] It was an old practice, although to the general public it seemed rare enough that news of it still possessed the capacity to shock. The impetus for the prohibition of torture in the Universal Declaration had been Nazi and fascist practices.[5] Standing moral principles and the experience of World War II made it relatively easy to gain the initial consensus on condemning torture. Still, the condemnation had no teeth. There was no provision for pursuing actual cases of torture through international norms—the single exception being that under the Geneva Conventions of 1949, the International Committee of the Red Cross (ICRC) was authorized to investigate prisoner treatment in situations of armed conflict. The ICRC's investigations were carried out privately, in mostly confidential exchanges with governments. In public, the international community had condemned torture only in general terms, never as actually practiced by a specific country. In sum, while states offered qualified endorsement of general human rights principles at the UN, there was very little institutional promotion of those principles and certainly no active implementation in the UN's first two decades.[6] Accordingly, international law prohibited torture in word only, and only in general terms rather than with reference to specific occurrences.

Amnesty's early leaders did communicate frequently with the ICRC, whose findings of torture in the course of its work were echoed in Amnesty's independent prisoner adoption inquiries. In 1966, just five years after AI was founded, its annual membership assembly approved cooperation with the ICRC to "establish the right to investigate alleged cases of torture" outside of situations of armed conflict, and directed AI's national sections to "give the problem of torture special attention."[7] Amnesty had always opposed the torture and other maltreatment of prisoners of conscience, but now it was beginning to decry the use of torture in general. Two years later, AI formally extended its mandate to include work against maltreatment of any prisoner.

The change broadened AI's concerns beyond the plight of prisoners of conscience: in 1968, the organization decided that, from then on, all use of torture should be subject to its watch.[8] The torture case thus provides us with an early view of phases in the emergence of international human rights norms, starting with Amnesty's efforts to report on torture as practiced by governments.

PHASE I, FACT FINDING: THE GREEK CASE

At the beginning of Amnesty International's self-appointed watch against torture, a military coup in Greece focused world attention on the use of torture in "the cradle of democracy." Torture in Greece, and the concurrent loss of political freedoms there after the coup, was particularly salient for onlookers in Europe and the West. Greece was a member of the North Atlantic Treaty Organization (NATO), a member of the Council of Europe, and an important strategic ally of the United States. In contrast to the distress over the coup expressed by most of the West, the U.S. continued to profess diplomatic support for the junta, given Greece's geopolitical position vis-à-vis the Communist bloc.[9]

When the Greek parliamentary government fell to the right-wing military takeover in May 1967, thousands of political prisoners were taken. Immediate arrests reportedly numbered between 2,500 and 6,000, including most prominent political leaders.[10] Coup leaders imposed martial law, clamping down on civil liberties and using terror tactics against suspected opponents of the new regime. Widespread arrests were made in the name of internal security and moral purification. In a broadly publicized example of purification efforts, the junta ordered mandatory Sunday church attendance for children and, in the schools, outlawed long hair for boys and miniskirts for girls.[11] "Beatnik" tourists were banned for a brief period.[12] More ominously, the rules of the state of siege imposed media censorship, prevented indoor and outdoor gatherings, permitted arrest and detention without charge, and replaced all ordinary trial procedures by courts martial.[13] Thousands of people suspected of leftist sympathies were detained and exiled to island prisons in the Aegean. Two weeks after the coup, the Greek minister of the interior estimated that 5,180 people were being detained as suspected leftists and militants on the island of Yioura.[14] Reports of torture also began to emerge soon after the coup.

The Scandinavian governments and the Netherlands brought charges against Greece through the Council of Europe. However, torture was not an immediate cause for Greece's condemnation in intergovernmental halls; in fact, the earliest censure of Greece was based on a technicality. Greece's failure to report and justify its state of siege through formal channels violated the terms of its membership in the Council of Europe, opening the way for Sweden, Norway, Denmark, and the Netherlands to file formal charges in September 1967. By failing to justify the state of siege, Greece had technically derogated from its responsibilities under the European Convention on Human Rights, but the charges made no mention of torture or other specific human rights violations.

Amnesty International sent its own mission to Greece in December 1967.[15] Greece was familiar and accessible for the small, relatively re-source-poor, London-based organization. According to Stefanie Grant, who organized Amnesty's delegation, AI recognized the need for reliable documentation of the then-unconfirmed accounts of torture.[16] Amnesty International's investigative team—two volunteer lawyers, Anthony Mar-reco and James Becket—set up a small office in Athens for four weeks, to receive statements from the relatives of people who had been detained and former detainees themselves. The repeated accounts suggested a pattern of severe mistreatment by Greek authorities. On 27 January 1968, AI publicly released Marreco and Becket's report, *Situation in Greece,* which included first-hand accounts of torture.[17] AI also circulated the report to Council of Europe members' foreign ministries.[18]

Amnesty International's investigation of Greece served as a catalyst for further European governmental action. The Amnesty report's documen-tation of torture substantiated less systematic press reports and prompted the Scandinavian governments to add charges of torture to the "Greek Case" in the Council of Europe. The official Scandinavian memo in the case noted that the countries had acquired new information on torture in Greece.[19] AI's *Situation in Greece* headed the list of documentation ac-companying the memo.[20]

Marreco returned to Greece on a second visit for AI with Dennis Geoghegan in March 1968, this time with the official cooperation of the Greek government. His second report, *Torture of Political Prisoners in Greece,* confirmed the earlier findings and was cited in addition to the first report at a follow-up hearing in May.[21] Reports and private state-ments from trial observers representing AI and the International Com-mission of Jurists (ICJ), as well as international press and television re-ports, supported the allegations at the follow-up hearings.

The new charges alleged not only that torture had occurred, but also that it had been official policy. According to the charges, "the evidence seemed to confirm" that Greek administrative practices "permitted, or even systematically made use of, torture and inhuman or degrading treatment."[22] Further, "complaints confirming torture remained unanswered" as part of a larger pattern, in which "political prisoners and their relatives were subject to constant pressure" and "lawyers were afraid to assume the defence of such prisoners."[23]

Later in 1968, a subcommission of the European Commission on Human Rights published the results of its own investigation, which confirmed and extended Amnesty's findings from Athens by documenting the use of torture in rural areas.[24] The subcommission heard further testimony that year in hearings at Strasbourg, the seat of the Council of Europe, and in Athens in 1969. Marreco, Becket, and Geoghegan testified at the Strasbourg hearings. They were the only witnesses listed who were identified by their NGO affiliations.[25] The pursuit of the allegations in the European Commission forced Greece to withdraw from the Council of Europe in December 1969 under threat of expulsion.

The Greek case provides a dramatic example of how information supplied by Amnesty International enabled willing European governments to act on human rights. By comparison, it also demonstrates the poor development of *global* human rights norms. The UN was by no means poised to act on Greek human rights concerns in 1967. However, it was not completely inactive on apartheid. In that context, ECOSOC adopted Resolution 1235 in 1967, authorizing its Commission on Human Rights and the Commission's main subsidiary body, the Sub-Commission on the Prevention of Discrimination and the Protection of Minorities (referred to below as the Commission and the Sub-Commission)[26] to "examine information relevant to *gross violations of human rights and fundamental freedoms*, as exemplified by apartheid as practiced in the Republic of South Africa . . . [and] racial discrimination as practiced notably in southern Rhodesia."[27] Despite the specific intent to address racial discrimination, the fact that the language framed the issue in human rights terms permitted a broader interpretation.[28]

Some NGOs, including Amnesty International and the ICJ, took advantage of the loophole to submit information on Greece, even though official protocol did not permit them to make oral or written criticism of the human rights records of UN member governments in UN proceedings.[29] AI submitted its January 1968 report to the UN Commission on Human Rights. Greece defended itself before the Commission by saying that its situation should not be compared to South Africa's human rights violations, but that the junta had implemented temporary measures to "save a country that was 'one step from the abyss.' "[30] No significant action in the UN resulted from the reports on Greece. Indeed, ECOSOC reacted to the NGOs' attempt to widen the application of Resolution 1235 by passing a second resolution, Resolution 1503, to make its human rights reviews confidential.[31] In 1972, a UN panel did, for the first time, consider submissions on Greece under the procedure specified by Resolution 1503. The panel had been inundated by 27,000 separate human rights complaints in the preceding year on numerous countries. The bulk of information on Greece was submitted jointly by Professor Frank C. Newman, a noted scholar of human rights law who was acting as voluntary legal counsel for Amnesty International, the ICJ, the International Federation for the Rights of Man, the U.S.-based International League for the Rights of Man, and some individuals.[32] Although the procedure itself was confidential, Amnesty made the contents of its submission public, and Newman spoke with the press. However, the UN took no further action on Greece.[33] The country returned to democratic rule in 1974.

Although only governments could officially challenge Greece's violation of human rights in the Council of Europe, Amnesty's fact finding placed a specific human rights concern at the core of the European case against the Greek government. But the evidence against Greece met a dead end in the UN Commission on Human Rights, the only global arena that could have censured Greece on human rights grounds.

The fate of the Greek case at the global level points to two conclusions about the global status of human rights norms at that time. First, while the UN was beginning to put pressure on southern Africa, the resolution intended to enable submission of information on "gross violations of human rights" only made a pretense of generality. Both Resolution 1235 and Resolution 1503 were controversial at their inception.[34] There was little intergovernmental consensus as to the appropriateness of applying the same general principles to other situations when information became available. Second, merely finding and publicizing information directly to intergovernmental bodies was not sufficient to secure action. Some governments, such as those in Scandinavia and the Netherlands, would act on human rights if they had the right information; many more would not. In general, human rights principles met with spotty acknowledgment and spottier application because corresponding norms were underdeveloped and not well supported by procedures.

Work in the Greek case raised Amnesty's profile among governments and the general public, particularly in Europe. AI also had begun to distinguish itself from the ICRC and the ICJ, the two main globally active rights-related groups with which it had communicated in the previous decade. While the ICJ and the ICRC had stronger ties to international organizations and were better known at the diplomatic level in the 1960s, neither of those organizations had comparable on-staff research arms or the grassroots membership based in national sections that Amnesty could mobilize on behalf of human rights. In order to insure continued direct access to prisoners, the ICRC conducted prison visits in consultation with governments and presumed confidentiality, unless governments chose to release its reports or released a distorted version of its findings.[35] The ICJ, an organization of lawyers with broader concerns pertaining to the rule of law, did not have an ongoing research department or links with the public. Thus, while those three organizations were active on Greece, Amnesty's reporting initiatives in Greece and its ability to coordinate publicity, communication with governments and other NGOs, and sustained research portended its future strengths as an organization.

In these early stages of transnational action on human rights, the NGOs sometimes cooperated to make up for their limitations. For example, circumstantial evidence suggests that AI and the ICJ were able to publicize information that the ICRC was bound not to disseminate. In a joint response to the U.S. ambassador to Greece's claim that the ICRC did not find evidence of systematic torture, the ICRC declined to comment. AI and the ICJ, however, issued a statement saying, "We have evidence that when the Red Cross asked to see prisoners who had allegedly been tortured, they were moved to other prisons to avoid the Red Cross being able to see them." They added that the Greek government had then refused to authorize the ICRC to continue to visit the prisons.[36]

The Greek case did provide a strong reminder, if one was needed, that despite universal condemnation of torture in the abstract, there were very few international-level checks on torture or other human rights violations as practiced by governments. Conversely, Amnesty's ability to monitor and investigate events in Greece also demonstrated that intergovernmental condemnation of torture could be carried out if governments could be convinced to act. Although AI's reports were not particularly welcome at the UN, the Greek case demonstrated that NGO initiatives on human rights at the intergovernmental level had potential. In other words, while facts alone did not necessarily produce action, there might be untapped potential for facts combined with pressure on the UN to implement the moral principles of human rights.

PHASE II, CONSENSUS BUILDING: THE CAMPAIGN FOR THE ABOLITION OF TORTURE

In December 1972, on the twenty-fourth anniversary of the signing of the Universal Declaration of Human Rights, AI initiated a Campaign for the Abolition of Torture (CAT) that was intended to raise public awareness of torture and the need for stronger international norms. A campaign against torture had the potential not only to create renewed international awareness of torture, but also to revive, deepen, and extend the international normative consensus against it. The campaign, Amnesty's first internationally coordinated publicity and lobbying effort, charted a new course for Amnesty International and for the development of international human rights norms.

The plan for an international campaign against torture originated with AI's International Executive Committee (IEC) under Sean MacBride and Eric Baker's leadership. As already noted, MacBride had been a skilled and energetic coalition builder for Amnesty and in his professional capacity as head of the ICJ. He had broad experience working with NGOs and governments at the UN level.[37] Baker, one of AI's founders, had served as interim head of Amnesty for several months after Benenson's resignation. Martin Ennals took over as secretary-general in 1968, and Baker then joined the IEC.

MacBride, Baker, and their colleagues envisioned a unique way to use Amnesty's resources—international public pressure based on information generated by careful research—to press for stronger human rights norms. MacBride wrote in Amnesty's 1971 annual report that "from now on each national section of AI should seek to persuade the government of its own country" to sponsor proposals at the UN that could strengthen Articles 5, 9, 18, and 19 of the Universal Declaration, the articles on torture, arbitrary arrest, detention and exile, freedom of conscience, and freedom of expression, which formed the basic reference points for Amnesty International's mandate. MacBride seemed well aware that such nationally based lobbying could not be promoted by the ICJ and ICRC, which had different members, different working styles, and different mandates, even though they all could agree on the importance of stronger norms to support human rights. In the 1971 report, MacBride noted candidly that the ICRC was "unable and unwilling" to work in such a way.[38]

Consensus Building through Publicity

The campaign strategy was threefold: it included dissemination of information on the international use of torture; enhancement of international legal means to fight torture; and development of new techniques of action to help victims of torture. In accord with the first part of the strategy, Amnesty initiated an international "information programme" on torture.[39] Amnesty planned to publish a thorough, widely distributed report on the worldwide use of torture in order to build public awareness of torture as a problem that occurred worldwide. The publicity was intended both to educate the public and to generate a climate of public support for action on torture. At the same time, Amnesty mobilized its own members to contact their own governments to ask them to support on action against torture in the United Nations.

The core document of the worldwide publicity effort was Amnesty's book-length study, *Report on Torture*.[40] The report, released 3 December 1973, represented "the first attempt by AI to identify a single problem which was global."[41] It described the characteristics of torture, reported on its global use, and cataloged the status of international legal remedies, maintaining AI's characteristically cautious, understated, objective tone. The researchers had ruled out some information as unreliable; in other cases, information was simply unavailable. For example, the report acknowledged that for several countries "believed to practise torture on a large scale as an administrative policy," information was not included because the facts simply could not be corroborated.[42] Despite the investigative obstacles, the report was geographically balanced to the extent possible. It chronicled torture and ill-treatment in sixty-one countries, although several Asian countries were missing: China, Thailand, Burma, and parts of Southeast Asia.

Consensus Building on the Need for Norms

In the second component of the campaign strategy, Amnesty advocated the pursuit of changes in international law at the UN in order to shore up the UN's rhetorical commitment to human rights. To that end, AI enlisted the help of experts and the public.

Through a series of regional expert study conferences during the campaign year, Amnesty initiated expert discussions on how to combat torture legally, medically, and politically. For example, Niall MacDermot, who had succeeded Sean MacBride as head of the ICJ, addressed a meeting hosted by AI's British section on the "present laws and remedies, and their inadequacies" with regard to torture.[43] In Norway, physicians and mental health professionals gathered to discuss physical and mental aspects of torture. The Belgian AI section hosted a conference on torture's socioeconomic and political aspects. Other meetings took place in West Germany, Ireland, Canada, Mexico, Switzerland, New Zealand, the United States, and Australia. The meetings included representatives of seventy-five different organizations, including the ICRC, the ICJ, the United Nations Economic, Social, and Cultural Organization (UNESCO), the UN Information Office, and numerous religious organizations.[44]

AI's legal efforts were necessarily incremental. If the United Nations could agree on a statement explicitly condemning torture, a small first step, it would be reaffirming the prohibition of torture in the Universal

Declaration of Human Rights. The long-term significance of such a change was unpredictable at the time; it was a fact of life that, like much of international law, its implications would have to be determined through later interpretation and application. Further, governments were unlikely to oppose a symbolic reaffirmation of resolve against torture. AI knew, however, that more ambitious political and legal efforts would have to be built on the earlier steps, meaning that a new UN statement against torture could provide an opening for constructing more specific norms on the basis of reaffirmed moral principles. Through some sort of "continuing international machinery," said an AI newsletter during the campaign, the organization hoped to "establish the Campaign for the Abolition of Torture as a world concern, thereby breaking through the popular conception that the treatment of the citizen is the concern of the sovereign state alone."[45]

Legal efforts at the UN took place at the level of government diplomats and legal elites. However, Amnesty planned not to depend on convincing governments through private consultation, an approach twentieth-century NGOs had taken before on sensitive and, for governments, potentially embarrassing issues such as slavery or prison conditions. For Amnesty, members of the public were important participants in the development of norms on human rights, since public opinion mattered to government leaders. Accordingly, AI sought to educate and involve the public in order to support elite-level efforts to develop stronger UN norms.

The main project for members during CAT was a very public campaign for a UN resolution that would be a first official step in articulating global concern about torture.[46] As part of the drive, Amnesty members gathered one million signatures on a petition, entitled "International Appeal to President of the General Assembly of the United Nations," imploring the UN General Assembly to "outlaw the torture of prisoners throughout the world." The singer Joan Baez publicized the opening of the petition drive at a London concert on April 4, 1973, and became its first signatory.[47] The appeal was delivered to the UN with a certificate signed by the conference officers of AI's Paris Conference on Torture, attesting to the number of signatories.[48] Amnesty estimated that the petition was the first contact with Amnesty for most of the individuals who signed it. Signers came from eighty-five countries.[49] The petition served both as a publicity tool and as a tangible indicator of consensus about the need for UN action on torture.

All of AI's national sections participated in the 1973 campaign.[50] Although Amnesty groups at that time often communicated directly with AI's International Secretariat, London charged the national offices with directing and coordinating the thematic activities on torture in each country. The national sections advised members how to lobby their own governments to support international action on torture. In CAT and other Amnesty campaigns to follow, recalled Nigel Rodley, AI's former legal adviser, the strategy of enlisting the public in lobbying their own governments enhanced Amnesty's ability to influence governments: "by being a grassroots movement, we essentially had embassies in a large number of countries, . . . which . . . could, and did, approach their governments on our concerns. And not only that, it was not just like any other embassy, but it was an embassy which reflected a constituency in their own countries. So they weren't just talking about this foreign body, Amnesty, to their foreign ministers; they were talking about themselves."[51]

CAT thus raised the issue of torture worldwide among governments and the public. The emphasis on using AI members to lobby their own governments fostered the growth of the Amnesty organizations within countries, and helped to build a membership base in each national section. Thus, the publicity efforts of CAT did not only help to build a broader consensus for new legal norms, but they also increased AI's links with the public, governments, and other rights-related groups, and broadened AI's capacity for lobbying.

New Action Techniques against Torture

In the third component of CAT, Amnesty organizers devised practical techniques to help members fight the use of torture. Amnesty's emphasis on the welfare and freedom of individual victims of human rights abuse had not diminished. Thus, AI used the expert conferences and other meetings throughout the campaign to continue searching for concrete techniques that could help protect individuals at the point of arrest and soon afterward. Amnesty needed some way of monitoring, responding to, and, if possible, preventing torture in individual cases, but faced a stiff challenge given the slow pace of its established research and group adoption processes.

The techniques used in preparation for and during CAT built on AI's traditional ways of supporting prisoners. Throughout the campaign, reports on individual countries highlighted the use of torture.[52] Amnesty's monthly newsletter for members also featured the stories of prisoners of conscience who had been tortured. During Amnesty's annual "Prisoner of Conscience Week," in October 1973, the cases of ten prisoners of conscience who had been tortured were highlighted for increased letter writing by the wider membership in addition to the prisoners' adoption groups.[53]

Further innovation was required to respond to the individual suffering that resulted from torture. AI members endorsed the need to expand the organization's tactics. At AI's 1973 International Council Meeting, members endorsed a report on techniques which recommended that the "old" techniques of letter writing and postcard campaigns should be expanded and updated through the use of "publicity and pressure techniques" and the development of "fast-working and effective national lobbies."[54] A consensus formed within Amnesty during the CAT year that a swift response was essential to dealing with torture, since torture frequently occurred during the first hours or days of detention. Group adoption took too long to have much effect on the use of torture. Moreover, AI was committed to working against all use of torture, but not all torture victims would qualify for adoption by groups as prisoners of conscience. Edy Kaufman, a scholar from Israel who first became involved with Amnesty during CAT, recalled that Amnesty had learned that "when you work on cases of torture you have to work quickly." He said that the original idea was to develop a "network of participants" who would send telexes to relevant government authorities when AI received word of individual cases of torture or potential torture—"there were no faxes yet."[55]

As a result of its discussions, AI developed and implemented an "Urgent Action" network in mid-1974 as a quick-response method. Amnesty sent Urgent Action (UA) bulletins directly to participating AI members, who would immediately muster "cables and express letters from individual participants around the world on behalf of a person known by name who is at risk of being tortured."[56] The Urgent Action process bypassed the potentially time-consuming process of investigating a case for potential group adoption. That could come later, if adoption by AI would help the individual. All that was needed to set Urgent Action in motion was a reliable report that a person had been, or might be, tortured.

The process that originated with CAT had potential for use in other kinds of cases. In 1976, AI expanded the scope of the UA technique to address a broader range of situations under AI's mandate when a quick response by the membership might protect a person.[57] Now, many Urgent Action participants receive Amnesty's bulletins via electronic mail and can respond by fax, shortening response time dramatically.

Torture in World Politics: The UN's Response to CAT and a Coup in Chile

The anti-torture campaign had a noticeable "impact on the media, public opinion, and the sensitivity of governments" to torture.[58] International interest intensified even further amid reports of a violent coup in Chile against President Salvador Allende's government in September 1973, just as CAT was in full swing.

Allende's idealism had drawn international interest in whether his democratic socialist "experiment" would be able to accomplish radical social change in Chile through democratic means. Despite bitter contestation, Allende's party had managed to maintain its congressional majority at the three-year midpoint of his presidential term in March 1973.[59] However, the level of behind-the-scenes conspiracy, terrorist incidents, public protests, and counterprotests remained high. Then, on 11 September 1973, the military coup led by General Augusto Pinochet produced an immediate wave of government-sponsored arrests, executions, and disappearances. Allende died during the coup. The violent ouster of the democratically elected president "profoundly shocked international public opinion."[60]

THE EXPERIENCE OF A CHILEAN PRISONER OF CONSCIENCE

A pattern of repression emerged in Chile as a result of the government's strategy, which targeted a wide range of suspected opponents. Coca Rudolfi, a young actress working in Santiago, opposed the coup and was active in the actors' union in Santiago, but did not consider herself any more involved in politics than most of the people she knew. She had been pouring her energy into a nascent acting career. A few months after the coup, she was arrested and tortured without knowing what she had done to draw the attention of authorities.[61]

Men dressed as civilians appeared at Rudolfi's apartment one night after the 11 P.M. curfew that had been imposed under the coup. They searched the place, turning everything upside down, and took her away to a military barracks. There, they took her to a small room and made her undress. Rudolfi remembered that she surprised the soldiers by taking off all of her clothes, even underwear, voluntarily—but on the way to the barracks she had sneaked an address that she did not want them to find from her purse into her underpants, and she knew that they would see it if she did not remove everything herself. The men blindfolded Rudolfi and fastened her legs and wrists to a kind of bed with a surface of wooden slats, threatening her with rape. They did not carry through with that threat, but there, for the rest of the night, they touched her private parts and tortured her with electric shocks.

Ruldolfi lost consciousness three times during the night of torture. At one point she felt herself having an out-of-body experience; despite the blindfold, she felt she could look down and see her own body in the room and the faces of the men who were torturing her. The seizures produced by the electrical shocks caused her head to thrash against the hard "bed" upon which she was restrained, leaving her with a permanent hearing loss in one ear that eventually required an operation. She remembers thinking that she was probably going to die. But in the morning, the torture stopped, and she was put in a dark cell the size of a small closet, where she was held in solitary confinement for a week. She was then moved to a women's prison to await her *consejo de guerra*, the military trial to which many political detainees were subjected after arrest in Chile. She later learned that there was a group of about eight actors in her circle who had been arrested at about the same time.

Somehow, through a route unknown to Rudolfi, word of her situation traveled from Chile to London, and a German Amnesty International group adopted her as a prisoner of conscience. Amnesty's records on its adoption cases are kept confidential. However, in keeping with Amnesty's commitment to shining light on human rights violations while protecting the victims, the appeal for Rudolfi's release was broadly public: in October 1974, Rudolfi was included in a group of twelve people from all over the world whose cases Amnesty publicized during its annual Prisoner of Conscience Week.[62] Prisoner cases featured in wider Amnesty publicity, whether as part of Prisoner of Conscience Week or "Prisoner of the Month," a regular feature of the newsletter at the time, could generate heavy action by the membership. Such efforts were often mounted to boost action in difficult or long-term cases. While in a typical prisoner adoption only one or a few groups would act, a "massive letter-writing campaign" could be set in motion by a special feature.[63]

During the imprisonment, Rudolfi was unaware of her adoption by Amnesty. She had not even heard of Amnesty International. Her father, a retired Admiral, visited government officials on Coca's behalf to try to speed her release. He was told by a navy captain that there was a "problem" in Rudolfi's case: there were people outside who were making "such a big noise" about her that it was causing "difficulty." Rudolfi's father, who was able to visit her twice weekly once she had been moved to the women's prison, told her on one visit that the officer had said that she should "tell Amnesty International to stop," and that if Amnesty kept making such a fuss, they would not let her free. But there was nothing Rudolfi could do, since AI's adoption campaign seemed to come out of thin air.[64] Her case was also publicized by smaller solidarity groups in the United States.[65] Eventually, according to Rudolfi, her father told her that "this pressure, these people outside were making such a big noise that apparently the only thing [the authorities] wanted was to get rid of us in one big trial." Rudolfi and her acting colleagues were brought before a military tribunal, with no stated crime, and were released in early 1975, after fifteen months of confinement.

The Pinochet government regularly made legal arrangements to deport people whose sentences by military courts had been commuted.[66] Ruldolfi was not forced to leave, and did not really want to leave Chile, but she was offered a visa to Britain through Equity, the actors' union.

Her father advised that she go, lest she be detained again, and she decided to accept the visa.

A week after her arrival in London, a fellow exile suggested a visit to AI's headquarters in London. She was curious to see and thank her mysterious guardians, although she still knew almost nothing about Amnesty International or its prisoner adoption process. Staffers stopped their work to celebrate her arrival as soon as she announced herself at the front desk. She recalled their exclamations as she was introduced: " 'You are Coca,' " they said, looking at her as if she were a walking miracle. Only then did she realize that "they had followed everything" about her case. Even though she was an actress, Rudolfi knew of few photographs of herself that might have been publicly available, yet Amnesty had somehow even gotten her picture.

Rudolfi never figured out how her case became known to Amnesty. She gave public talks for Amnesty during her exile in Britain, but her acting opportunities there were limited since English was not her native tongue. She was photographed standing outside Amnesty's London headquarters for a fifteenth-anniversary profile of Amnesty International in the London *Times* in 1976.[67] When Chile returned to a democratic government in 1990, she was able to return home, and by 1992, she was acting on television in Santiago.

Rudolfi's experience highlights both the strength and the weakness of prisoner adoption, which is still a core activity of many AI members, but was practically Amnesty's only method of public mobilization before CAT. The genius of the adoption method lies in its attention to the individual. Authorities find it difficult to ignore numerous cordial but persistent inquiries about specific prisoners. On the other hand, adoption only works one-person-at-a-time. It was not fast enough to prevent the torture Rudolfi experienced early in her detention. Further, it does not address the sources of widespread patterns of abuse. In contrast, CAT emphasized a categorical prohibition of torture through its focus on norms. At the individual level, AI's new Urgent Action technique expanded both the range of methods for fighting torture and the number of cases AI could take on.

TORTURE IN CHILE

As in Greece, NGOs took the lead in bringing the facts out of Chile. Although delegations from the International Red Cross, the UN High Commissioner for Refugees, and the Inter-American Commission for Human Rights visited Chile almost immediately, Amnesty and the International Commission of Jurists initiated their own investigations as they had done after the Greek coup. Amnesty quickly sent a three-person team on a week-long investigative mission that began on 1 November 1973.[68] Its findings of torture, summary executions, and detention without trial were confirmed by an ICJ visit in April 1974. AI sent two more representatives to Chile in the spring of 1974 to observe military tribunals.

While AI's research scope was not yet truly global, its coverage of Latin America was intensifying in the early 1970s. On their early visits, Amnesty and the ICJ established contact with the leaders of the Chilean human rights groups that were forming. One of the first was the Comité de Cooperación para la Paz en Chile (Committee of Cooperation for Peace in Chile, referred to below as COPACHI or Comité), an ecumenical group organized in October 1973. At its core was a small group of Chilean lawyers. Their contacts with outside groups helped get human rights information out to international observers, and this external attention helped to protect the domestic actors. Roberto Garretón, a founding member of COPACHI, recalled almost daily telephone contact with AI, and regular, but less frequent, contact with the ICJ. Amnesty "used to call at nine in the morning," he said. The Comité kept track of arrests on a national scale and helped relatives to prepare petitions of *amparo*, the Chilean version of habeas corpus, to seek information through the courts on the detained and disappeared. The Comité regularly exchanged information with Amnesty about detainees and new arrests, both by phone and by mail. Garretón estimated that about 90 percent of the information mailed from Chile actually arrived at AI headquarters, which he viewed as a fairly high percentage. Nevertheless, "it was a mystery, sometimes, how they knew about arrests," he affirmed. At times, Amnesty had information before he did.[69]

José Zalaquett headed the legal department at COPACHI before he was arrested and exiled in 1975. Zalaquett, who later joined Amnesty's International Executive Committee, recalled his first acquaintance with AI through COPACHI. He was not present when the AI team first visited Chile, but he said, "I remember that Amnesty sent [their] draft report for us to correct it, any mistakes, before they published it, and I was impressed by that . . . we established a working relationship with them whereby we would send them information and they would sometimes funnel, through us, relief money for families. Because they trusted that we would do that in a non-partisan, serious way. And information, support, relationships, and so forth developed over about two years."[70]

The confluence of events in Chile melded with AI's public campaign against torture to spur international interest in torture at the UN in late 1973. At the global level, Amnesty raised the torture issue before the public and government officials using its research for the *Report on Torture* and the ongoing stream of information from its routine contacts with Chile and other countries. The information AI commanded belied international adherence to the principles articulated in the UDHR and reinforced the need for stronger norms at the global level. Through CAT, AI was engaging governments not just over their practices or treatment of prisoners, but also in direct pursuit of new international legal mechanisms to respond to torture.

Observers widely acknowledged that AI's campaign served as the stimulus for the decision of the sponsoring governments to bring torture before the General Assembly at that time.[71] The Swedish delegation, together with those of Austria, Costa Rica, the Netherlands, and Trinidad and Tobago, submitted the initial resolution. Galvanized by events in Chile, the General Assembly adopted the first UN resolution on torture on 2 November 1973, only two weeks after the Chilean coup. The resolution, adopted unanimously, expressed "grave concern" over the continuing practice of torture, reiterated the rejection of torture expressed in Article 5 of the UDHR, and urged all governments to become parties to international instruments outlawing "torture and other inhuman or degrading treatment or punishment."[72] UN condemnation of torture at that time was strongly associated with "the expression of world-wide disgust at the brutality of the overthrow of the Allende government."[73] Numerous official statements at the UN referred to Amnesty International's initiatives.[74]

Such focus was rare for UN human rights discussions. The resolution itself was introduced under an agenda item not originally intended to permit discussion of specific human rights problems. When the sponsors were criticized for using a general agenda slot to discuss the specific problem of torture, the Dutch delegate replied that directing attention to real problems was "the only way we can ever escape from the abstract vagueness which so often tends to turn our discussions on human rights into academic and frustrating debates."[75]

While the resolution did not commit the UN to monitoring efforts, it paved the way for further consideration of torture by expressing the General Assembly's intention to examine the issue again in the future. Afterwards, torture was brought annually before the UN in a variety of venues, frequently with reference to facts in the high-profile case of Chile. AI was a guiding force behind many of those efforts.

THE PARIS CONFERENCE

The campaign year culminated in the World Conference on Torture, hosted by AI on 10–11 December 1973 in Paris. The conference was to be a summing up of the year's efforts, to include experts, government representatives, AI staff, and Amnesty members. Its purpose was "to establish the strategy for a continuing campaign against torture and to draw up an effective program to eradicate it."[76] However, last-minute governmental trepidation almost wrecked the conference plans when UNESCO, which had contracted to let AI use its Paris headquarters for the meeting, canceled the contract. UNESCO claimed that the *Report on Torture* was a conference document, thus placing the upcoming conference in violation of a UN rule prohibiting direct criticism of member governments.[77] Sean MacBride blamed the decision on pressure from some governments mentioned in the report.[78] The French AI section had to scramble to locate a new venue in time for the conference.

Between 250 and 300 invited experts and delegates were divided into four "commissions" for the duration of the conference, each with the task of constructing "detailed proposals on how best to stop the use of torture."[79] The commissions were arranged thematically to follow up on and advance the findings of the regional conferences on torture that had preceded the conference. Commission A tackled problems of identifying the persons and institutions responsible for torture. Commission B looked at socioeconomic and political factors contributing to torture. Commission C assessed the legal features of the problem of torture. Commission D was charged with the consideration of medical aspects, both physical and psychological, of torture. The conference recommendations, published in the report of the conference, set AI's agenda for future norm construction on torture.

In this way, the second, consensus-building phase of norm generation on torture was essentially engendered and defined by Amnesty's Campaign for the Abolition of Torture and its series of international conferences. AI not only reported on torture, but presented information in the context of a public demand for normative change. AI built consensus about the need for attention to torture through several routes: consultation with experts; collaboration with sympathetic governments and nongovernmental organizations; and public pressure. However, as the earlier case of Greece had shown, widespread disapprobation of torture did not produce normative change by itself. From that point on, when a demand for action was implied by the problematic facts, AI stepped in with ideas—and sometimes draft texts—for incremental normative change as part of the solution.

CAT pioneered a way for NGOs to become major players in setting the UN's human rights agenda. Initially, only AI, a few fellow NGOs, and a limited number of sympathetic governments actively worked for normative change on human rights, but CAT blazed a trail for future attention to torture by creating an international consensus that the problem of torture required norm-building action.

In ensuing years, CAT provided a prototype for AI's campaigns on other human rights problems. Coordinated by an organization that relied on politically nonpartisan, objective investigation, CAT confirmed the potential power of using facts and principles to inform communication with governments and the public over actions previously hidden from public view. CAT also demonstrated the usefulness of planned conferences and workshops to bring officials, activists, and legal experts together to study a human rights problem and formulate a response that could be implemented both at the elite level and through the members. Further, CAT demonstrated that, even in an intergovernmental body like the UN, political will could be mustered to deal with human rights abuses.

Although it was only an early point in the broader time line of norms on torture, CAT is one of the most clearly documented examples of the positive impact of NGO activity on global norm emergence. Theo van Boven, director of the UN Human Rights Division from 1977 to 1982, commented that CAT was a major component of a "process leading to a series of international instruments on the protection of persons subjected to detention or imprisonment in the UN General Assembly."[80]

PHASE III, NORM CONSTRUCTION: BUILDING A NORMATIVE FRAMEWORK FOR TORTURE

Based on recommendations made at the Paris Conference, AI decided to continue its campaign against torture. A major part of its continuing work would now include "[lending] its expertise where possible and relevant to the work of the United Nations to abolish torture."[81] The IEC established the CAT as a permanent department of AI's International Secretariat, to be known as the Campaign Department, early in 1974.[82] The Campaign Department began as a two-person operation, working with the Research Department and AI's other new department, the Legal Office, not only to further mobilize members of the public on behalf of prisoners, but also to apply AI's knowledge and experience of human rights problems to efforts to develop legal norms at the UN.

The Legal Office at the International Secretariat was, at first, one person: Nigel Rodley had advised AI throughout most of the original campaign after his hiring as legal officer and part-time researcher on North America on January 1, 1973.[83] The Campaign and Legal departments, while modest in size, anticipated a global audience, both public and governmental, for Amnesty's concerns. While previously Amnesty's researchers had collected and managed information primarily for the purpose of prisoner adoption, the decision to continue CAT required major adjustments for the Research Department, noted Dick Oosting, a former staff member of AI's Dutch section who joined the International Secretariat staff to establish the permanent Campaign Department in 1974.[84] In addition to the prisoner work, AI researchers now had to prepare information to be shared more broadly as well as to inform Amnesty's efforts to influence the construction of new norms on torture. The integration of CAT into Amnesty's organizational structure was more or less complete by 1975.[85]

Amnesty stepped up its activity in the UN in tandem with its new goals for CAT and the continuing crisis in Chile. The increasing interaction with the UN required close attention to the annual cycles of the UN calendar. The main human rights body under the UN Charter, ECOSOC's Commission on Human Rights, meets in Geneva during the first three months of the year. Its Sub-Commission on the Promotion and Protection of Human Rights (then known as the Sub-Commission on the Prevention of Discrimination and the Protection of Minorities) meets in August. The Commission makes recommendations to the whole Economic and Social Council, which meets for a week in May and then convenes for a full session in June and July, in preparation for the General Assembly session that lasts from September through December.

Thus, in early 1974 AI submitted to the Commission on Human Rights the report on its November 1973 delegation to Chile. AI and other NGOs also testified on Chile before the Sub-Commission that year. The next autumn in New York, the UN General Assembly adopted a second resolution on torture, which was drawn up by the Netherlands and Sweden in consultation with Austria and Ireland. The Dutch government, especially, had been in close touch with Amnesty on the torture issue. The UN's 1974 resolution concerning torture followed upon the previous year's resolution by emphasizing the need to develop legal recourse and protection for victims. Without naming Chile, the resolution characterized the need for normative remedies as a response to "the increase in the alarming reports on torture."[86]

The efforts to get the UN talking about torture did not stop with resolutions pertaining to the UN's routine annual meetings, however. In a move that drew some criticism at the time for extending human rights concerns to UN bodies outside of the Commission on Human Rights, the 1974 resolution directed the World Health Organization (WHO) and the upcoming Fifth UN Congress on the Prevention of Crime and Treatment of Offenders (referred to below as the Crime Congress) to address the practical issues related to torture that lay within their purview.[87] In the resolution, General Assembly directed WHO to draft a code of medical ethics for the treatment and protection of prisoners against torture. The General Assembly directed the quinquennial Crime Congress, whose next meeting was approaching in 1975, to consider adding a prohibition against torture to the Standard Minimum Rules for the Treatment of Prisoners, which had been adopted at the first Crime Congress in 1955, and to develop a new code of ethics for law enforcement personnel.[88]

The use of technical conferences within the UN system to develop ethical and professional standards for law enforcement officials and medical professionals was Amnesty's idea.[89] AI staff and the other participants in the CAT year's conferences on torture were familiar with the detention conditions in which torture takes place. Certain occupational groups—doctors, police, prison officials—were most likely to have contact with detained persons. That is why AI's Paris Conference had recommended the articulation of standards that, in practical ways, could prevent or mitigate torture and other cruel and maltreatment by medical practitioners and law enforcement officials. UN endorsement would add legitimacy to such standards, which could potentially form important legal reference points for the conduct of any government's civil servants. And, not to be overlooked, UN articulation of such standards would give Amnesty International yet another basis for putting pressure on governments in the fight against torture.

The 1974 General Assembly resolution therefore offered a new opening for the development of international legal standards on torture, although their substance was yet to be determined. With that in mind, AI prepared assiduously for the Fifth Crime Congress, drafting written proposals and organizing preparatory seminars for law enforcement officials and interested NGOs and governments. In its work preparatory to the Crime Congress, AI occupied—especially for that time—an unusually prominent position for an NGO working with sympathetic governments. A law enforcement–ethics conference in the Hague for Western European police officers prior to the Crime Congress was cofinanced by the Dutch government and law enforcement unions, and cosponsored by AI's International Secretariat and the Dutch AI section.[90] The "Declaration of the Hague," drawn up at the AI-sponsored conference, was presented by the Netherlands for consideration at the Crime Congress and became one of two main working documents there.[91] It contained ethical principles for law enforcement officers, including the right to disobey orders that contradicted principles of human rights and the duty to disobey orders to torture, execute, or otherwise harm a person in custody. AI and the Internation Commission of Jurists also collaborated to draft a code of ethics for lawyers prior to the Crime Congress.[92]

AI sent its secretary-general Martin Ennals, legal adviser Nigel Rodley, CAT organizer Dick Oosting, the president of AI's French section, and two other representatives to the 1975 session of the congress.[93] They lobbied governments and participated to the full extent permitted by UN conference rules. Amnesty submitted sixteen pages of recommendations, including a proposal that the congress ask the UN General Assembly to declare torture to be a crime under international law. AI distributed the proposals directly to fifty governments prior to the congress and asked AI national sections to press their governments to support the proposals in the UN.[94] As part of the official program, Amnesty also held two seminars during the congress to discuss legal, ethical, and professional aspects of torture and prospects for strengthening the Standard Minimum Rules for the Treatment of Prisoners.[95]

The Crime Congress demurred from adopting any proposals on professional conduct, but recommended that the General Assembly appoint a committee to study the matter. At its session later in 1975, the General Assembly directed the ongoing UN Committee on Crime Prevention and Control (referred to below as the Crime Committee) to do so.

Amnesty wanted to influence the content of the code with regard to torture. It submitted a statement to the Crime Committee pointing out what it felt were the "most salient features" of the Declaration of The Hague—the declaration that had been drawn up at AI's cosponsored conference—for the committee's consideration.[96] Language in the Declaration of The Hague, for example, addressed not only civilian police, but members of other kinds of security forces that may be involved in arrest and detention in some countries.[97] This broadened language, which found its way into the UN code, was important because security forces frequently became involved in torture of prisoners.

Over a period of years, the Crime Committee drafted what became the Code of Conduct for Law Enforcement Officials, adopted by the General Assembly on 17 December 1979.[98] According to one source, Rodley and Margo Picken worked alongside the committee on the draft.[99] At several points, the code incorporates principles from the Declaration of The Hague, although all of Amnesty's concerns were not addressed, as Rodley has pointed out elsewhere.[100]

The same strategy helped to translate the consensus developed earlier among experts and NGOs into UN standards on the medical front. For its part in following up on the 1974 General Assembly resolution, the WHO cooperated with the two nongovernmental professional groups, the World Medical Association and the Council for International Organizations of Medical Sciences, to draft "Principles of Medical Ethics Relevant to the Role of Health Personnel, Particularly Physicians, in the Protection of Prisoners and Detainees against Torture and Other Cruel, Inhuman, or Degrading Treatment or Punishment," which was adopted 18 December 1982 by the General Assembly.[101]

The Declaration on Torture

The 1975 Crime Congress spent most of its time sowing seeds for more general norms in the form of a draft UN declaration against torture. A working group met at the outset of the congress to plan for how further to carry out the General Assembly's 1974 resolution to explore legal protection for victims of torture and to create guidelines for professionals in contact with detainees. The working group was "informal" in the UN sense, meaning that participation was open not just to governmental participants but to relevant NGOs with consultative status who, in contrast, could only be observers at the formal sessions. This meant that Amnesty International could, and did, participate actively.[102]

Members of the working group agreed that a more authoritative articulation of the Universal Declaration of Human Rights' prohibition of torture was needed, to provide a "cornerstone" for "any action within the United Nations structure to combat this evil."[103] The working group therefore commenced work on a draft of a proposed UN declaration against torture to be forwarded to the UN General Assembly for consideration. If adopted, a declaration would become a strong recommendation that, technically, would not be legally binding, but would at the same time confer the presumption of obligation on all members of the United Nations. Declarations are understood to have a stronger hortatory force than simple resolutions, and declarations often form the basis for follow-up work to elaborate a binding convention, or treaty. Hans Danelius, a Swedish diplomat and lawyer who was then under-secretary for legal and consular affairs of the Swedish Ministry of Foreign Affairs, authored the initial draft of the declaration that became the basis for discussion.[104]

The informal working group delegated its task to an ongoing drafting group, also "informal" and open to all members of the informal working group, that would continue drafting discussions for the duration of the congress. Nigel Rodley attended for AI. According to Oosting, "the Swedish government took it upon itself to initiate the drafting process and we, as it were, fed into that, texts, and bits of texts, and, and our own ideas, and pushed them back and discussed them to see what was compatible . . . with their assessment of what was, in the end, possible to get through."[105]

The draft declaration was adopted by the congress and sent to the General Assembly for consideration. AI again organized support for the declaration through its national sections and through other NGOs with UN consultative status before the declaration was to come up for a vote in the United Nations.[106] AI's secretary-general, Martin Ennals, together with Andrew Blane, of AI's International Executive Committee, lobbied UN delegations in New York before the vote.[107] The draft was officially adopted by the General Assembly on 9 December 1975, as the Declaration on the Protection of All Persons from Being Subjected to Torture and Other Cruel, Inhuman or Degrading Treatment or Punishment.[108]

For the first time, this declaration provided a definition of torture in international instruments. Substantively, the declaration reaffirmed the gravity of torture as a violation of human rights, and proposed specific actions that states should take to prevent torture. It did not explicitly classify torture as an international crime, as AI had originally wished. The Crime Congress, in creating the resolution to explore international legal protection for victims of torture, recognized that although a declaration would be an important step in outlawing torture, an international convention against torture was the ultimate goal.[109]

The structure of the UN Crime Congress and the Crime Committee in this period kept discussions somewhat sheltered from the political conflicts that plagued UN organs more directly connected to the human rights mandate. The geopolitical divides that could obstruct the Commission on Human Rights were only latent at the Crime Congress, and the state representatives to the Crime Congress were, in general, national-level bureaucrats and experts on techniques of law enforcement. They did not necessarily bear the diplomatic mandate to place national interests in the balance as they considered the impact of human rights issues.

The Convention against Torture and Other Cruel, Inhuman or Degrading Treatment or Punishment

While negotiations over a declaration began with a degree of unity about what should be included, work on a binding norm against torture began with several competing drafts. As it had done for the declaration, the Swedish UN delegation initiated work on a convention by organizing broad cosponsorship of an authorizing resolution that was adopted by the UN General Assembly in December 1977. Danelius then authored and submitted a preliminary draft to the Commission on Human Rights on 18 January 1978. His draft was based largely on the declaration, with some additions.[110]

However, a separate, NGO-sponsored draft was already in circulation. The International Association of Penal Law (IAPL) had submitted a draft prepared in consultation with AI and the ICJ on 15 January 1978. Numerous experts on torture had been consulted in the preparation of the IAPL draft, which was more focused and more demanding than the Swedish draft.[111] For example, the IAPL draft had no statute of limitations for the crime of torture, and focused only on torture, while the Swedish draft considered "other cruel, inhuman or degrading treatment or punishment."[112] A third NGO-sponsored draft also circulated. Au-

thored by Jean-Jacques Gautier of the Swiss Committee Against Torture
(SCAT), it primarily addressed the inspection of places of detention.

For NGOs, negotiation to avoid the distracting presentation of competing drafts in an intergovernmental forum was imperative, both strategically and politically. The very process of agreement on a starting draft
could waste valuable time in the UN calendar. Moreover, although NGOs
could participate in consideration of the drafts at the Commission, disagreement about priorities could dilute their influence. The secretary of
SCAT, François de Vargas, later reflected that "this multiplicity was . . .
unfortunate because of the dispersal of efforts which it provoked."[113]

All three drafts were discussed at an NGO meeting of experts in Switzerland in the summer of 1978.[114] Prior to the NGO meeting, Niall Mac-
Dermot, the head of the ICJ, proposed that the SCAT draft be tabled and
considered later, as an optional protocol to the full convention. Gautier
agreed. In the end, the Swedish draft served as the basic document in
the drafting process, and parts of the IAPL draft were incorporated.

The official drafting discussions began in March 1979 in Geneva. In
consecutive years until 1984, an open-ended working group met in tandem with the Commission on Human Rights for one week prior to each
session of the Commission and with occasional meetings during the sessions. Under Commission rules, "open-ended" meant that any of the governments represented on the Commission could attend, and consultative NGOs or other states could participate as observers. (The
Commission had a rotating membership of thirty-two states from 1978–
79 and forty-two from 1980–84.) Thus, NGOs had relatively free access,
if not at the level of member states.

Amnesty had preferred stronger language than that of the Swedish
draft chosen as the basic negotiating document. Perhaps for this reason,
Amnesty exercised a "more limited role" in the drafting of the Convention against Torture than it had during work on the declaration.[115] Still,
AI and ICJ took "an active part" as NGOs in the working group, while
only twenty or thirty member or observer states were usually present.[116]
Decisions in the drafting group were made by consensus.

In line with AI's allegiance to principles as opposed to the practical
efforts of governments to limit their obligations, Amnesty emphasized
the preservation of existing standards while making the convention as
strong as possible. AI's representatives exercised an informed watchdog
role, aware that small turns of phrase could eventually be used to open
or close loopholes of state accountability. For example, Jan Herman
Burgers and Hans Danelius recalled that during the 1983 session, AI
objected to the preamble phrase that ostensibly indicated states parties'
desire "to convert the principles of the Declaration into binding treaty
obligations and to adopt a system for their effective implementation."[117]

Such a phrase could be interpreted as implying that the declaration on its own was not binding. While that would have been true, technically, since the declaration was not treaty law, to compare the declaration implicitly to treaty law could vitiate its customary force, which by then was indeed almost universally accepted (and which AI referred to repeatedly in its work on torture). To eliminate ambiguity, the drafters settled upon final wording that cited the international community's desire to "make more effective the struggle against torture and other cruel, inhuman or degrading treatment or punishment."[118]

Amnesty's otherwise substantial role in constructing norms on torture was circumscribed by UN rules. In informal UN meetings and in nongovernmental meetings, Amnesty played an active preparatory role and was a close consultant in the drafting process. However, during the formal, official portions of the drafting process, small, neutral, and committed government delegations exercised the greatest leadership, often aided in their efforts by NGO expertise, lobbying, and information. The Netherlands and Sweden were critical links between nongovernmental and intergovernmental arenas in the construction of norms on torture. In this way, AI took on an indirect role when norm construction became official.

The political neutrality of Sweden and the Netherlands, like the third-party status of Amnesty, made them effective facilitators of international norm generation at the governmental level. For example, Sweden consulted with governments behind the scenes to initiate the call for a convention in the General Assembly and ensure that a resolution to that effect would pass. Sweden's representative, Hans Danelius, had also held informal consultations on the draft with interested government delegations after the initial drafting session in 1979.[119]

Sweden's brokering status permitted it to help solve the question of how treaty compliance should be monitored. Agreement had been difficult during the first four meetings of the drafting group.[120] The solution was to establish a monitoring body, the Committee against Torture, that would not only receive reports from countries that accepted the treaty, but could also investigate reports of the systematic use of torture. In addition, NGOs were empowered to submit such reports to the monitoring body.

Amnesty later celebrated the innovation for giving NGOs access to the supervisory process. Nigel Rodley, speaking for AI, emphasized the potential for NGO contributions to intergovernmental organizations: "Certainly, the evidence is, in terms of many other international human rights mechanisms[,] that non-governmental organisations that do have the possibility of initiating action by such organisms have been able to contribute mightily to the activities of those organisms."[121] What he did not say was that his own organization had helped create and maintain the channels through which such contributions had been made.

Meanwhile, a draft text of an Optional Protocol to the convention, which would strengthen the enforcement measures of the treaty for the states that chose to sign on, was formally submitted to the UN Commission on Human Rights on 6 March 1980 by the government of Costa Rica. The draft had been developed by the ICJ and SCAT, based on SCAT's tabled convention draft of two years earlier. The SCAT proposal's enforcement measures exceeded those in other international treaties, while the enforcement measures contained in the convention draft chosen for debate were based on similar procedures found in existing conventions.[122] That similarity was considered a strength, since parallel treaty procedures might be more immediately acceptable to states. To avoid delaying the adoption of the convention itself, consideration of the Optional Protocol was postponed again until after adoption of the convention.[123]

By the early 1984 drafting session the draft convention was more or less complete. In a brokering role similar to that played earlier by Sweden, the Dutch chair of the drafting group, Jan Herman Burgers, consulted informally with government delegations to resolve remaining questions and prepare a report, which included the draft convention, for the whole Commission on Human Rights to consider that same session.[124]

It highlights the importance and efficacy of the NGOs and state "brokers" to note that the superpowers were not particularly supportive of the convention. Although the United States participated in the drafting committee of the Commission and strongly advocated the principle of universal jurisdiction, it never became a cosponsor, nor did it sign the convention immediately after it was opened for signature. More pointedly, the USSR led a group of countries that wanted to allow signees not to recognize the supervisory authority of the Committee against Torture, often referred to as "supervisory competence," described in Articles 19 and 20 of the draft convention.[125] During debate before the Commission, NGOs continued to demand nonoptional implementation mechanisms. The secretary-general of the ICJ urged agreement on supervisory competence. He pointed out that although the USSR had rejected on principle "any attempt by intergovernmental organisations to concern themselves with . . . violations," the USSR had recognized in its statements on Chile that the UN had the authority to inquire into cases of "gross and systematic" human rights violations, as outlined in Resolution 1503. The ICJ statement drew an analogy between the principle underlying Resolution 1503 and Article 20 of the Convention on Torture, arguing that the practical difference was only that "Article 20 is more informal and more speedy and therefore better adapted to the international crime of torture."[126] Addressing the commission on the same day, AI's secretary-gen-

eral Thomas Hammarberg stressed the importance of effective enforcement power for the convention given Amnesty's knowledge of torture:
"All governments are nowadays prepared to state that they oppose torture . . . [but] while government after government condemns that practice, Amnesty International and other non-governmental organizations
continue to receive alarming testimonies on what goes on in the interrogation centres in country after country. . . . Not only is torture widespread. It is also systematic in many countries."[127]

The Netherlands' delegate, Alphons Hamer, led the sponsors in making a crucial compromise, conditional upon the withdrawal of other
amendments, that allowed countries to declare upon signature or ratification that they did not recognize the committee's authority to supervise
compliance with the treaty. The draft of the convention was adopted in
the Commission without a vote on 6 March 1984.

To summarize, for torture, formal norms were built and strengthened
sequentially, starting with indications of concern in UN resolutions and
continuing with a more formal declaration, professional guidelines, and
finally the Convention against Torture, which is legally binding for the
countries that sign it. These formal norms serve as markers of international agreement about the reprehensibility of torture, but wide application and behavioral acceptance of the principles behind the norms is
still needed. In applying norms on torture, Amnesty has played a continuing role. In the case of the draft convention, Amnesty began to call for
a stronger enforcement capability as the convention went forward from
the Commission to be considered by the General Assembly.

PHASE IV: NORM APPLICATION, PUSHING FOR
PRACTICAL SAFEGUARDS AGAINST TORTURE

Once the drafting was completed, AI began publicity efforts to support
the passage of the convention by the wider UN. In April 1984, the month
after the convention draft was adopted by the UN Commission on
Human Rights, Amnesty International launched a second Campaign for
the Abolition of Torture. Concurrently, AI published the book-length
report, *Torture in the Eighties*, which reported on the global incidence of
torture from the beginning of 1980 through mid-1983. Approximately a
decade had passed since the origination of CAT.

The outsider identity of Amnesty allowed it to remain a steadfast voice
advocating the principles behind the norms that were being constructed
even as it mobilized support for the convention. In the introduction to
Torture in the Eighties, Amnesty actually criticized the draft convention.
Welcoming stronger norms in principle, Amnesty outlined the points it

held to be "essential" for the draft convention on torture about to be considered by the General Assembly.[128] Since AI would not be able to speak or take part in the government negotiations in the General Assembly, it was now essential that Amnesty influence the debate over a binding convention by eliciting international public pressure and educating the General Assembly members.

The discussion of the convention in Amnesty's new campaign report presented a principled counterpoint to the compromises in evidence in the convention's final draft. AI used the report to address an expanded, public audience, following its consultation with governments responsible for the official construction of norms. Amnesty's familiarity with the drafting discussions informed its criticisms of the weak points of the proposed convention.

Amnesty's criticisms covered four main issues. First, AI said that the unqualified use of the phrase "lawful sanctions" in Article 1 was a loophole for governments, since a government might legislate punishments that might otherwise qualify as torture or other cruel, inhuman, or degrading treatment. Second, AI called for universal jurisdiction involving "no safe haven for torturers."[129] Third, the convention wording did not make its breadth of application explicit. AI urged that *all* articles of the convention apply to torture and other mistreatment. Finally, echoing the comments that the ICJ had made before the commission, AI called for effective, nonoptional implementation mechanisms. In the body of the report, AI invoked the standards against torture that had already been developed internationally, many of which it had helped to create. As part of the campaign, Amnesty also publicized its own "Twelve-Point Program for the Elimination of Torture," a list of recommended actions for governments that prescribes a range of measures such as "safeguards during interrogation and custody" (Point 4) and "ratification of international instruments" (Point 12).[130]

Meanwhile, at the General Assembly, the Netherlands delegation again made sure that the convention survived debate. Within the Third Committee of the General Assembly, to which the draft convention was assigned, some governments wanted to postpone further consideration of the proposed convention on torture. The Netherlands, a newly democratized Argentina, and Sweden cooperated to advance a proposal for adoption before the sentiments for postponement could gel into firm stands.[131] They were eventually joined in sponsoring the resolution for adoption by nineteen delegations.[132] Amnesty's statement at the next year's meeting of the Sub-Commission on Prevention of Discrimination and Protection of Minorities called for ratification of the convention as a matter of urgency.[133]

Special Rapporteur on Torture

After the progress in the creation of formal norms on torture, there still was no formal way for the UN to monitor torture everywhere. The convention would impose a reporting requirement, but only on the signatory countries. The UN Human Rights Commission had sometimes appointed a special expert, called a special rapporteur, charged with monitoring countries experiencing human rights trouble. In the early 1980s, there was an innovation: the monitoring concept was extended to apply to particular problems occurring all over the world, such as disappearances and extrajudicial executions.[134] The special procedures, now referred to as "thematic mechanisms" for their focus on categories of human rights problems rather than on countries, have since proliferated in the UN system.[135] Soon after the completion of the UN convention, the idea was broached to establish a Special Rapporteur on Torture.

Amnesty International, the Netherlands, and Sweden, described by one commentator as the NGO "godmother" and diplomatic "godfathers" of the convention, had some private doubts when the director of the UN Centre for Human Rights suggested that torture needed its own thematic monitoring mechanism, according to the Dutch international lawyer who became the first special rapporteur on Torture.[136] After years of work for a binding treaty, they wanted to see as many countries as possible ratify it as soon as possible. A certain number of ratifications were necessary before the treaty could enter into force, and all other things being equal, there was some question whether establishing a special rapporteur as a separate mechanism would delay ratification, perhaps by reducing the perceived need to sign on to a binding treaty.[137] An argument for a special rapporteur, however, was precisely that the convention would take some time to enter into force,[138] and the kind of monitoring the special rapporteur could provide was not covered by any existing human rights mechanism.

The latter arguments proved persuasive, and Amnesty became a strong supporter of the establishment of the Special Rapporteur on Torture.[139] At the next session of the Commission on Human Rights, in May 1985, the Commission created this position,[140] which was, in effect, a new universal monitoring mechanism.[141] Right away, AI emphasized the preventive possibilities for the new post in its UN statements. While the special rapporteur is not a permanent office, its mandate has been renewed regularly since 1985. Unlike the treaty bodies, which simply receive reports at regular intervals, the special rapporteur can make immediate inquiries to governments as soon as allegations of violations are received. The special rapporteur may also visit the countries of inquiry, which is essential for direct investigation and permits direct UN contact with senior government officials.[142] Menno Kamminga, a former member of Amnesty's Legal Department, wrote in a scholarly article that "human rights workers welcomed the fact that violations could be more easily exposed," while "oppressive governments appreciated the fact that they were not the only ones to be singled out for criticism."[143]

The thematic strategies, which do not depend on a binding treaty for their validity, have reinforced the declaratory norms against human rights violations by creating a means for official UN action based on the collection and interpretation of facts in light of norms. Some of the procedures for UN communication with governments echo AI's Urgent Action technique.[144]

The mandate of a special rapporteur is not highly specific as to exactly what procedures should be followed, so that the strength of the position depends to a great extent on the individual who holds the post. An active individual in the post can broaden the effective mandate. A weak special rapporteur will likely be ineffectual, as has happened occasionally with country rapporteurs. For the thematic mechanisms, however, capable and NGO-friendly experts have often been appointed. The second Special Rapporteur on Torture, appointed in 1992 and still serving as of 1999, was Nigel Rodley, AI's former legal adviser who was centrally involved in standard setting on torture, starting with the UN Declaration against Torture.

Optional Protocol to the Convention

UN consideration of the Optional Protocol to the Convention against Torture, which would offer stronger implementation of the convention through regular visits by UN experts to detention centers, had been postponed during the construction of the convention. It was not forgotten. The UN Special Rapporteur on Torture recommended the adoption of such a system in his second annual report in 1987, as a preventive mechanism.[145] But since, in November 1987, a similar mechanism in the European system was opened for signing as part of the European Convention against Torture,[146] the UN Human Rights Commission adopted a wait-and-see approach, hoping to observe how well the European system of investigation operated before taking further action on the Optional Protocol.

The Optional Protocol was modeled on the work of the International Committee of the Red Cross. The ICRC's visits to Greece in 1971 and to Iran in 1977–78 were cited explicitly by the ICJ as having had the effect of reducing torture in those countries. In the case of UN inspections under the protocol, the experts would report confidentially to governments, but the Optional Protocol reserved the right for the committee to publish its findings if they were not accepted in good faith by the government itself. This last provision, in theory, would provide an incentive for swift remedial action by offending governments upon receipt of findings of torture.[147]

Amnesty joined arguments in favor of the protocol. Arguing before the Commission in 1992, AI argued that there was no need to wait any longer, since "the European Committee for the Prevention of Torture['s] . . . vigorous and thorough work is already well accepted . . . and its detailed working practices could serve as a useful model for a universal system."[148] Progress has been slow, but AI and other NGOs have participated in the Commission's open-ended working group to develop the draft, which as of this writing has continued to meet for yearly sessions since its establishment in 1992.[149]

Conclusion: A Template for Norm Emergence

Amnesty International provided a driving force behind the emergence of norms on torture. One government official involved in the construction of norms against torture reflected that AI served as the "starting motor that brought the whole process [of the UN consideration of torture] into being."[150] Without the antitorture campaign of AI, he said, there would have been no UN Convention against Torture.[151]

The Campaign for the Abolition of Torture was a new kind of endeavor for AI, and its success provided a blueprint for the emergence of norms in the United Nations. The fact that torture was a hidden practice and a serious charge to level against governments required uncompromising standards of informational accuracy. AI's traditional technique relied on addressing governments about specific cases. Thus, when it took on torture, it had to be able to confirm the likelihood or threat of specific instances of torture. For to propound poorly founded allegations in communications from its membership to government officials would impugn AI's credibility and endanger its ability to come to the aid of torture victims.

Understanding the recent history of norms against torture in light of the campaigning techniques forged by AI suggests that NGOs can become influential as third parties in the creation of sets of international norms. Consistent and persistent loyalty to their causes becomes a component of their effectiveness, but political and geographical impartiality also matter with respect to application of their proposed normative agenda. Such characteristics enhanced AI's legitimacy in the fact-finding and consensus-building phases of norm emergence. AI's research served as both an informational resource and the bulwark of its reputation for independence and impartiality, enabling Amnesty to influence and build on consensus about the need for norms in the light of politically high-profile cases. In calling for action in real cases of torture, Amnesty occupied the moral high ground, in that it was invoking a principle that had already been accepted in the Universal Declaration on Human Rights. Amnesty could not be as directly involved in actual norm construction because of the difference in authority between NGOs and states at the international level. Technical expertise mattered most during the norm construction phase, when NGOs had to work with governments to achieve new formal norms. The contacts formed with elites during consensus-building activities also enhanced Amnesty's ability to promote norm emergence. In the final phase, norm application, governments learned from the techniques developed by NGOs in their struggles to promote human rights. Fact finding, impartiality, and independence took on new salience once new norms were drafted; as newer cases could then be framed in light of the norm endorsements already accomplished. Human rights violations, illuminated in large part through NGO-generated information, could then be interpreted by way of stronger international norms.

Chapter Four

DISAPPEARANCES

WHEN DISAPPEARANCES began as a technique of state-sponsored repression in the 1960s, the phenomenon straddled known categories of human rights violations without really fitting into any. The word "disappearance" was a newly coined term for what seemed to be a new governmental tactic. International law did not articulate the idea that a government would kidnap its own people, do them further harm during detention, kill them, and dispose of their bodies—all in secret and without official acknowledgment. But that is what began to happen in Latin America and other regions of the world, beginning in the 1960s and intensifying in the 1970s. The secrecy and the compound nature of the abuses that characterized disappearance stymied existing legal principles pertaining to human rights. A disappeared prisoner might be tortured under detention or deprived of life, but disappearance could not be equated with unlawful detention or with execution because, although abductions were often witnessed, governments refused to acknowledge the disappearances themselves or any participation by authorities in the activity. Physical proof of the fate of the victim of a disappearance was rarely available. There was only government silence, the absence of the victim, and the unresolved grief of those left behind. The legal and human rights dilemmas became apparent as prominent cases of disappearances came to world attention.

FORCED DISAPPEARANCE: A VIOLATION WITHOUT NORMS

Something like disappearances had been practiced by Nazi Germany. Amnesty International traced disappearance-like tactics to a 1941 Nazi policy, the *Nacht und Nebel* ("Night and Fog") decrees of the German High Command, by which Nazis captured suspected resisters in France and elsewhere and secretly transferred them to Germany.[1] Although the Fourth Geneva Convention of 1949 was meant to address the *Nacht und Nebel* crimes by prohibiting cross-border kidnapping during wartime,[2] no one envisioned government-sponsored abduction, secret detention, and denial as a widespread tactic.

In the 1960s and 1970s, military governments throughout Latin America began to use disappearances and politically motivated, extrajudicial killing on a large scale in the name of fighting leftist insurgency. Disappearance had characteristic ideological and institutional roots as a component of state terror. Institutionally, it happened in states where there were close links among government institutions, the military, and a powerful economic elite. Ideologically, disappearances were framed by the doctrine of counterinsurgency or the desire to do away with perceived enemies of the state.[3]

The first named use of "disappearances" took place as part of counterinsurgency tactics employed by the Guatemalan military in response to guerrilla activity, beginning about 1966 in Guatemala's rural highlands.[4] Guatemala's mainly indigenous rural population, as well as trade union members and suspected communists, were killed and "disappeared" in violence that was to escalate in ensuing decades. No systematic governmental or nongovernmental protest came forth internationally when the early abuses occurred. On the contrary, the U.S. presidential administrations of John F. Kennedy and Lyndon Baines Johnson pumped military aid and counterinsurgency training into Guatemala.[5] UN monitoring mechanisms were not established, and even Amnesty did not mention Guatemala until its 1971 annual report. AI then reported that at the request of international trade unions it had written to Guatemala's Pontifical Commission of Justice and Peace and the Organization of American States (OAS), to point out the "recent arrests, disappearances, and murders" of purported opponents of the government.[6] AI's first report on Guatemala was not published until 1976, ten years after the use of disappearances began.[7] Even by that time, "nobody [at the UN] wanted to do anything" about Guatemala.[8]

Thus, the earliest disappearances took place with little international protest. Some of the obstacles were political: especially in the 1960s, international security strategists might have perceived Guatemala as a country strongly linked to U.S. security interests in the hemisphere, but Guatemala contrasted with Greece, for example, in that it did not have a high international political profile, either strategically or symbolically. Although such political considerations were not of great import to AI, AI was a young organization with limited resources when disappearances broke out in Guatemala. It lacked contacts in Latin America at first, and international press coverage of Latin America was sketchy. In addition, from the perspective of Amnesty's prisoner adoption guidelines, human rights violations in the presence of armed guerrilla movements posed a challenge. Armed resisters themselves could not qualify as prisoners of conscience, since Amnesty did not adopt those who had participated in or advocated violent tactics. Further, the guerrilla fighting that characterized conflict in many Latin American countries itself "made adoption and identification" of prisoners of conscience difficult.[9] AI had not yet worked out direct techniques for opposing the newer kinds of human rights violations that were occurring in Guatemala.[10]

The subtle differences between disappearances and political detention made disappearances even more difficult to address by way of existing international principles. In contrast with torture, there was not even a rhetorical prohibition of disappearances in international law on which to build intergovernmental monitoring efforts, and the clandestine nature of detention repudiated habeas corpus remedies, the standard legal method of protecting prisoners against unwarranted detention. Most countries' legal systems have some version of habeas corpus, which enables lawyers to learn the charges against a prisoner and where the prisoner is being held.

While Amnesty took a different approach to human rights than some older, more experienced NGOs, AI had learned from the experience of the International Committee of the Red Cross (ICRC), for example, and acquaintance with ICRC procedures helped to orient Amnesty's very early approach to torture in a way that was not possible for disappearances. Disappearances were new for everyone.

Phase I, Fact Finding: Bringing Disappearances to Light

This study separates disappearances from torture and other forms of human rights abuse for the purposes of tracing the emergence of human rights norms as they apply to different forms of state-sponsored violence. It should be emphasized that this is a false division to some extent. Events and norms pertaining to disappearances emerged at a different rate from those on torture, but some of the same events were proving grounds for norms on several human rights issues. Accordingly, AI's Campaign for the Abolition of Torture, (CAT), by enhancing the organization's capacity for research, lobbying, and direct appeals to governments, had ramifications for work against disappearances. Even though CAT was focused on torture, Amnesty soon applied similar techniques to disappearances. The Urgent Action technique, for example, was broadened from its original focus on torture and applied to other issues starting in 1976.[11]

The need for ways to address disappearances internationally intensified as the use of disappearances spread through Latin America and elsewhere. An explosion of disappearance cases in the 1970s provided new reason for AI and the rest of the international community to examine the shortcomings of international norms on human rights. Pinochet's Chile provided a prominent focal point.

Disappearances in Chile: An International Focal Point

It is sobering to note that, in retrospect, fewer disappearances took place in Chile than in Guatemala or Argentina. After Chile returned to democracy in 1990, the country's Truth and Reconciliation Commission documented 957 cases of disappeared prisoners (*detenidos desaparecidos*), most of which had occurred between the 1973 coup and 1977.[12] However, Chile's high international profile drew criticism not only for the use of torture but for a range of human rights violations, including disappearances.

As explained in the previous chapter, events in Chile served as a central referent for UN action on torture. Collected information, however, did not engage action in the same way with regard to disappearances. Torture had been, like the Prisoner of Conscience, a compelling focus around which to mobilize public concern. The concept of torture was familiar to most people and had required even less interpretation to the general public than had the concept of the prisoner of conscience. Torture was a graphic form of violation; although secretive, it was not mysterious. Torture frequently left victims alive to attest to their experiences. Therefore, on a basic level, Amnesty's task had been to raise awareness that torture was occurring globally. AI offered a way for ordinary people to help, through the letter-writing system it had set up to help free prisoners of conscience and others under threat. Disappearances were a more complex phenomenon, and more needed to be learned, even by the time that *desaparecido* (disappeared person) became a new word in the international vocabulary as a result of the Pinochet coup.

In the flurry of international visits to Chile by Amnesty, the International Commission of Jurists (ICJ), and representatives of the Inter-American Commission on Human Rights that took place in late 1973 and 1974, some complaints of disappearances surfaced. In addition to its anti-torture efforts, Amnesty began a special publicity campaign on behalf of disappeared prisoners from many countries in 1974.[13]

Much fact-finding in Chile was already being performed by Chile's active network of lawyers. Chilean human rights groups sent copies of their case lists to AI, the Inter-American Human Rights Commission, and the UN human rights division in Geneva. Amnesty and the ICJ also made their own efforts to collect testimony and to contact Chilean administrative authorities and the Supreme Court.[14] In most cases of disappearance, rather than deny the arrest, the government simply did not respond: only four of five thousand writs of *amparo* (a rough equivalent of habeas corpus) were granted by Chilean courts in the six years after the coup.[15] Through such filings, however, Chilean human rights activists also cre-

ated documentation of suspected disappearances that could be dissemin-
ated outside Chile with the help of Amnesty and other groups.

The fact gathering on disappearances happened in Chile at a level
which was not possible in Guatemala, for example, where disappearances
were still occurring. The legal procedures available to Chileans, and
Chile's long-standing jurisprudential tradition, provided an active internal network of experienced lawyers who gathered evidence and maintained ongoing communication with external organizations. Guatemala,
on the other hand, had been under continuous military rule since 1954.
Strong, independent judicial institutions, an educated populace, and
other features characteristic of a strong civil society had simply not been
permitted to develop in Guatemala, so similar internal networks and external links were weak or nonexistent there.

While the OAS, the regional intergovernmental organization for the
Americas, issued four successive special reports on Chile between 1974
and 1985, repeatedly condemning disappearances in strong terms,[16] the
OAS met with steadily decreasing cooperation of the Chilean government.[17] The UN was quick to condemn the Chilean coup on 6 November
1974, but its first resolution on Chile did not specifically mention disappearances.[18] The United Nations Ad Hoc Working Group on Human
Rights in Chile, created by the Human Rights Commission 1975, provided a venue for the reception of information on human rights violations, including disappearances.[19] The establishment of the working
group indicated a shift in the UN's approach to human rights. It represented a public focus on a "problem" country, and an implicit call for
international accountability that had rarely been made before. Previously, only southern Africa had been the subject of a UN ad hoc human
rights investigation.

The Ad Hoc Working Group had to pursue its mandate from outside
Chile, however, because Chile refused to cooperate with the UN inquiry.
Chile denied entry to the working group in June 1975. At about the same
time, the Pinochet government released to newspapers internationally a
list of 119 people whose relatives had reported them disappeared, but
who it maintained had been killed "by their own comrades" or in violent
confrontations with police. The report was also published in the Chilean
press. The arrests and suspected disappearance of almost half of these
persons had earlier been reported to Amnesty International. In some of
the cases Amnesty had already asked its members to send "inquiries to
the Chilean authorities" about the missing prisoners.[20] After the discrep-
ant reports came to light, Pinochet ordered an "investigation" into the
matter in August 1975.

The incident described above shows how independent monitoring
could highlight discrepancies between a government's account of sus-

pected human rights violations and independent fact-finding efforts. It shows, at the least, that even governments like Augusto Pinochet's could be interested in preserving at least a pretense of telling the truth. For the international audience, the facts shed light on what was happening in Chile.

Still, the information about specific cases of disappearances did not immediately create a demand for norms that might be applied in later cases. Principles regarding disappearances were only weakly generalized: discussion of disappearances in the UN then was essentially part of high-profile fights over Chile, and soon, Argentina, that were not to be matched in many other cases. More information and greater consensus about the nature of disappearances were needed before new norms could be constructed.

The Case of Argentina

Two-and-a-half years after the coup in Chile, a military coup in Argentina on 24 March 1976 drew further attention to disappearances. Although the coup was no surprise to those following Argentine politics, the coup unleashed repression on a "completely unexpected" scale.[21] While Argentina under the previous leader, Isabel Perón, had experienced a great deal of internal conflict, the right-wing coup brought a dramatic increase in political killings, arrests, kidnappings, disappearances, and torture. The coup makers' Proceso de Reorganización nacional, or Process of National Reorganization, was designed to whip the economy into shape, reduce political corruption, and get rid of "subversives" as part of the process. To that end, the junta under the presidency of General Jorge Rafael Videla implemented a plan that combined severe economic restructuring measures with a policy of purging the country of potential enemies, including categories of people thought to contribute to a climate of subversion, "which could easily include any kind of critic or dissident," or even people with certain occupations, such as teachers, university students, or labor leaders.[22]

The documented number of disappeared persons in Argentina— 8,961 people—exceeded that of Chile by a factor of nine. Over 85 percent of the disappearances occurred from 1976 to 1978.[23] Two other military presidents would succeed Videla in the armed forces' efforts to preserve the Proceso before Argentina's return to democratic rule in 1983, but, as in Chile, the worst of the violence took place in the period initially after the coup, under Videla's leadership.

The kidnappings were carried out by agents of the Argentine armed forces, who secured clearance from local police when an abduction was planned.[24] A disappeared person in Argentina was typically interrogated and tortured in one or more clandestine detention centers. Although a few were released, many others were transferred from one detention center to another. "Transfer" was also a euphemism for illegal execution; prisoners' bodies were disposed of in the ocean, in lakes and reservoirs, and in anonymous graves.[25]

Realizing that a prompt visit to Chile had established essential contact with domestic groups and promoted immediate attention to human rights there, Amnesty consciously applied the Chilean model in its response to the Argentine coup.[26] Patricia Feeney of Amnesty's research department, Fr. Robert Drinan of the U.S. Congress, and Lord Avebury of the British House of Lords comprised an AI delegation that visited Argentina from 6 to 15 November 1976. It was routine for Amnesty to secure official permission for its visits, and the Argentina mission was no exception. However, in sharp contrast with the previous experience of Amnesty delegations on their visits to other countries, where they were usually treated cordially, members of the AI mission to Argentina experienced a threatening level of harassment. "Every single interview we did, every place we went, was staked out," said Feeney.[27]

As in Chile, domestic human rights groups had organized to collect information and search for remedies to human rights violations. Feeney, Drinan, and Lord Avebury met with numerous people and groups working for human rights in Argentina, as well as with government officials. The AI mission established some important personal contacts with people who were beginning to collect information within Argentina on human rights violations and working to coordinate human rights efforts within Argentina and internationally. As a result, Amnesty became an important conduit of information and source of solidarity for Argentine human rights groups, including the groups representing relatives of the disappeared.[28]

The authorities contacted by AI refused to "divulge the identity or number of political prisoners" in Argentina. It was difficult for the investigators to tell whether people who had been arrested were "disappeared," and consequently feared dead, or whether they were still being held as prisoners. The best figure on the number of prisoners available at the time to Amnesty was the estimate of the Argentine minister of the interior, who told journalists on 18 November 1976 that the number of political prisoners was somewhere in the wide range between two and ten thousand.[29]

Despite the lack of precision, it had become evident that the scale of disappearances in Argentina was far beyond that of Chile. International pressure began to mount for an accounting as to the whereabouts of disappeared persons in Argentina. The report of Amnesty's mission to Argentina came out in March 1977. The Madres de Plaza de Mayo, the famous group of mothers of the disappeared who walked in their white scarves every Thursday at noon in downtown Buenos Aires in silent protest, were attracting international attention. Some of the Madres made international trips of their own to the United States, Canada, and Europe in 1978, and testified before the OAS, the UN, and the U.S. Congress in 1979.[30]

The 1978 soccer World Cup, held in Argentina, put the country in the world spotlight. Argentina seemed to regard it as an opportunity for positive public relations, but others saw it differently. AI released a collection of quotes from athletes, journalists, and sports officials. An Argentine official was quoted as saying that the World Cup would be "just the occasion to show the Argentine's real way of life," while players and sports commentators evidenced a range of opinions about the relationship between international sport and politics. Some favored focus on soccer alone, while an Italian athlete eloquently observed that "football is a beautiful jungle where people can live hidden" but "at this moment, the people of Argentina need help."[31] The World Cup prompted debate on Argentina wherever there were avid soccer fans. By that time the Argentine government had completely stopped answering OAS requests for information on individuals.

Chile was also engaged at that time in a kind of standoff with international organizations regarding the facts of human rights abuses. A report on prisoners in Chile's secret detention camps came out in March 1977, and comprised Amnesty's first research report on disappearances as such.[32] Although the Pinochet regime had gained unwanted notoriety for human rights violations, international inquiries only seemed to fuel more Chilean denials. Chile finally permitted a visit by the UN's Ad Hoc Working Group on Chile in 1978. The UN's report of that visit prompted the UN General Assembly to express concern "at the refusal of the Chilean authorities to accept responsibility or account for the large number of persons reported to have disappeared for political reasons, or to undertake an adequate investigation of cases drawn to their attention."[33]

The International Climate: Human Rights Crisis

Because disappearance was a relatively new phenomenon without clear reference points in international law, Amnesty and other human rights NGOs faced difficult work at two levels. At one level was the effort to denounce the situation in Chile, Argentina, and other countries through direct criticism of the governments and aid to human rights victims and their families. At the second level was the need to raise awareness on disappearances and push for new legal norms of international human rights protection.

Amnesty had developed experience mounting global efforts for new norms and action on human rights through the Campaign for the Abolition of Torture in the early 1970s. In the late 1970s, AI expanded its efforts. Stefanie Grant, AI's former head of research, in 1977 signed on again to establish and direct Amnesty International USA's (AIUSA's) Washington Liaison Office. Margo Picken had been officially installed as AI's UN representative in New York by the end of 1977. The Legal, Campaign, and Research Departments at the International Secretariat were staffed and active. Amnesty was poised to participate in newly rich forms of NGO networking and influence in the U.S. capital and internationally that grew out of the U.S. Congress's and the Carter administration's focus on human rights in foreign policy.[34] And Amnesty's receipt of the 1977 Nobel Peace Prize lent it new prestige and attention.

Amnesty maintained frequent contact with many of the Argentine groups. Some important contacts were maintained through AI's U.S. section. One Amnesty member, who prefers to remain anonymous, played a critical role. The former Spanish teacher and specialist on Argentina and Brazil helped to advise and direct the activities of U.S. Amnesty members who worked on issues related to Argentina through AIUSA's internal advisory network for local groups, known in Amnesty parlance as a Coordination Group (Co-Group). Based at her home in the United States, the Co-Group leader used the telephone day and night to keep up direct communication with many of the Argentine groups, including the Mothers of the Plaza de Mayo, who had organized in Argentina to protest the disappearance of their sons and daughters, and the Grandmothers of the Plaza de Mayo, who traced the secret adoptions that were the fate of babies born to some of their daughters who were pregnant when they were arrested. She relayed information to Amnesty's International Secretariat, the Amnesty International—USA offices, and other external activists on Argentina during this period. She "*was* the telephone to us," said Nélida Navajas, a leader of the Grandmothers, in Buenos Aires. "If there were a thousand [of her], there would be no human rights violations."[35]

Facts to Action: Creation of the UN Working Group on Enforced or Involuntary Disappearances

The Campaign for the Abolition of Torture had emphasized a UN response to violations as well as a public response. A campaign to raise awareness and set up legal prohibitions of disappearances internationally faced additional challenges. Given the fact that disappearances were, by design, incompletely understood, the ambiguity of disappearances might be met with a similar vagueness in UN statements, unless the concept could be clearly framed as a distinct form of human rights violation. With regard to torture, AI had managed to help foster a UN resolution in 1975 that set the stage for a formal declaration and more detailed and binding legal standards, but those had hearkened back to strong pronouncements against torture in earlier international instruments. No such pronouncements existed for disappearances. The UN response to disappearances as they reached epidemic proportions was to focus on the countries where they occurred, in particular on Argentina. That included calling for special inquiries into the "fate" of the disappeared.

Despite a level of international attention comparable to that devoted to the Chilean situation, Argentina was largely successful in avoiding explicit condemnation in the UN. It did so through skillful use of diplomatic tactics that included aligning itself with the USSR and developing countries in the UN Commission on Human Rights. Argentina flouted the fact that President Jimmy Carter of the United States was backing intergovernmental pressure on it.[36] But Argentina's calculated evasion of UN censure was an open secret. In a 1978 resolution aimed at Argentina, the UN General Assembly mentioned no country by name, but expressed concern about "reports from various parts of the world relating to enforced or involuntary disappearances."[37]

The resolution represented the first time the U.N. General Assembly had condemned disappearances as a category of human rights violation and not with reference to any specific country. However, Argentina's keen feel for UN politics, which had enabled it to avoid direct public criticism there, also meant that the import of the resolution was not lost on its diplomats. The resolution was understood as a threat.[38] Still, the UN was not dealing overtly with Argentina. The 1979 meeting of UN Commission on Human Rights postponed deeper consideration of disappearances until the next year's session.[39]

At the regional level, representatives of the OAS's Inter-American Commission on Human Rights (IACHR) conducted a mission to Argentina in September 1979. Nongovernmental organizations of widely varying ideological stripes were active in Argentina, documenting human rights violations and maintaining external contact.[40] A measure of the Argentine government's perception of threat from the human rights groups at home, perhaps, was the fact that prior to the IACHR's visit, the offices of four human rights groups were raided and files were seized.[41] Those groups were the Marxist Argentine League for the Rights of Man; its subgroup, the Commission of Relatives of the Disappeared and Political Prisoners; the church-based Ecumenical Movement for Human Rights; and the Permanent Assembly for Human Rights.

Meanwhile, after 1979's postponement of consideration of disappearances in the UN Commission on Human Rights, international NGOs undertook efforts to raise awareness of disappearances during the year before the 1980 session of the commission.[42] Amnesty, for its part, drew public attention by launching another intensive campaign on behalf of the disappeared in Argentina. It emphasized the pattern of disappearances in that country and the Argentine government's lack of responsiveness. AI described a "characteristic train of events in the lives of the *desaparecidos*," constructed from accounts of prisoners held for brief periods: "They are kept hooded and blindfolded; as a result they have great difficulty in recognizing their place of detention. . . . Systematic torture and summary executions are routine. . . . They are usually subjected to torture and physical abuse."[43] AI publicized what it had learned about the fate of the disappeared in Argentina: some were murdered and dumped "on waste-ground, in forests, or at the bottom of lakes," some kept in secret camps, some transferred to official prisons, and sometimes they were simply released after a month or less.[44]

AI published its own computerized list of 2,665 disappeared Argentines, which was a conservative count, since it represented only the cases that AI had been able to document fully.[45] The youngest person on the list was Simón Antonio Riquielo, a baby who had been arrested with his mother when he was twenty days old. His mother was known to have been transferred to a prison in Uruguay, but there was no trace of her child. AI shared stories like these with the public and submitted the list of the disappeared to the Argentine government and the OAS's IACHR prior to its 1979 visit to Argentina.[46] Pressure mounted on Argentina after the strongly worded OAS report on its mission cited disappearances as a major concern.[47] Amnesty also submitted its latest information on disappearances in Argentina, as well as in Afghanistan and Ethiopia, to the UN Sub-Commission in August of that year.[48]

Amnesty's list of Argentine disappearances was updated and published again in advance of the 1980 meeting of the UN Commission on Human Rights. By then, the number of documented cases had risen to 3,600.[49] The Commission took action on disappearances that year, but not in the way that human rights proponents had hoped. Just as the Chilean case was identified with the torture issue at the UN, the Argentina case had become identified with disappearances. However, instead of creating an ad hoc working group to focus closely on Argentina, the 1980 Commission on Human Rights created a five-person body of experts, charged only with investigating disappearances in general. The general mandate was a disappointment for those who wanted the UN to spotlight abuses in Argentina. The new group, the UN Working Group on Enforced or Involuntary Disappearances (WGEID), was given a one-year renewable term.

Amnesty routinely maintained an active presence as an observer at the meetings of the Commission, lobbying for strong measures against Argentina. Even though the resolution that set up the Working Group "was known informally in the corridors as the 'Argentina resolution,' " insufficient political support existed to put through a more direct repudiation of Argentina's human rights violations.[50] For that reason, the WGEID was seen by many, including NGO representatives, as a consolation prize. Direct censure of Argentina, it was thought, would have sent a stronger message against disappearances. The general, temporary mandate of the WGEID caused added concern: doubts remained about whether the group would actively pursue its mandate, or simply bide its time.

The WGEID could in theory investigate disappearances anywhere, but NGOs were understandably pessimistic. The Working Group's potential depended in large part on how its mandate was interpreted in practice, since the authorizing resolution had not been specific about how the Working Group should conduct its business. The noncontroversial approach would have been to institute a simple registry of alleged disappearances, but Theo van Boven, the director of the UN Division of Human Rights in Geneva, had bigger plans. Following upon his earlier experience establishing the Ad Hoc Working Group on Chile in 1975,[51] Van Boven was resolved to make the WGEID an active tool for investigation.

Although it had seemed that the WGEID might be less effective on Argentina, it had potential for establishing normative standards for action against disappearances everywhere, not just in Argentina. As soon as the creation of the WGEID was confirmed by the full Economic and Social Council, van Boven set up a special meeting to consult with Amnesty, the ICJ, and several other NGOs about the new working group. He envisioned that the WGEID should be able to take action as well as receive information, but unlike NGOs, the UN had no experience acting on disappearances. According to van Boven, he and his staff "wanted particularly to know what techniques they were using . . . so that we could learn from them." He continued, "[W]e were in the early stages. [The UN] had hardly dealt with these questions in any effective ways. And NGOs had been doing that."[52]

Menno Kamminga, then a member of Amnesty International's Legal Department, suggested to van Boven's staff that something like Amnesty International's Urgent Action procedure might be useful for the Working Group, because it would provide a channel for quick reporting, early inquiry, and direct communication with governments on specific cases.[53] Van Boven implemented a similar urgent procedure for the WGEID. Along with a slower "routine" procedure for making inquiries, the "urgent" procedure used telex to transmit details of an alleged disappearance to the involved governments, requesting information to clarify the case.

The procedures were introduced within months, at the WGEID's first session from June 9 to 13, 1980. Official documentation couched the urgent procedure in understated phrasing that nevertheless put governments on notice. The Working Group's report explained that, although the procedures were not directly mandated, they were "derived from the terms of reference and the debates" leading up to its creation. The Working Group announced in its report that those who "contemplated the detention of a person and his disappearance" should realize that, from then on, "the Group was continuously acting as the eyes of the international community, and acting with that sense of urgency which alone can save lives."[54]

Although it was not made explicit in the report, the group's preventative action was modeled on the kind of active fact finding that Amnesty and other NGOs were already doing. The report did explain that the investigative approach it had chosen carried "potential for intense scrutiny of information and flexible action," and made it possible, through country visits, to establish "direct contacts with those having first-hand knowledge of enforced or involuntary disappearances." These elements, the report went on, were likely to be key in "achieving a better understanding of the problem and reaching desired solutions."[55]

While little conceptual clarification of disappearances had yet occurred in UN discussions, a new intergovernmental fact-finding and investigation process had been crafted in spite of state resistance. Making the most of the opportunity, NGOs rallied to provide information, investigative techniques, and pressure to maintain the working group for its intended purpose beyond its initial one-year mandate. The urgent communication procedure of the WGEID was the first procedure empowering a UN group "to take action systematically and routinely in case of a feared violation of human rights."[56] Since its creation, the WGEID has become an ongoing part of the UN's work on human rights. Much of the information that comes to the WGEID is still channeled there by NGOs. In a scholarly analysis of the UN's thematic human rights procedures, Kamminga noted that the rate of response to the WGEID's urgent communication procedure was "much higher" than the 20 percent response rate to its routine requests for information on individual cases.[57] Nigel Rodley, head of AI's Legal Department when the WGEID was created, reflected that the WGEID "turned out to be a tremendous evolution of the UN's approach to human rights problems and an inroad into dealing with individual cases that we had never had before." He continued, "The UN often does the right things for the wrong reasons, and this was one of them."[58]

Phase II, Consensus Building: The Concept of Disappearances

The inherent conundrum in the concept of disappearances was a potential stumbling block to the achievement of a coherent UN approach to disappearances and to Amnesty's effectiveness in aiding prisoners. Arriving at a useful working definition of disappearances presented a challenge. Normally, the state assumes responsibility for each prisoner's fate, but when the state refuses to acknowledge detention, it abdicates responsibility. When detention is not even acknowledged, "all legal and moral constraint on official behavior is at once removed."[59]

Information on disappearances contributed to growing agreement among human rights activists, relatives of the disappeared, and legal experts that disappearance was a separate category of human mistreatment, not fully covered by existing norms. However, it was not clear how disappearances could best be described or conceptualized in formal human rights norms. Disappearances did not equate with the death penalty, although disappearance had sometimes been characterized as a form of state-sponsored killing.[60] There were special problems that arose in light of the indeterminate fate of the disappeared.

Neither was disappearance equivalent to secret detention. In its research, AI was no stranger to government secrecy in the Soviet Union, for example.[61] However, in contrast with imprisonment or even execution of suspected political opponents, disappearances generated a " 'hit and hide the hand' moral situation" with an emphasis on "deniability," according to José Zalaquett, the former member of Chile's COPACHI.[62] During the course of intensified efforts to counter disappearances in the late 1970s, Amnesty's leadership realized that further conceptual work was required in order to make progress, since the "traditional model [of political imprisonment] was beginning to break up."[63]

To explore how best to work on disappearances, the U.S. section of Amnesty began to work with the International Secretariat to initiate conceptual discussions about disappearances. The Washington Office of AIUSA was working closely with the Co-Group leader mentioned above, who communicated regularly with NGOs in Argentina, so U.S.-based AI staff had developed familiarity with disappearances through direct contact with Argentine NGOs as well as through AI's research at the International Secretariat.[64] According to Zalaquett, "there was a lot of uneasiness about . . . the need to sort out mechanisms" with reference to disappearances.[65]

Ann Blyberg and Patricia Weiss Fagen, AIUSA board members, were assigned to try to work out some of the questions that existed about the phenomenon of "disappearance." Those included a lack of clarity concerning the different words for disappearances being used in various geographical regions, and how to characterize the core elements of a disappearance.[66] Blyberg, then a young attorney, began simply by talking to a number of different people about disappearances. She quickly realized that there were areas of confusion and untested assumptions about disappearances among activists and others concerned with the issue. She drafted a questionnaire for Amnesty contacts to isolate and clarify the problems in need of further analysis. After experimenting with questionnaire a few times, Blyberg began to believe that some sort of mutual exchange—a conversation rather than individual questionnaires—would be beneficial. She contacted Stefanie Grant in the Washington AIUSA office to suggest "a meeting of people who have a lot of expertise on what's being called disappearances in different countries, . . . [to] get them to address these questions, and then see if, out of that . . . we [could] get some clarity."[67] Grant agreed. Once AIUSA decided to sponsor such a conference, Blyberg talked to many people, using a version of her questionnaire, in order to draw a bead on issues ripe for further discussion. At that point, the questions included basic issues like "what is the difference between disappearance and a kidnapping? What is the difference between disappearance and arbitrary killing? What is the difference between a disappearance and incommunicado detention? Those sorts of questions." A further conundrum was presented by the question of how to apply the term "disappearance" because of the implications in specific cases.

> Basically, what people in Amnesty or in Argentina were calling a disappearance, the Filipinos were calling a salvaging. But on the other hand, they were using "salvaging" for situations where somebody would disappear . . . and then would show up, either alive or dead. And so one of the questions was, how long does a person have to be [missing] . . . before you call it a disappearance? And once they show up, do you still call it a disappearance, or does it become something else? Because all of these have implications for . . . how you try to address the [cause] . . . and what you seek as remedy.[68]

Blyberg worked with AIUSA staff to organize a small, seminar-style conference for 22–25 June 1980 at the Wingspread Conference Center in Racine, Wisconsin. The timing was portentous, since the Working Group on Enforced or Involuntary Disappearances had only just been established. According to Blyberg, Amnesty wanted to get the definition worked out, "precisely because the UN was working on it," the feeling being that Amnesty ought to bring some of its experience to bear on the issue.

At Wingspread, a small number of participants gathered from AI, national human rights groups in countries where disappearances were occurring or had occurred, and international human rights groups to present and discuss conference study papers. Many of the papers were in-depth analyses of disappearances as they had occurred in different countries. The working papers served as starting points for conference discussions. A "conceptualization of disappearances as a working idea was hammered out" at the seminar, said José Zalaquett, who chaired the discussions.[69] Blyberg recalled that Zalaquett was able to play a leading role in the development of the conceptual chapter of the seminar report because of his experience and immersion in moral and legal issues relating to disappearances: "between thinking about it, being aware of [the issues involved] because he's from Chile, and then being at the seminar."[70] The seminar participants built a working definition of disappearances that would be valid both from a legal-normative perspective and an experiential one.

For a working definition of disappearances, the participants identified three common "bare facts" that, together, indicated that a disappearance had occurred:

1. There are reasonable grounds to believe that a person (the victim) has been taken into custody by the authorities or their agent.

2. The authorities deny that the victim is in their custody or the custody of their agent;

3. There are reasonable grounds to disbelieve that denial.[71]

From this, Amnesty's International Executive Committee (IEC) confirmed AI's working policy on the use of the word, "disappearance" at its next meeting in December 1980. The working definition that was adopted was precisely that which had been hammered out by the conference. The IEC decided that the term should be enclosed in quotation marks in AI materials, as a reminder that "disappearance" was not random or accidental, but a deliberate act by governments or their agents. The definition has lasted; a similarly worded definition appears in the organizing document of a recent AI campaign on disappearances.[72]

The conceptual work at the Wingspread seminar placed government denial and accountability at the center of a definition of disappearances and formed the basis for Amnesty's recommended international response to disappearances. One of the characteristics of disappearance that was particularly difficult to deal with was the sense of ambiguity concerning the fate of the prisoner. The observation that disappearance is rooted in government secrecy and deception, no matter what the fate of the prisoner, put the focus back on government accountability—a focus necessary for both legal norms and practical action against disappearances.

The language of the Wingspread conference was incorporated right away into AI's international statements. The rhetoric of AI's post-Wingspread UN statements stripped the air of mystery and confusion from the concept of disappearances and placed responsibility on governments. Just two months after the seminar, speaking at the 1980 meeting of the UN Sub-Commission, AI emphasized the importance of understanding the nature of disappearances: "As in the case of torture, it is important to know what we mean by the word [disappearances] and to know under what circumstances it is likely to take place. Because only then can appropriate recommendations for counter-action take place."[73] Amnesty then supplied its understanding of the critical elements of a disappearance. The term was not "mysterious," but "in fact, a 'disappearance' consists of nothing else but arrest and detention which is subsequently denied by the authorities."[74] The statement went on to distinguish disappearances from other types of human rights violations and to present a list of recommendations for intergovernmental consideration of reports of disappearance. AI asserted that disappearances is a "cynical" term that should always be enclosed in quotation marks.

Definitional issues were one reason that, earlier that year, the delegates to the 1980 Commission on Human Rights had encountered difficulty agreeing on a suitable draft resolution on disappearances. This would clear up the questions the Commission faced, such as how to exclude cases such as ordinary missing persons reports and how to invoke government accountability in serious disappearance cases. AI's statement delivered to the 1980 UN Sub-Commission implicitly answered those questions. According to Amnesty, disappearances should be considered to be acts of government authorities. It must be recognized that disappeared people have not simply disappeared; the disappeared should be assumed, by intergovernmental organizations (IGOs) and NGOs, to be alive until proven dead. Further, governments should be accountable even after a change in leadership, since families have a right to know about the fate of relatives.

Amnesty asserted that disappearances are exacerbated by "legislation permitting broad government discretion and the absence of judicial . . . controls," the same factors that also permit torture and extrajudicial killing by governments. Publicity was required to end disappearances, according to AI, since governments resort to it because they think they can get away with it. Therefore, governments should be forced either to acknowledge detention or to investigate disappearances cases.

In its next statement before the Commission on Human Rights on 17 February 1981, AI presented examples of disappearances that had just occurred in the days since the opening of the Commission session, then emphasized the rights of the families to know the fate of their relatives and the need for government responses to legal inquiries. The need and right to know was stressed as a "fundamental aspect of the 'disappearance' phenomenon."[75] The statement closed by calling for the continuation of the newly formed WGEID beyond one year. Although there was reason to doubt the prospects for a permanent WGEID in the first couple of years after its creation, the WGEID's mandate was renewed and has became a central part of the UN human rights apparatus.[76]

Applying the Urgent Action Technique

In the meantime, Amnesty continued to use its own Urgent Action technique in cases of arrest and possible torture or disappearance. AI's connections with local activists permitted effective use of speedy communications to try to put Argentina and other governments on notice that the world was watching their actions. For example, on 27 and 28 February 1981, little more than a week after AI's statement to the Commission, plainclothes police raided the office of the Centro de Estudios Legales y Sociales (CELS), the Buenos Aires human rights organization that had been founded in 1980, and arrested six prominent members of the group. CELS members had secretly completed and shipped a report on Argentine disappearances to be presented at an upcoming international meeting in Paris.[77] One of those arrested, Emilio Mignone, was a lawyer whose daughter had "disappeared" within months of the coup. Mignone had plunged into efforts to document human rights abuses and to organize international pressure on the Argentine government, and he had just returned to Buenos Aires after giving testimony on disappearances before the UN Commission on Human Rights in Geneva.[78] Mignone's son tried to accompany him as the authorities took him away, protesting that he didn't want his father to disappear as his sister had done. The arresting official reportedly said, "Don't worry, your father is now well known and so we can't do that."[79]

Angela Westerkamp's husband, José Federico Westerkamp, was another of the CELS founders who was rounded up. The Westerkamps were scientists whose son, Gustavo, had been imprisoned since 1975 under Argentina's Poder Ejecutivo Nacional (National Executive Power) decree, which allowed the government to detain people without specifying the reason for imprisonment. Gustavo had been adopted by AI as a prisoner of conscience. In fact, all but one of the six arrested had children who had "disappeared" or were imprisoned.[80] On the night her husband was taken, Angela Westerkamp phoned Amnesty's U.S.-based liaison with Argentina.[81] The Amnesty worker then phoned the International Secretariat and began calling her already well-used "emergency list" of the U.S.-based organizations monitoring Argentina.[82] Mrs. Westerkamp recalled that international telegrams began arriving in Argentina the next day. AI cabled the Argentine president right away. On 3 March, AI issued an Urgent Action bulletin, instructing AI members to send telegrams or express letters demanding immediate release, and on 4 March, AI issued a press statement on the case.[83] The CELS members were released shortly thereafter, on 6 March.[84] In court, the CELS members were charged with possession of materials affecting national security. In the office raid, the Argentine authorities had taken files documenting about six thousand disappearances.[85] After pressure through official channels, including expressions of concern from the United States government, the cases were formally dismissed.[86] French, Spanish, and English versions of the Paris report that CELS had compiled soon circulated internationally.[87]

Amnesty's response to the CELS arrests illustrates the potential of international attention to protect individuals from physical harm. However, disappearances still presented a challenge to conventional understandings of prisoner detention, which had yet to be fully addressed in international norms. The problem of how to conceive of disappearances that AI had solved for its own purposes at the Wingspread conference, and had shared with the relevant UN organs, was still not directly transferable to formal international norms.

Disappearances posed particular challenges for consensus building. Not all of those challenges had been met by the time deliberate construction of norms began to be considered in the UN. On the positive side, AI had led the development of an understanding of disappearances that insisted on government accountability. At the UN, opponents of disappearances had succeeded in getting the WGEID established as an indirect way of dealing with disappearances in Argentina, and it became a useful general mechanism. The WGEID also showed itself to be receptive to NGO methods and reporting. The bedrock of agreement now existed that disappearances comprised a singular matter of concern for international human rights organs. What remained was to work out its articulation in formal norms.

Phase III, Norm Construction: Building Norms to Deal with Disappearances

The establishment of the WGEID had been, in effect, a weak UN statement on Argentina that nevertheless formed a promising basis for an ongoing international response to disappearances wherever they might occur. Although it was a weak response to Argentina, it provided a strong opportunity to begin formulating international standards of response to disappearances wherever they might occur. The durability of the WGEID as a normative mechanism had yet to be shown, but an international tool was now available for official communication with the governments of countries where disappearances were occurring. AI mounted a two-month publicity campaign starting in December 1981, to publicly emphasize the distinct nature of disappearances, press for government accountability, and encourage wider recognition of the work of the WGEID. The fact that the UN was now monitoring disappearances could also provide a stronger reference point—and a new international outlet—for Amnesty International's reporting on individuals.

Once established, the WGEID was not viewed simply as a mechanism to deal with Argentine violations. Even in its first report, the WGEID had noted that it had received reports on disappearances in Argentina, Bolivia, Brazil, Chile, Cyprus, El Salvador, Ethiopia, Guatemala, Indonesia, Mexico, Nicaragua, Peru, the Philippines, South Africa, and Uruguay. Government responses were also noted. Among them, Ethiopia took the opportunity to scold Amnesty, which had provided a large amount of information to the Working Group based on its information on disappearances across the globe: "The information received by the group concerning enforced or involuntary disappearances in Ethiopia is baseless and unfounded. Our views about Amnesty International from which this information has originated are well known." Argentina condemned "terrorist" organizations for making allegations against the government.[88]

Drafting the Declaration on Disappearances

The Working Group on Enforced or Involuntary Disappearances had not actually needed to define disappearances to do its investigative work. The lack of a clear definition was a potential impediment, however, to elaborating more specific international statements to deal with disappearances. NGO support was needed to launch work toward a UN statement outlawing disappearances, but given the ambiguities evident in a disappearance case, NGOs themselves disagreed as to how, or whether, separate official standards to prohibit disappearances should be articulated. The disagreements arose not over whether disappearances were a pressing problem, nor even in whether stronger legal protection was needed at the international level. Even those who believed that the separate elements of disappearances were already minimally covered by international norms recognized that disappearances were a distinctly difficult problem to address because it was a "compound" violation that combined a number of separate features. This consensus had been cemented by the creation of the WGEID following world attention to disappearances in Argentina. The primary disagreement arose over how and whether to construct *new* norms concerning disappearances, given the possibility that legal side effects in the form of unwanted loopholes might arise if new laws were hastily constructed.

The urgency of the problem outweighed the risks in the view of some NGOs, particularly those that had organized to deal with the Latin American outbreak of disappearances. Regionally based organizations of relatives of the disappeared, for example, some of them newly active on the international scene, strongly favored creating an international convention against disappearances with binding legal force.[89] For symbolic as well as practical reasons, such a convention would reinforce the efforts of domestic NGOs to counter impunity in their own newly democratized or democratizing Latin American states, for example. Global human rights NGOs also wanted strong international statements against disappearances, but some individuals with more experience at the UN level, including people within Amnesty, feared that premature action risked creating unintended, and possibly detrimental, legal precedent.

It was one thing for Amnesty International to establish its own working definition of disappearances: it helped to clarify its work and push for the UN to deal with disappearances. It was another thing to establish an international legal standard that would place disappearances within a matrix of other kinds of human rights violations. The implications had to be very carefully considered. Disappearance often combined, but was separate from, torture, arbitrary detention, incommunicado detention, and extrajudicial executions (EJEs). To imply that UN statements regarding torture, for example, were not sufficient to deal with disappearances might undermine the strength of the norms on torture that Amnesty had worked so hard to promote. In addition, care had to be taken when situating disappearances within the existing international normative context. For example, it would certainly be a mistake to frame the statute of limitations and other jurisdictional issues pertaining to disappearances in such a way that it would then be in a state's interest to kill rather than release people who had secretly been detained.

Given the compound nature of disappearances, then, ill-considered drafts of formal norms could open terrain for unresolved political and semantic battles that could undermine disappearance norms or render them ineffectual. Further, a binding treaty would require a definition of disappearances, which was sure to be tricky for some of the reasons just mentioned. There certainly was evidence that some states would do all they could to vitiate the force of new norms on disappearances. In the meantime, the UN's dealings with Argentina and Chile had exercised other UN mechanisms for dealing with actual cases of disappearances, such as the procedure under Resolution 1503 for investigation of alleged "gross" and consistent violations, ad hoc committees, and the WGEID. That progress was not to be dismissed.

Such issues were debated within Amnesty and among NGOs and human rights activists in the years following the creation of the WGEID. One normative step seemed feasible: a UN declaration on disappearances might clarify the UN prohibition of disappearances without requiring a definition in the text. Further, it was clear in the UN context of the development of norms on torture that, whether or not NGOs agreed to pursue a convention on disappearances, a declaration was a prerequisite for a convention.

The chance to advance a declaration on disappearances arose in 1988. Reed Brody, Ingrid Kirschner, Nigel Rodley, and David Weissbrodt were sitting together to observe the proceedings of the UN Sub-Commission's Working Group on Detention. Brody was representing the International Commission of Jurists (ICJ) at the time, Rodley and Kirschner were observing for Amnesty, and Weissbrodt was there on behalf of the Minnesota Lawyers' Committee for Human Rights but had worked before with Amnesty both as a volunteer and as a professional. During the meetings, one of the officials in the working group suggested that some sort of declaration would be useful. Taking the comment as an invitation, the NGO representatives produced a first draft "literally overnight," taking the language of the UN Convention against Torture as their model.[90] Reed Brody, for the ICJ, then collaborated with Sub-Commission expert Louis Joinet to put the draft before the Working Group on Detention.[91]

A definition of disappearances was notably absent from the original draft. "No satisfactory definition . . . had yet been proposed" due to the "flexible and compound nature of the phenomenon,"[92] and the drafters considered it a bad strategic move to attempt a definition for the UN declaration. As Rodley pointed out during the process, "It [would] be extremely difficult, if at all possible, to find a satisfactory definition of enforced or involuntary disappearances. . . . It is a characteristic of the horrible phenomenon that it tends to elude precise definition: thus, any attempt at finding a definition risks seriously undermining the drafting process."[93]

With such provisos in mind, the International Commission of Jurists took on the primary coordinating role in the preparation of the draft UN declaration against disappearances, working closely with AI and other NGO experts.[94] The draft went through several rounds of analysis and revision. The ICJ sent copies to "governments, NGOs, the Working Group on Enforced or Involuntary Disappearances, and others" for comments.[95]

A strongly worded first draft of a regional Inter-American Convention on the Forced Disappearances of Persons was already in circulation in the Organization of American States. At a 1988 colloquium held in Buenos Aires, Latin American human rights groups had supported working for a UN declaration only because it was an intermediate and necessary step in developing a UN convention.[96] Views were mixed within global human rights groups and within AI itself as to the advisability of proceeding with efforts to prepare an international convention against disappearances, and the caution of global groups was not particularly appreciated by some Latin American activists. However, there was agreement that a UN declaration should go ahead. In preparing the declaration for the UN, the coordinating group also looked to the early wording of the draft Inter-American convention for guidance.[97]

The Working Group on Disappearances chimed in with proposed additions to the draft UN declaration on disappearances that were inspired by the draft Inter-American convention. The WGEID advised that even though a full-fledged definition of disappearances was not strictly warranted in the declaration, the typical elements of a disappearance ought to be included in a preamble to the declaration to strengthen "the normative content of the declaration."[98] Those typical elements could be identified from the cases which had been submitted to the WGEID, which by then had eight years of experience dealing with reports of disappearances. Its report suggested language for that segment of the preamble: "In many countries persons are detained or abducted against their will, for whatever reason, by officials of any branch or level of government or by organized groups or private individuals acting on behalf of or in connivance with the government, followed by a refusal to disclose the fate or whereabouts of the persons concerned or a refusal to acknowledge their arrest or detention, and . . . as a result such persons are placed outside the protective precinct of the law."[99] Thus, some of the cautions that had been anticipated in debate over a new UN statement on disappearances were echoed by the WGEID, but in the process of avoiding such pitfalls, the draft could be kept strong by describing the elements of a disappearance in direct language. The working group's recommendation explicitly avoided a judgment on motives behind disappearances, because a grand strategy for the use of disappearances would often be difficult to prove. Rather than characterize disappearance as a systematic, premeditated practice, which it was in its most sinister form, the preamble simply described disappearances as the sum of component actions. In that way, whether disappearances were carried out randomly to hide evidence of "routine torture," or authorized at the highest level of government as part of a premeditated strategy, authorities could still be held accountable.[100]

The ICJ produced a revised draft for the 1989 meeting of the Working Group on Detention. That group gave extended consideration to the revised draft and produced a second revision. To accomplish a final draft in time for the next year's session, the ICJ convened an expert meeting, chaired by Brody, to assist the chairman of the Working Group on Detention, Alfonso Martínez. The Expert Meeting on the Draft "Declaration on the Protection of All Persons from Enforced or Involuntary Disappearances" took place in Geneva, 21–23 March 1990. The list of participants included NGO representatives from AI, ICJ, the Minnesota Lawyers Committee for Human Rights, the Federation internationale des droits de l'homme, the UN Centre for Human Rights, and the Latin American Federation of Associations of Relatives of Disappeared Persons (FEDEFAM), as well as several participants invited by virtue of their membership in UN working groups: four members of the Working Group on Detention, two more members of the Sub-Commission on the Prevention of Discrimination and the Protection of Minorities, and two members of the UN Working Group on Enforced or Involuntary Disappearances.[101] For three days, the participants worked on all parts of the draft declaration. Because the UN Commission on Human Rights works on a yearly calendar cycle, the intensive efforts of NGOs to finish the draft probably sped up progress on the declaration by a few years.[102]

The chair of the Working Group on Detention, the French diplomat Beatrice le Frapper du Hellen, ironed out remaining disagreements among governments and human rights organizations in 1991 and early 1992 so that the draft could be passed through the Sub-Commission's Working Group on Detention, the Sub-Commission itself, and the Commission on Human Rights.[103] The Economic and Social Council on July 20, 1992, adopted a resolution to transmit the declaration, officially entitled "Declaration on the Protection of All Persons from Enforced Disappearance" to the General Assembly for consideration, where it was adopted at the 1992 session.[104]

The draft declaration was a potentially important step in the establishment of international law regarding disappearances. It was the first UN statement to characterize disappearances as a crime. It was true that Amnesty International's own working definition had been unstinting in attributing responsibility to governments, but until the Declaration against Disappearances was adopted, the UN's WGEID had been forced to rely on a mélange of related international standards to lend moral and legal force to its inquiries. As the WGEID observed in its 1990 report, no "internationally accepted characterization of the phenomenon and its particular status as a crime in international law" was present in any one instrument. Moreover, states had no guidelines telling them what concrete measures to take at the domestic level to investigate and document disappearances.[105] The declaration, if adopted by the General Assembly, would accomplish those steps fairly quickly. In the meantime, the strong first draft of the Latin American regional convention, which had preceded the UN declaration, had been delayed and drastically watered down by governments. NGOs had been shut out of portions of the drafting process on the Inter-American Convention, and that draft's implementation mechanisms had been gutted to make it acceptable to member governments.[106] As written, then, the draft UN declaration stood as the strongest existing international normative statement on disappearances.

NGOs had played a role in the construction of the declaration and in helping the WGEID gather the information that helped it fulfill its mandate. Thanks to the cues provided by NGOs, the new UN declaration actually contained enough guidelines and specifics to be useful for norm-based action against disappearances.

PHASE IV, NORM APPLICATION: THE UN IS NOT "MERELY A SOURCE OF RULES"

In 1992, in the midst of the General Assembly session that would consider adopting the draft declaration, Amnesty held a study conference. AI was preparing for a new campaign on disappearances and political killings to start in 1993. The conference, entitled "Elimination and Terror: International Conference on Political Killings and Disappearances," was hosted 4–6 September 1992 in Noordwijkerhout, The Netherlands, by the Dutch section of Amnesty International. It had been twelve years since Wingspread, and the Dutch section had sponsored a similar conference on political killings a decade earlier.[107]

The Noordwijkerhout conference was not an "expert meeting" like the one that had been organized by the ICJ for the purposes of drafting the declaration. Instead, as the title suggests, conference participants studied disappearances and political killings from an activist perspective. Amnesty invited 140 people from fifty countries to review the experiences of the victims and their families, study and evaluate summaries of the historic responses of domestic and international communities to the violations, and to set an agenda for future work against the violations.[108] The conference was timed as an opportunity to discuss how to stop disappearances and political killings, and strategies for strengthening national laws and international norms in the lead-up to the 1993 UN World Conference on Human Rights, set for June in Vienna.

Various Amnesty staff and professionals in the field of human rights had produced study papers on their areas of expertise for discussion at an expert conference held in Britain near Beaconsfield, in November 1991. Several of those papers were revised and presented at the Dutch conference.[109] At Noordwijkerhout, participants divided into five separate working parties: Action by Intergovernmental Organizations, which covered issues related to international norms and their implementation; Bringing the Perpetrators to Justice, on the problem of impunity and domestic legal standards; Campaigning from Abroad, covering how to apply outside pressure effectively in the context of differing country situations and geographical regions; Action within the Countries, which focused on ideas for groups working to influence their own governments; and Campaigning against Abuses by Nongovernmental Entities, which discussed the considerations involved in working to limit human rights violations by opposition groups rather than governments.

The 1992 conference, in many ways, illustrated the maturing of the international human rights community. Many of the participants had been involved in work on disappearances for a decade or more, either within Amnesty or in other organizations, perhaps changing jobs but still pursuing human rights questions. Many of the participants in the working party on Action through Intergovernmental Organizations, for example, had represented NGOs for years and were accustomed to collaborating. Discussions exhibited an awareness not only of the need for cooperation among international colleagues, but also of the importance of working with those closest to the atrocities, the victims and the domestic human rights NGOs themselves. Experience had shown that fact finding and consensus building were most effective when local groups existed that could be supported by international observers. Furthermore, when conditions permitted, domestic groups could attack the roots of abuses through education, protest, and lobbying for the establishment of strong domestic human rights laws.

Some of the papers presented at the Dutch conference dealt with specific country situations; others with particular themes.[110] Papers prepared for the intergovernmental organizations working group included one chronicling the UN's failure to act on disappearances in Iraq in the 1990s, and several analytical papers on subjects such as the strengths and weaknesses of the WGEID in its dozen years of operation, the UN's approach to dealing with political killings. Others analyzed the history and significance of legal norms on disappearances—the then-draft declaration in the UN, the Inter-American Convention on disappearances in the Latin American regional system, and the upcoming year in the United Nations, which would include the 1993 UN World Conference on Human Rights. The four other conference working parties discussed how governments themselves were coming to terms with past human rights violations, the use of international pressure on governments, internal action for human rights by domestic groups, and a new and newly controversial subject: how to address political killings by opposition groups. A representative from each working party at the conference made a presentation concerning either what Amnesty should do, or what the UN and the wider international community should be encouraged to do to strengthen and implement existing rules.

In contrast to the Wingspread conference, the focus of the Netherlands conference was no longer on conceptual clarification and consensus building about the makeup of disappearances. Instead, the theme was much more strongly focused on how Amnesty and other NGOs could work with the UN and with each other to stop and prevent disappearances through international prohibition and positive action. The conference participants reiterated the idea that strong legal norms were needed to provide a basis for effective application.

It was felt that the draft declaration, which was close to being adopted at the concurrent General Assembly session, could serve as an adequate baseline document if adopted without dilution. On the other hand, it was noted that the Inter-American convention was damaging to the cause in its then-current form because of the compromises entailed in getting the document accepted by governments. Many felt that the shortcomings of the Inter-American Convention on the Forced Disappearance of Persons stemmed from the fact that NGOs had *not* been involved at every stage of the drafting process. The conference's working party on intergovernmental organizations concluded that, from the perspective of a desire to strengthen protection against disappearances, human rights advocates should wait for adoption of the draft UN declaration before taking further action in the UN toward a possible convention against disappearances.

Amnesty's book based on the conference proceedings asserts that the UN "should not be thought of merely as a source of rules on human rights." Instead, "the need for action is inherent in the existence of the United Nations."[111] Although it was premature to initiate work on a global convention before seeing how the problems with the Inter-American Convention and the draft UN Declaration were resolved, an evident trend toward use of disappearances by more, rather than fewer,[112] states during the 1980s confirmed the view that, whatever the problems with formal norms, some kind of action was needed. The day after the conference, Amnesty held an additional meeting for representatives from Amnesty's national sections to use the conference recommendations to help shape plans for its public campaign on disappearances, set to begin the following August. The campaign would press for implementation of the UN rules that *did* exist.

The General Assembly adopted the declaration on 18 December 1992 without a vote.[113] After that, it served not just as a source of guidelines for governments, but as a reference point for human rights proponents as the Inter-American Convention drafting was completed. In those negotiations, some of the power of the original OAS draft was restored.

In August 1993, Amnesty set in motion its second international campaign against disappearances and political killings, with the theme, "The Lives behind the Lies." Twenty-five people who had been disappeared or killed were featured in publicity materials, to emphasize the human impact of government use of disappearances and killing. Despite the broadening of Amnesty's approach over the years, in its public campaigns the organization still emphasized specific human rights violations against individuals in particular countries. But much had been learned about disappearances, and much accomplished by way of normative prohibitions, since Wingspread, and a thematic centerpiece of the new campaign was preventive action. To that end, Amnesty introduced a set of recommendations for preventing disappearances, and a separate set for prevention of political killings.[114] The 14-Point Programs, as they were called, were modeled after the similar guidelines AI had adopted at the ten-year anniversary of its Campaign for the Abolition of Torture in 1983.

Amnesty's 14-Point Programs were suggestions for how governmental authorities should show commitment to preventing disappearances by putting the UN's condemnation of disappearances into practice. The 14 points on disappearances were brief, calling for government to make clear their condemnation of disappearances and to establish domestic mechanisms ensuring that any arrests and detention were carried out in accordance with regular standards. For example, governments should indicate to their military, police, and security forces that disappearances "will not be tolerated under any circumstances" (Point 1). Commanding officers should be held responsible for acts by those under their command (Point 2). Information about the location of prisoners should be released to relatives, lawyers, and the courts, and those persons as well as doctors should be given access to prisoners (Points 3 and 7). Finally, governments were urged to ratify and implement formal international norms containing "safeguards and remedies" against disappearances (Point 13); and to recognize their responsibility not to aid or abet disappearances in other countries through arms transfers or forcibly returning people to countries where they may be at risk of "disappearance" (Point 14).

The 14-Point Programs were distributed to AI members with charts showing how each point of each program had a basis in existing international law. The international legal norms mentioned included the Declaration on the Protection of All Persons from Enforced Disappearances, the Body of Principles for the Protection of All Persons under Any Form of Detention or Imprisonment,[115] the Declaration of Basic Principles of

Justice for Victims of Crime and Abuse of Power,[116] the International Covenant on Civil and Political Rights, and the Standard Minimum Rules for the Treatment of Prisoners.[117] In this way, the program for the prevention of disappearances urged governments to take preventative and remedial action, but it also fostered public education and involvement.

A Convention under Construction

While agreement existed among NGOs and government officials sympathetic to human rights that current international norms and laws still provided insufficient protection against disappearances, views remained mixed concerning the desirability of a binding UN convention against disappearances. Amnesty had actively participated in the ICJ's coordinating work on the draft UN declaration, but as international debate had taken place concerning the draft declaration and the draft Inter-American Convention, AI had adopted a wait-and-see attitude toward a possible UN convention. Amnesty's attitude was important because of its experience, reputation, and public membership. Any fundamental disagreement among the large, global human rights NGOs would not go unnoticed by governments and would dilute the influence of those who sought to be involved in the drafting process.

With the adoption of a restored Inter-American Convention in 1994,[118] the landscape of international norms on disappearances was brought into better focus, and Amnesty set aside some of its earlier hesitations. Amnesty, the ICJ, and other NGOs cooperated to create a draft international Convention on the Protection of All Persons from Enforced Disappearance. Meetings concerning a possible convention began in conjunction with the 1994 session of the UN Sub-Commission. AI convened an expert meeting in 1996 to produce a first draft for submission to the Sub-Commission.[119] In 1997, several representatives of nongovernmental organizations met with the WGEID to discuss issues related to the draft, including how the proposed convention should be monitored.[120] Work continued on the draft in a sessional working group of the Sub-Commission, and a full draft text was presented in 1998.[121]

A major recent question at the close of the 1990s was how to limit the number (and accompanying bureaucratic requirements) of new treaty-monitoring bodies at the UN, as the number of binding human rights norms grew and UN resources shrank or failed to grow.[122] In lieu of a binding convention, the WGEID monitored states' compliance with the declaration on disappearances, but its 1999 report noted that its resources had been so constrained that it was unable to include compliance information or comments on the draft convention.[123] The draft convention would take the route of previous binding human rights treaties by creating its own monitoring body, the Committee against Forced Disappearance, composed of experts. In 1998, AI urged that the Commission on Human Rights act quickly to facilitate adoption of a convention that "preserves and enhances" the draft's strengths,[124] and continued to warn against the danger that its provisions could still be "weakened by governments as the draft proceeds through the UN system."[125] The draft convention kept its place on the agenda of the UN human rights organs in 1999, and was scheduled to be considered again by the Commission and the Sub-Commission in 2000.[126]

Conclusion

The case of disappearances suggests that the international normative response to human rights violations can be slowed by lack of information, international indifference to particular country cases (e.g., Guatemala), lack of conceptual tools with which to classify the violation itself, and the active resistance of states to censure. To the extent that Amnesty made a significant difference in norms on disappearances, it was through the early discovery and reporting of violations, exchange with domestic NGOs and other international groups, faithfulness to its own findings, and interpretation of the violation in terms consistent with existing normative provisions.

Amnesty's collection and publication of the facts surrounding disappearances in Argentina helped lead to international recognition that a method to grapple with disappearances was needed at the UN. Still, the concept of disappearances had not yet been explicitly delineated in the wording of legal standards of international human rights. That lack did not keep international bodies from expressing official, rhetorical concern over the facts of disappearances, but it did leave such statements without a conceptually refined basis in international instruments. The ability to link disappearances to the actions of states as moral agents remained at an investigative, case-by-case level.

Although disappearances seemed to mock existing human rights norms, AI devised a strategy of demanding that states live up to their own claims of legitimacy by accounting for the disappeared. In this regard, the AI urgent action procedure served as a model for the "urgent procedure" of the Working Group on Enforced or Involuntary Disappearances. International NGOs also aided relatives of disappeared persons by helping them bring their concerns to international attention, thus playing a networking role between the public and international experts.

The emergence of a conceptual basis for norms on disappearances was greatly facilitated by contacts among NGOs and through conference settings where ideas could be tested and developed among experts. But, while AI's conceptual and campaigning work influenced the development of norms on disappearances, Amnesty's methods themselves were influenced by changes in the environment. The increased concealment inherent in the use of disappearances forced AI to adapt its methods to cope with cases that fell outside its traditional prisoner adoption model. In its work against disappearances, Amnesty continued to insist that governments be accountable for their treatment of citizens. Amnesty's hesitation to proceed with the construction of formal norms when the concepts and potential loopholes could not be fully known exhibited the caution that accompanies movement into uncharted territory, but also a sophistication that encouraged continuing debate among regional NGOs, global NGOs, governments, and the UN human rights apparatus over how the contemporary web of human rights norms could best be developed.

Chapter Five

EXTRAJUDICIAL EXECUTIONS

AMNESTY INTERNATIONAL has occasionally reinterpreted its mandate to address new forms of human rights, but always with special consideration reserved for its original focus on prisoners. The abuses discussed in previous chapters—political imprisonment, torture, and disappearances—fell on a continuum of ways that *prisoners* could be mistreated by governments. Victims of political killings, on the other hand, might never even have been held in custody. Therefore, political killings provided another unique challenge to AI's focus, mission, and structure—and to existing international norms.

Until the mid-to-late 1970s, the international community had not confronted the broad realm of government behavior between large-scale, planned killing of civilians and the use of the death penalty as a judicial punishment. At that time, it became apparent that governments were increasingly using extrajudicial executions (EJEs), that is, lethal violence that was not judicially imposed, to target internal, political threats. A 1981 scholarly article by two analysts connected with Amnesty International noted a "dramatic increase" in EJEs in Latin America.[1] Despite the existence of formal norms protecting the right to life and prohibiting genocide, UN member states did not hold one another accountable for such behavior. Many governments framed the use of lethal force in the terms of national security, a realm reserved from international interference. Thus, principles existed against political killings, although norms of behavior—both legal and customary—lagged behind before Amnesty International decided to adopt the issue in the late 1970s.

Many governments in the 1970s began to resort to political killing as an alternative or adjunct to political detention. Some of the same countries— Chile, Argentina—that had raised international attention to torture and disappearances also used outright killing to silence dissent. It was not clear at first how Amnesty International should deal with the phenomenon. First, as already noted, outright political killing was not explicitly addressed by Amnesty's stand against prisoner abuse, although it was clearly a technique that was increasingly being used to squelch freedom of expression, the principle at the core of AI's purpose. Second, AI was unsure how effective group adoption techniques or even the Urgent Action network could be with respect to EJEs, when the "adopted" person had already been killed. Third, government use of lethal force was a complicated issue, since some force in police conduct and armed conflict were accepted internationally as legitimate. The difficulties in information gathering that existed for other human rights violations were compounded by the additional ambiguities inherent in states' use of lethal force.

EJEs: Behavior at the Extremes of Earlier Norms against Killing

International law prohibiting some forms of state-sponsored killing had been articulated very soon after the UN was founded. Norms against large-scale killing by states, such as genocide, emerged rapidly after World War II in response to the killing of civilians on a massive scale during the Holocaust. The international community incorporated the individual's "right to life" in the Universal Declaration of Human Rights in 1948, and adopted the Convention on the Prevention and Punishment of the Crime of Genocide the same year. Thus, at Amnesty International's founding in 1961, the notion that governments or their agents would target individuals for killing as a means of repressing dissent was conceivable, but extrajudicial executions seemed to lie beyond the pale in comparison to regular reports of political imprisonment and torture. Like disappearances, governments employing political killings often hid behind a veneer of silence and deniability through the use of paramilitary "death squads." But, on the other hand, unlike political imprisonment, torture, or disappearances, the international community acknowledged that governments sometimes had a legitimate claim on the use of lethal force. The police's resort to force during crowd control may result in deaths, for example, but are hard to classify as politically targeted deaths. In other situations, governments using political killings could claim they were in a state of war, where different rules applied. Further, many states did and still do reserve the right to use the death penalty as a legal form of punishment for certain crimes. Although EJEs could be unambiguously classified as acts of terror, on the surface some of their characteristics blurred the lines between internationally legitimate and illegitimate uses of power.

Phase I, Fact Finding: Human Rights Violations "Outside the Prison Cell"

One of the earliest examples of political killing on a wide scale after World War II happened in 1965, when the Indonesian army, blaming the Communist party of Indonesia for a coup attempt, wiped out between

500,000 and one million people in less than a year.[2] It was a deliberate effort to eliminate opposition. During the next decade, politically motivated killings on a similar scale took place in Cambodia under the Maoist Khmer Rouge regime, 1975–79, and in Uganda, 1971–79. Government-affiliated "death squads" became active. Killing was used as a counterinsurgency tactic in countries of Latin America in this period, for example, in Guatemala after 1966, and in El Salvador after 1979. Although some of these examples of killing might, after some study, have fallen under the Genocide Convention that had been adopted by the UN in 1948, in many cases the serious charge of genocide is not easy to show conclusively, especially while the abuses are going on. To be classified as genocide, acts must be "committed with intent to destroy, in whole or in part, a national, ethnical, racial or religious group, as such."[3] Ways needed to be found to investigate, stop, or prevent killings before they reached the scale of genocidal murder.

Amnesty International's information-gathering capacity on human rights had, with the Campaign for the Abolition of Torture (CAT), expanded for all practical purposes to a global scope. Knowledge of human rights violations, of course, did not emerge in neat compartments. Experience showed that governments used political imprisonment, torture, and disappearances in combination. Those same governments also used political killings in one form or another. Every disappearance that ended in death could be considered a concealed political killing. Massacres to repress dissent were political killings. A full understanding of the context in which political prisoners were being held inevitably confronted other forms of punishment that might be meted out by states. There was a clear sense among AI's staff by the late 1970s, if not before, that Amnesty needed to address the issue of political killings. However, disappearances and torture were offenses committed while a person was under detention in the prison cell. Even the death penalty as a judicially imposed punishment treated prisoners rather than people on the street.

Amnesty started to consider working against political killings reluctantly, said José Zalaquett, because it "took Amnesty outside of the prison cell." To deal with extrajudicial killings, Amnesty would also have to move beyond the prison cell: "Amnesty concerned itself only with prisoners: . . . Don't torture people in prison. Don't [sentence] people to the death penalty, and give them a fair trial. But when, from [the] death penalty you start looking at the killings in the streets—Amnesty . . . came out of the prison and into the street and the battlefield. But it came . . . with the arsenal of human rights concepts." Despite that arsenal, extrajudicial killing was difficult to address conceptually. According to Zalaquett, it was "enormously more complex" than disappearances, "although it looks more clear-cut."[4]

Even as Amnesty began to grapple with extrajudicial executions, for AI and other human rights experts there appeared to be a haunting possibility that the apparent effectiveness of prisoner adoption techniques had caused governments to impose more final, and secret, ways of dealing with opponents. Political prisoners now attracted sustained international attention; outright killing and disappearances ending in death were more deniable—and irreversible. Further, after a political killing the victims were no longer able to tell their story, so officials could claim that the perpetrators of EJEs had first been attacked by the victims. If true, such a claim placed the incident within the realm of rules of armed conflict, where standards on killing were different from peacetime and governments were permitted to use force against opponents. In any case, governments knew very well that if they could frame an incident in a certain way or create doubt about the circumstances, they could put a damper on any international public outcry that might be generated.

It was undeniable that the patterns of abuse were changing for the worse. For example, Amnesty reported in 1978 that "no prisoners of conscience were adopted . . . from July 1977 to June 1978, but the organization recorded over 300 cases of people who had 'disappeared' after being abducted by official or semi-official paramilitary groups—death squads. Most were murdered within a short time of their detention."[5] The leader of Human Rights Watch remarked decades later that governments' turn toward "deniable" abuses with "blurred" connections to official government authorities was at least partly a response to the remarkable earlier successes of human rights groups in getting prisoners freed.[6]

Whether people were imprisoned, tortured, disappeared, or murdered, Amnesty International was learning about it through its now-global research activities. Grasp of the facts of human rights abuses brought AI to a point where it had to decide whether and how it would deal with the growing problem of extrajudicial killings. Of course, Amnesty was already "dealing with" such killings in a limited way, simply by reporting on them. In the course of research on Latin America, for example, extrajudicial killings could hardly be ignored. In 1976, Amnesty reported that "figures for the number of political prisoners are misleading if they fail to take into consideration political assassinations . . . particularly prevalent in Guatemala and Argentina. . . . The Research Department intends to devote much of the forthcoming year to analyzing this phenomenon."[7] In 1976, as well, Amnesty expanded the Urgent Action program, established the year before to mobilize speedy letters and telegrams, to include "cases of urgency other than torture," such as "threats of execution."[8] AI's 1978 annual report noted that although the death penalty had been all but abolished by law in Latin America, the region's ongoing political violence was characterized by "abductions, disappearance, torture, and extra-legal executions or assassinations," which AI had dealt with "by sending numerous telegrams" and Urgent Action.[9]

As AI staff were grappling with how to address EJEs more effectively, news came that one hundred indigenous *campesinos* had been shot by Guatemalan soldiers on 29 May 1978 in the village of Panzós. The army claimed that they were responding to a violent challenge by the peasants, who were in the village discussing a "land tenure problem." However, Amnesty had "reliable sources" who maintained that the army fired on them without provocation.[10] Clayton Yeo, then Amnesty's deputy head of research, recalled a meeting at that time, in which someone exclaimed, "We really ought to be dealing with these killings." AI staff fully recognized the irony that, taken literally, Amnesty's mandate covered those who were detained or tortured for their beliefs, but not those who were being killed outright. "There were no doubts that there were murderous governments," said Yeo. "The concern was with what one worked on," given the broad scope of human rights violations. Reporting and other kinds of work that attention to political killings necessitated had to be intensified if they were to be prevented.

Amnesty itself was challenged by the very information about human rights abuses that it had helped to channel to the public. It could hardly ignore the information from local NGOs—and national AI sections who were hearing from solidarity groups in contact with Latin American countries—that something more needed to be done. Such considerations seemed to shout out for stronger international norms on what governments would and would not be permitted to do in the name of internal security. They also strengthened the pressure within Amnesty to redefine the scope of its work.

PHASE II, CONSENSUS BUILDING: THE NEED TO ADDRESS EJEs

The step "outside the prison cell" entailed considerable consensus building within Amnesty International as well as within the international community. While political killings made an awkward match with AI's prisoner-adoption mandate, no other organization was as well equipped to address the issue. Although the right to life was already a core human rights norm, there were obvious gaps in protection. The problem of "murder by governments" had yet to be named in a way that called states to account.

Amnesty's first statements about political killings linked them both to the death penalty and disappearances, two kinds of prisoner treatment that Amnesty already opposed.

Amnesty began to pursue better international norms against political killings in a little-known branch of the UN: the Crime Prevention and Criminal Justice Office, headquartered in Vienna. The Crime Prevention and Criminal Justice Office administered the quinquennial governmental Congress on the Prevention of Crime and the Treatment of Offenders (Crime Congress), which AI had begun attending regularly in 1975 to pursue norms against torture. The Crime Congress addressed concrete issues related to judicial punishment and reported to the General Assembly. It was logical, then, to ask the Crime Congress to consider international norms to prohibit both the death penalty and extrajudicial killing. The Crime Congress became the target of Amnesty's strategy to develop a consensus for abolition of the death penalty, and on the need for norms against EJEs. AI planned its first international campaign against capital punishment—not political killings, except as they were then understood by Amnesty as part of the "death penalty" issue—to coincide with the 1980 Crime Congress.

In the lead-up to the 1980 meeting of the Crime Congress, AI organized public pressure on governments to act. The program at AI's 1977 conference on the death penalty, held at Stockholm, included a workshop on extrajudicial executions. Although AI's normal work against capital punishment did not include political killings, a state's use of extrajudicial executions was described at that conference as part of the death penalty.[11] There were some at the Stockholm conference who felt that Amnesty should address EJEs more fully in its work. Echoing the techniques of the antitorture campaign, AI collected signatures on an international petition against capital punishment.[12]

The period between the Stockholm conference and the 1980 Crime Congress was a time of conceptual definition within Amnesty International as well. Amnesty's 1978 International Council Meeting, meeting in Cambridge, England, asked a special Mandate Committee to prepare recommendations for developing AI's methods and approach toward EJEs. The committee recommended that, as a "prisoner-oriented movement," AI should continue actively to oppose the extrajudicial execution of any *prisoner*. This was not new. The committee expanded the focus, however, adding that AI should oppose any other political killings if the facts showed that the killings formed part of a consistent pattern of abuse, or if the government was deliberately targeting an individual.

Amnesty's commitment to political impartiality and nonviolence was evident in the Mandate Committee's recommendations. The committee concluded that "the mandate would not cover the shooting of someone on his way to kill people, or who might shoot back, or [who might] be part of a situation in which a police officer might simply mistakenly shoot someone too quickly. . . . [T]he idea was, if it was murder by the government, then AI would oppose it. But only in the political context."[13]

In 1980, AI's International Council Meeting, its worldwide gathering of delegates from the membership, affirmed the AI Mandate Committee's earlier findings by expanding AI's opposition to the death penalty and prisoner mistreatment to encompass extrajudicial executions. This was a big step. It meant that Amnesty should act using all techniques available when it had facts to show that governments were killing people for deliberate, nonspontaneous, political reasons.

AI's expanding capabilities and responsibilities brought new questions as to how far it should expand its scope of work. Because AI was a membership-driven organization, it *could* shift or expand its focus relatively easily, within certain limits. Some of those limits were dictated by the personal and financial resources of the organization. Other questions about focus were defined by the debates about how to approach political killings and disappearances in the late 1970s. Together, the questions called for internally as well as externally oriented discussions within AI.

The International Secretariat and the International Executive Committee (IEC) now had to decide how to implement the expanded policy. The International Secretariat was cautious of expansion, already conscious of its own limitations given the enormous tasks that its members already mandated. The new mandate would require all of the same attention the earlier issues required: research, international conceptual exploration, consensus building, and norm construction. The busy International Secretariat staffers, in particular, were acutely aware that Amnesty was, in Yeo's words, "an organization with limited resources, taking on an enormous task." He continued, "Amnesty is just human beings! These are people who get tired, who are new or experienced, young or old, having babies, sometimes sick, sometimes worried about something else, trying to apply international standards with a very particular form of impartiality, to a very specific set of local facts."[14] The urgency and the expanding scope of AI's work seemed to pull against the need to maintain clarity and focus.

Conferences, for example, had become a proven way for AI to "bring together a lot of concerns, knowledge, ideas on an issue, and . . . provide a platform from where it actually is easier to take it up in the UN, take it up with other organizations, motivate your own membership," said Dick Oosting, Amnesty's first Campaign Department head. A conference "basically provides] a focus for an issue." But despite their efficiency and usefulness, conferences and campaigns also represented a large amount of added work for the International Secretariat. Campaigns "draw on the same research time, effort, and capacity. . . . They are officially very much interlinked with each other, you draw on the same campaigning structures, and then, target groups, governments, *et cetera*."[15]

One solution that partially relieved the International Secretariat in conceptual exploration and consensus building was for national sections to adopt responsibility for certain issues. National sections also provided the funding base for the central operations of Amnesty. Therefore, national sections both augmented the capacity of AI's International Secretariat and provided a source of internal change for AI since, in practice, influential national sections not only aided the central work, but sometimes also pressed the Secretariat to adopt certain policies. The larger and wealthier national sections of Amnesty, particularly in the United States and Europe, possessed significant staff, volunteer, political, and financial resources. The involvement of AIUSA on disappearances, its research contacts with Argentine groups, and sponsorship of the Wingspread seminar in 1980 are examples.

In a similar way, the Dutch section of Amnesty International was particularly interested in advancing AI's work on political killings. Argentina's use of disappearances and EJEs was a high-profile issue in the Netherlands after the Argentine coup. Dutch groups in solidarity with Argentina put pressure on the Dutch government to act. The Dutch parliament was in the process of defining a Dutch bilateral foreign policy on human rights. On the popular front, Holland played Argentina in the finals of the World Cup soccer match, which Argentina hosted in 1978 at the height of military rule.[16]

At the 1980 Crime Congress, Amnesty and forty-one other NGOs submitted a joint statement calling the death penalty a violation of the right to life and the provisions against cruel, inhuman, or degrading treatment or punishment, urging all human rights NGOs to campaign for its abolition, and asking the assembly to go on record as opposing it.[17] But that and AI's public campaign against the death penalty failed to catalyze the congress to condemn judicially imposed capital punishment. "We appealed to the United Nations for the abolition of the death penalty, and we were circulating this appeal and getting signatures for it, while this Congress was preparing and was held. So there was a lot of pressure on them to adopt that, [but] they didn't—there was a clash at the conference."[18] The congress did, however, resolve that the General Assembly should take up the issue of political killings. In strong language, it condemned "murder committed or tolerated by governments," referring to the "incidence in different parts of the world of summary executions as well as of arbitrary executions."[19] The term *summary* refers to government-sponsored killings in lieu of any legal process, and *arbitrary* characterizes executions violating established legal protections.[20] But, against

AI's urging, such qualifications left intact the assumption that executions are legitimate when imposed with judicial safeguards.

The next General Assembly followed with a resolution urging states to respect relevant articles of the International Covenant on Civil and Political Rights (ICCPR), and asking the UN secretary-general to use his "best endeavors" when it appeared that minimum legal safeguards were not respected.[21] The UN resolutions regarding "summary and arbitrary" executions rhetorically reinforced the ICCPR's pronouncement against the arbitrary deprivation of life, encouraging states to circumscribe the use of executions with legal safeguards. Further, the General Assembly expressed concern "at the occurrence of executions which are widely regarded as being politically motivated." The resolution urged states to follow basic procedures and urged the secretary-general to ask for "views and observations" from states, regional intergovernmental organizations, and consultative NGOs about such executions. The secretary-general's subsequent report, issued on January 22, 1982, cited Amnesty International's concerns about the "intentional execution of persons for political reasons."[22] However, the 1980 General Assembly resolution established no way of actually reporting on states' violation of legal safeguards.

Given Amnesty's goals on the death penalty, the outcome was a frustrating one; again, the nod toward "summary and arbitrary executions" was a consolation prize for the Amnesty campaign on the death penalty. Still, the 1980 Crime Congress did open the way for strong AI statements on state-sponsored killings, providing a reference point for AI to address the UN on the issue. Following the General Assembly's first resolution on EJEs, AI made a strong statement on the political use of the death penalty at the 1981 meeting of the Commission on Human Rights, entitled "Murder by Governments." In it, AI expressed concern over killings "systematically ordered and executed under the auspices of the government," and proceeded to give specific examples of reports of extrajudicial killings that referred to seven governments by name in Africa and Latin America.[23] To name countries went beyond diplomatic convention in the Commission, but it was a convention that was beginning to be breached with regard to other forms of human rights violations at about the same time. The UN General Assembly adopted a second resolution regarding EJEs later in 1981.[24]

Through the sixth Crime Congress and through resolutions at the General Assembly, political killings were established on the UN agenda. The 1982 session of the Commission on Human Rights (1 February–12 March) was characterized by strong talk on political killings. Theo van Boven, the director of the UN Division of Human Rights, opened the session with a statement emphasizing the right to life and naming countries where political killings had been reported.[25] Other speakers echoed his remarks. Amnesty addressed the commission on "The Political Use of the Death Penalty." The emphasis on political killings prepared the way for the Human Rights Commission to recommend stronger UN action.[26]

Amnesty had not yet held a public campaign on political killings, although it had spoken out on the topic in various UN venues and had publicized the problem of political executions in its country-level work. AI worked closely with the Danish government with reference to the political killings issue at the 1982 session of the Commission on Human Rights. (Amnesty had a history of collaboration with the Scandinavian governments, and Denmark was the Scandinavian government then on rotation at the Commission on Human Rights.) Working with Denmark, Amnesty representatives helped to draft the language to create a significant new monitoring mechanism, the Special Rapporteur on Summary or Arbitrary Executions. Publicly, in its statement at the Commission, Denmark cited Amnesty International information as it introduced the resolution to create the new special rapporteur.[27]

The creation of the special rapporteur was a major step forward in the UN's approach to EJEs. Before the special rapporteur was established in 1982, the only other "thematic" UN mechanism for monitoring specific forms of violations of human rights was the Working Group on Enforced or Involuntary Disappearances. Until then, special rapporteurs had only been assigned to countries, for a limited period of time.[28] The politics surrounding the thematic emphasis this time did not reflect an effort to avoid incisive criticism of an acute case, as had happened with Argentina and the WGEID. There seemed to be a general consensus that an emphasis on categories rather than country cases was called for in order to make progress on dealing with EJEs.

The Danes, again with some input from Amnesty International, advanced the name of Amos Wako of Kenya, who was chosen as the first special rapporteur.[29] As soon as Wako took office, Amnesty began communicating information on EJEs that it had collected and urged the special rapporteur to investigate, and not just describe, the facts of EJEs. The first person in such an office could set precedents conducive to upholding human rights, just as van Boven's initiative had helped to establish the WGEID as an active international monitoring tool on disappearances.

Indeed, Wako proved active in his first year. Even though his mandate did not formally give him the authority to question governments about information he gathered on summary and arbitrary executions,[30] he communicated allegations to governments anyway, requested responses, and printed many of them in his first report. For that, he was criticized by governments at the 1983 meeting of the Commission on Human Rights.[31] He subsequently moderated his actions somewhat, but just as the WGEID had taken a page from AI's urgent action technique, Wako implemented an urgent communication procedure with governments for use when he received information about individual cases.[32] By his fourth report he had revived his original practice of naming governments and reporting their replies to allegations.[33]

With the creation of such a mechanism, it was important for AI to continue to build its own internal focus by sorting out the conceptual issues pertinent to the consensus necessary for effective use of UN mechanisms and the development of international norms. In that spirit, Amnesty's Dutch section hosted an international conference in Noordwijkerhout, The Netherlands, 30 April–2 May 1982, for AI to study the nature of extrajudicial executions and discuss efforts to combat them.[34] The timing of the conference was similar to that of the Wingspread conference on disappearances, in that the UN had just created a new mechanism. The conceptual work, therefore, would be useful not only for defining how Amnesty might work effectively on EJEs, but also for clarifying the possible emphasis with relation to human rights norms endorsed by governments and the UN. About 120 people attended, including AI staff, representatives of national human rights organizations, international human rights groups, and UN representatives. The conference came up with a conceptualization of political killings that, for the first time, separated EJEs, disappearances, and torture as phenomena. AI had already decided to treat them separately in its public campaigns, but the people at the conference—some of AI's International Secretariat staff, some more accustomed to practical campaigning for human rights "on the ground," and some UN officials—articulated the distinction. In the opening section of the conference statement, the "Declaration of Amsterdam," AI set forth "a miniature description of extrajudicial executions and their institutional settings, the things that occur, what happens to the rest of society, and the connection to torture and disappearances."[35] The statement noted that extrajudicial executions are often accompanied by suspended constitutional rights and the failure of independent judicial safeguards, and that governments try to keep EJEs secret. Disappearance and torture often precede the killing, and such killings take a range of forms, from "assassinations to the wholesale liquidation of political opposition." The "miniature description" concludes by emphasizing governmental accountability.[36]

The conference deliberations worked out and preserved a consensus within AI on how to understand EJEs and how to communicate about them during its campaigns when pressing for prevention and investigation of the phenomenon. For example, at this conference participants decided to use the term "extrajudicial" rather than "extralegal" to describe this type of killing, in order to avoid confusion about governments' use of a legalized death penalty.

Amnesty's statement at the next meeting of the Sub-Commission summarized the findings and recommendations of the Dutch conference and expressed AI's desire for the special rapporteur to address the problems of extrajudicial executions, and not just irregularities in judicial executions, as might be implied by the phrase the UN was using, "summary or arbitrary executions."[37] In 1992, the name of the special rapporteur was changed to include "extrajudicial, summary, or arbitrary executions."[38] While the mechanism has its limits, the special rapporteur has since become even more specific in monitoring governments, visiting countries, and communicating via questionnaires and follow-up correspondence regarding individual cases.[39] Most of the information about cases comes from NGOs. The special rapporteur has noted that information from NGOs is "indispensable" to carrying out the mandate of the office.[40]

In the following year, on the public side, Amnesty organized its first campaign on EJEs, focusing on the theme of "Political Killings by Governments." Some experienced Amnesty staff had serious doubts whether the public would respond to the idea of approaching governments on behalf of people who had been killed. Amnesty had stretched its prisoner adoption techniques to deal with torture and had begun to work against disappearances: it had not tried applying its approaches in the context of political killings before. Groups that had investigated such cases, for example, found it even more difficult and frustrating to work on behalf of someone who had already been killed or had disappeared and was thought dead. Work for those who had been unlawfully executed with the involvement or acquiescence of the government did not hold out the same possibility of relief for the victims, and so the hope that permeated prisoner adoption work would be more difficult to sustain, it was feared.

The campaign publicity, for that reason, needed to interpret and explain the problem of political killings, educating the public and Amnesty groups on the issue in order to facilitate further Amnesty efforts for stronger norm implementation and practical prevention.[41] Amnesty wanted to emphasize government responsibility for political killings, giving the lie to popular attitudes that terrorists committed most political violence, that political killings were primarily the result of armed conflict or clashes between the political "right" and "left," and that therefore no public pleas could be effective.

A concrete mechanism for monitoring extrajudicial executions emerged from the UN without a long period of consensus building on the issue. Thus, the phase was telescoped to a greater degree than for the norm-building process on torture and disappearances. This is attributable to three factors. First, despite Amnesty International's mandate-driven needs for internal consensus building about how to work against EJEs, the emphasis on government accountability that AI had fostered for torture and disappearances almost certainly contributed to the international community's readiness to establish a monitoring mechanism for political killings. Second, and relatedly, given the prohibitions against deprivation of life that were already set down in the International Covenant and other international norms, there was little need for a UN declaration on extrajudicial executions to provide a basis for further norm developments. From a legal perspective, that meant that the international community could be moved more quickly to the development of monitoring mechanisms and advisory guidelines. Third, through its earlier work, Amnesty International had established productive links with sympathetic governments, which facilitated the movement from principles to concrete standards where consensus building was not an obstacle.

PHASE III, NORM CONSTRUCTION: PRINCIPLES AND A PROTOCOL

A feature of fully elaborated norms in the United Nations is that the establishment of binding norms often opens the way for further elaboration on the agreed-upon principles through nonbinding auxiliary standards. Such standards recommend specific measures that states may take to support human rights principles in different issue areas. Political killings is one area where such elaboration has taken place since the special rapporteur was established. Interestingly, as both human rights norms and human rights NGOs proliferated in the 1980s and 1990s, the NGO role in norm generation has not diminished. What has happened, however, is that norm-building techniques and expertise have diffused to other NGOs, often with a division of labor among NGOs or active collaboration among them. The development of principles to investigate political killings provides an example of how AI's fact-finding and norm-construction expertise provided a model for a smaller NGO that could take on part of a task that Amnesty might have attempted had circumstances been different.

The political killings issue raised the question of how facts might be gathered to show maltreatment and government culpability after the fact. Indeed, if political killings represented political murder, then criminal investigation techniques were an obvious place to start. Amnesty International carried out its own survey of how various states and countries deal with autopsies of arbitrary killings in 1984.[42] David Weissbrodt, a professor at the University of Minnesota Law School, was spending his 1982–83 sabbatical leave on the staff the Legal Office of Amnesty International at the International Secretariat in London when the idea for the project arose. At the same time back in Minnesota, Sam Hines, a Twin Cities attorney, and Don Fraser, then the mayor of Minneapolis,[43] were forming a local organization of attorneys to work on human rights, the Minnesota Lawyers International Human Rights Committee (Lawyers Committee).[44] Hines and Fraser wrote to Weissbrodt in London asking for ideas on possible projects for the group.[45]

Given the pressure on AI to take on more and more issues, and given AI's awareness of the increasing need to work against extrajudicial executions, "it was pretty clear that [research on autopsy procedures] this was really an Amnesty project," but that a thorough research project was more than the office could take on internally.[46] However, there was some precedent for requesting assistance from legal contacts in various parts of the world who were willing to volunteer some time for AI to work on discrete projects. From London, Weissbrodt asked the Lawyers Committee president, Sam Hines, to research the legal procedure followed in Minnesota to obtain an autopsy when there was a suspicious death. Weissbrodt asked a few contacts in other parts of the world to write similar memos for AI, with the purpose of beginning a catalog of domestic standards that might be used as reference points for the development of an international standard for the investigation of suspicious deaths. At the end of Weissbrodt's sabbatical, the research on domestic autopsy standards was unfinished.

The potential usefulness of such research was highlighted when, in August 1983, Senator Benigno Aquino was assassinated in the Philippines. Despite promises to the contrary, the government of the Philippines under Ferdinand Marcos failed to conduct a thorough investigation of the assassination. At that time, there were no internationally standardized death investigation procedures. There was no external norm, therefore, that could be used as a basis for criticism when governments failed to implement proper investigation of political killings in a case like the death of Aquino.

The Minnesota Lawyers Committee considered further involvement in the project as it formed project committees in the fall of 1983. Weissbrodt suggested the need for research on death investigation and autopsy standards in order to develop a general set of recommended standards that could be applied internationally.[47] The Lawyers Committee decided to take on the project.

The research had two necessary components: legal and medical. Legally, law enforcement procedures necessary for a thorough investigation of extrajudicial executions had to be clarified. On the legal side, it would be important to ensure evidence was not wasted through mistakes in legal procedures or shoddy evidence protection techniques, whether by design or simple lack of knowledge by local authorities.

The medical aspect involved articulating the steps required for a valid forensic autopsy. A forensic autopsy does not immediately come to mind as a tool of human rights advocacy. However, an examination of the body could be an important tool in establishing the facts of a case. It could establish a person's identity, thus aiding the search for disappeared persons. It could identify signs of torture on the body of an extrajudicial execution victim. Sometimes, by matching the circumstances under which a person was last seen with identification of his or her body and signs of ill treatment, government culpability could be established scientifically.

Barbara Frey, one of the early organizers of the Lawyers Committee, became its executive director in 1985. As a volunteer participant on the autopsy project, and later as head of the Lawyers Committee, Frey recruited professionals outside the Lawyers Committee with the expertise to assist in developing a protocol. The first phase of the project focused on autopsy and what to do medically with the body of a person who dies as the result of probable or possible illegal activity. This portion of the project was referred to as the "Protocol." The intent, according to Frey, was to make the protocol general enough that "first-world standards" were not a prerequisite for conducting a thorough autopsy. Then, feeling that they needed to include standards for conducting a police investigation of a suspicious killing, the focus expanded to investigatory procedures. The second portion of the project was referred to as the "Principles."

The Lawyers Committee began at home, with the resources at hand in Minneapolis. Frey recruited the Hennepin County Attorney, Thomas Johnson, to research investigatory procedures, and looked to a local pathologist and to the County Medical Examiner's Office for medical expertise. Frey invited Lindsey Thomas, M.D., to join the project as a volunteer medical consultant. Thomas had been performing autopsies for four years, but had no forensic training, so she and Frey also enlisted the participation of the chief medical examiner of Minneapolis's Hennepin County, Dr. Garry Peterson. In consultation with a newly formed treatment center, the Center for Victims of Torture located in Minneapolis, Thomas began work on the Protocol by reviewing the existing medical literature on torture. She also reviewed standard autopsy protocols, such as those published by the U.S. organization, the National Association of Medical Examiners. Thomas then extended the implications of the literature, asking herself, "Given what the medical world knows about torture, what specific things would be helpful" in an autopsy investigation?[48] Thomas then constructed a draft protocol, with forensic advice from Peterson. The draft included instructions on the kinds of evidence an examiner should look for and collect in order to document the circumstances of death, including torture.

When she began her research, Thomas knew of no forensic pathologists with whom she could consult who had experience in the documentation of torture as part of an autopsy. "At that time," she said, "there really wasn't anybody that did, except in Denmark."[49] AI had asked some Danish doctors to investigate torture in Spain and other countries, and the doctors had formed the ongoing Danish Medical Group in 1974, partly as a result of AI's Paris Conference on Torture's call for doctors' involvement in "the documentation and verification of torture."[50] An AI forensic medical group formed two years later.

Dr. Jorgen Thomsen, a Danish pathologist, was a member of the Danish Medical Group. Thomas corresponded with Thomsen when she began working on the project, and met him when she attended the Cross-Channel Conference, an annual cross-national conference of forensic pathologists from Britain, Holland, and Belgium in May 1986. Thomsen was at that time an assistant professor in forensic medicine at the University of Copenhagen, and Denmark had been invited to attend. As she worked on the international autopsy standards, Thomas learned from other medical specialists involved with the issue. Some doctors were beginning to recognize the need for international standards. There had been calls, in particular, for the establishment of international procedures concerning investigation of deaths that took place outside the deceased's own country.[51] Thomsen et al. noted in 1984 that "it would be a major step forward to establish international rules" to allow foreign specialists to investigate cases of alleged torture.[52] Several people from the American Association for the Advancement of Science were also becoming interested in this topic.[53]

In 1985, three successive drafts of the autopsy protocol were circulated internationally to medical, legal, and human rights groups for comment. A series of forensic sciences conferences provided further opportunity to develop expert contacts who were interested in human rights topics. Thomas and Frey presented the Protocol in New Orleans at the February 1986 meeting of the American Academy of Forensic Scientists, in a special forum on human rights issues. At that meeting, Clyde Snow, the Oklahoma forensic anthropologist well known for his work exhuming graves in Argentina, and his colleague, Karen Ramey Burns, offered to contribute to the protocol. Burns, then a research associate at the Center for Archaeological Sciences of the University of Georgia, contributed a model protocol for disinterment and analysis of skeletal remains. Thus, the final version of the Protocol actually contained three model protocols: a model protocol for a legal investigation, including procedures for a sufficient inquiry and for establishing a special Commission of Inquiry; a model autopsy protocol, including steps that would document signs of torture or mistreatment; and a protocol for excavation and analysis of remains.[54]

The Lawyers Committee devoted a considerable proportion of its time and resources to the development of the Protocol. Before September

1985, when Frey became the paid executive director of the organization, all the work on the Protocol had been done by volunteers. A Legal Fellow joined the staff in the fall of 1986, to spend most of her time on work related to the protocol. The Lawyers Committee decided to schedule a conference on the Protocol for 1987, and Frey began to raise money to hold the conference.

Applying to "every organization that the Committee could think of for funding for the conference," said Frey, "we came up dry." Knowing that the Danish government had worked with Amnesty on the EJE issue, the Lawyers Committee wrote to Christian Hoppe, the Danish UN representative who had helped to sponsor a resolution on forensics in human rights work at the Human Rights Commission.[55] Hoppe helped to secure a gift of $10,000 from the Danish Ministry of Foreign Affairs, which made up the bulk of the funding for the Minnesota conference.[56] Frey remarked, "Without them we wouldn't have been able to do it, and even with them it was quite remarkable" that the Lawyers Committee managed to bring off a productive conference with minimal financial resources.[57]

Participants in the conference, held at Spring Hill conference center in Minnesota, included twenty-six persons from six U.S. states and six countries. AI, the Ford Foundation, the AAAS, the UN Centre for Human Rights of Geneva, the UN Centre for Social Development and Humanitarian Affairs of Vienna, the International Service for Human Rights of Geneva, and the International Human Rights Law Group of New York were among the intergovernmental and nongovernmental organizations represented.

The conference convened both a legal and a medical working group, with the shared goals of "reviewing the Minnesota Protocol and reaching a consensus on principles for international adoption."[58] Participants were briefed by Slawomir Redo, of the UN Centre for Social Development and Humanitarian Affairs, on the status of the draft "Principles on the Effective Prevention and Investigation of Extra-Legal, Arbitrary and Summary Executions," in anticipation of the Principles' being taken up by the UN Committee on Crime Prevention and Control at its tenth session in August 1988. The office of the Special Rapporteur on Summary or Arbitrary Executions sent a staff member to the meeting. The legal working group prepared a final draft of the Principles, "based on drafts prepared by the UN Secretariat, in pursuance of resolution 11 of the Seventh United Nations Congress on the Prevention of Crime and the Treatment of Offenders and ECOSOC resolution 1986/10, section IV, and the Minnesota Lawyers Human Rights Committee."[59] Based on the efforts of the two working groups, the protocol and the principles were combined into a single document to be advanced at the United Nations.[60]

The UN Route

The Lawyers Committee had found an area ripe for research and international standard setting. But the Minnesota Project had to be known and used by governments to be effective. At that time, the Danish government was on rotation as the member of the United Nations Commission on Human Rights from the Scandinavian group. Weissbrodt contacted Christian Hoppe, the Danish representative who had helped secure funding for the Spring Hill conference, asking him to sponsor a resolution at the Commission urging attention to the uses of forensic science in human rights work. In Weissbrodt's letter to Hoppe, he suggested language for a General Assembly resolution at the 1988 session, expanding on language in a resolution on EJEs that Hoppe had introduced at the 1987 General Assembly.[61] At the Commission on Human Rights and before the General Assembly, Denmark introduced language that mentioned the Minnesota Protocol and urged the special rapporteur to devote attention to the Minnesota project.[62] At the General Assembly, the Danish delegation presented what was by then known as the Minnesota Protocol, resulting in a resolution recognizing and encouraging the effort to establish international minimum standards for death investigations. The resolution could provide a basis for further consideration of the Minnesota standards in the human rights bodies of the UN.

Having secured Denmark's cooperation, the Lawyers Committee planned the official introduction of the document into the United Nations machinery.[63] Although the project had been recognized by the UN, it had not been adopted as an official UN standard. The Lawyers Committee hoped at the beginning that the special rapporteur, Amos Wako of Kenya, would use his position to help advance the Protocol and the Principles. The Danes had been instrumental in Wako's appointment. Wako was based in Geneva, where the UN Commission on Human Rights meets annually, and it had been assumed that the Lawyers Committee would work through the office of the Special Rapporteur on Summary or Arbitrary Executions.

Instead, it became apparent that the same purpose could probably be achieved more quickly through the Crime Prevention and Control branch of the UN in Vienna. Political haggling could delay initiatives originating in the Geneva-based Commission on Human Rights. The Vienna staff were able to pay more attention to the project, and the Crime Prevention and Control Branch of the UN was much less politicized concerning human rights issues at that time than were the UN organs in Geneva. Members of the Committee on Crime Prevention and Control, the first hurdle for the Protocol and Principles, tended to take a technical and legal approach to its agenda.[64]

Wako later referred to the Lawyers Committee's efforts in the annual report of the special rapporteur to the Commission on Human Rights. However, "the real work was done out of Vienna."[65] In Vienna, staff experts under Slavomir Redo, the UN official who had represented the UN Office of Social and Humanitarian Affairs at the Spring Hill conference, drafted a resolution and sent the proposal through the Crime Commission and on through the Economic and Social Council (ECOSOC) to the General Assembly. Amnesty International became involved again at this later stage of the process and readopted the issue to lobby ECOSOC in New York when the resolution reached that level.[66]

Redo later spoke warmly of his contacts with the Minnesota Lawyers Committee. He noted that the work on the Principles "started concurrently in two places": Geneva's UN Centre for Human Rights (now known as the Office of the UN High Commissioner for Human Rights); and the Crime Prevention Branch of the United Nations in Vienna. The interests of both commissions in such a set of principles, in his words, "somehow merged."[67] Both were interested in the development of investigatory guidelines. The mandate for their development originated in UN's human rights program at the Centre for Human Rights in Geneva, the branch of the UN Secretariat that then administered human rights programs for the Commission on Human Rights and the Sub-Commission.[68] Later efforts to finalize the draft text came out of the Crime Prevention branch in Vienna.

This route has since become politicized, at least temporarily.[69] But from 1984, when safeguards against the death penalty successfully emerged from the Crime Prevention branch,[70] there were indications that the guidelines on investigation of extralegal killings could also be developed and ushered through the Vienna process. At the time that the death penalty safeguards were approved, Redo remarked, it was thought that they would also apply to extralegal killings. Nigel Rodley, then head of the AI International Secretariat's Legal Office, had masterminded the death penalty safeguards passed in 1984. As it turned out, further discussion among UN staff and other interested parties revealed that something beyond the death penalty safeguards was needed.[71] Therefore there was impetus within the Committee on Crime Prevention, along with the Commission on Human Rights, to proceed with the extralegal killings project, and the Commission experts conferred on the issue.

Redo acknowledged the heavy effort involved in drafting new norms. He noted that Amnesty International and the Minnesota Lawyers Committee were the NGOs most involved in work on the principles and protocol, with the Minnesota people having been more heavily involved on the newer issues relating directly to extralegal executions. In the long drafting process for what eventually became the UN's *Manual on the*

Effective Prevention and Investigation of Extra-legal, Arbitrary, and Summary Executions, drafts were "worked back and forth endlessly."[72] The general UN procedure of distributing the text of the *Manual* to every member state, coordinated through UN channels, was supplemented with an arrangement by the Minnesota Lawyers Committee to distribute the manual to its constituents.[73] Amnesty International also cites and occasionally distributes copies of the Principles in its communications with governments.[74]

Redo deemed the contribution of the Lawyers Committee to be "tremendous," particularly their development of the autopsy protocol, "now known as the Minnesota Protocol for evermore." It is not unusual for NGOs to work on draft instruments, noted Redo, but the "Minnesota people" were "really enthusiastic," he said. They put their "heart and mind" into the project.[75]

The Danes, in their financial assistance for the Minnesota conference, were key contacts for the Lawyers Committee, and Danish doctors like Jorgen Thomsen were clearly important for both the Lawyers Committee and AI. Redo's offices had less contact with the Danes, however. In the main, Minnesota "coordinated the work for us."[76]

Phase IV, Norm Application: Using the Guidelines

As for the potential effects of the guidelines, Redo remarked diplomatically that these guidelines serve as a "thoughtful and practical approach to the issue, if one wants to follow the guidelines." He sees their significance as an illustration of the checks and balances that are needed for government investigations, for governments that wish to follow the guidelines.

Guidelines as Prevention?

What was the purpose of drawing up a *Manual on the Investigation and Prevention of Extra-legal, Arbitrary, and Summary Executions?* Investigatory guidelines for an alleged crime that has already occurred could hardly be called a preventive measure. Indeed, this cuts to the heart of an apparent irony for human rights work. An organization like AI must react to events: a human rights abuse occurs; the organization investigates; the organization acts. When the organization does encounter a violation, it has no power to punish human rights violators.

Deterrence must come from some other source, and several members of the Minnesota advocates saw the preventative aspect of the guidelines in their potential as deterrence measures, if weak ones. "In other words, the logic was that if you had adequate death investigation standards, that they would be used to investigate and prosecute the actual perpetrators, which would put a damper on military- or governmental-sponsored deaths or assassinations, because there would be some understanding that their chances of getting prosecuted would be higher."[77] Despite the presumed intention of the drafters, there was some feeling within AI that the title's reference to "extra-legal, arbitrary, and summary executions" comes on a bit strong in practice. James Welsh, an AI staff member who has worked with the *Manual,* pointed out that to send a government the guidelines, or even to cite the title when pressing for a thorough investigation of a death involving possible illegal activity can be awkward. AI did not object to the title during the drafting process, but found that in use, the title may be clumsy or accusatory:

> It's a very charged title. . . . [It] isn't something neutral, like, "Investigation of Deaths in Custody," or, "Investigation of Unexplained, Sudden, Violent Deaths." . . . I can think personally of some cases where *we have not been sure* why the person died. We would have found it a little bit more comfortable to write to the government and say, "We don't know why this person died. We're writing to find out. Has this death been investigated in accordance with the UN Standard?" . . . It's saying, "You might have murdered this person." We don't necessarily want to say that. What we want to say is, "Have you investigated the death?[78]

Welsh concluded that "we live with that, and we do use the standard, and we do write," saying, "Have you investigated this death, taking into account these elements?" His comments emphasize the role of objectivity and respect for procedures necessary for norm application. AI uses the principles in its own correspondence, although the guidelines ultimately call for adoption of the Principles into a country's own domestic law. In 1994, correspondence with the Lawyers Committee about the new proposals, AI, as a result of its broader contacts, was in a position to offer comments for possible improvements to the Protocol and Principles.

As a legal mechanism, the guidelines had to be specific about legal principles that governments should incorporate into domestic law. As a practical investigative mechanism, the guidelines had to be available, easy to understand, and applicable in situations where investigators might possess only very basic technology. Amnesty's comments to the Lawyers Committee emphasized that the legal protocol should recommend mandatory and binding domestic mechanisms that would force governments by law to investigate cases of extrajudicial executions. Further, AI suggested that later editions should streamline the autopsy protocol to highlight the principles behind the recommended procedures, specify the minimum desirable criteria of the autopsy examination in a checklist form, and simplify language related to specialized nonmedical procedures. It also noted that the first edition had lacked a good distribution strategy.[79]

CONCLUSION

This case study provides a close view of the results of a large NGO's capacity to foster the development of normative instruments based on its own discovery of gaps in the international normative framework. When the larger issue of extrajudicial killing showed up as a problem, AI had learned through its previous campaigns that a thematic approach to a human rights problem could be effective. A conceptual conference, as with the disappearance issue, clarified Amnesty's focus and enriched its campaign work. The unavailability of information concerning possible domestic remedies for cases of extrajudicial killing, however, led to the joint AI and Lawyers Committee efforts to catalog domestic investigative procedures.

The involvement of the Lawyers Committee initially consisted of supporting a larger AI project. However, its growing involvement, and its success in creating new normative guidelines, offers support for the notion that the importance and success of a third party role in the instigation of international norms is not limited to a large, historically unique NGO. The Lawyers Committee successfully employed the strategies learned from the larger NGOs. The norm-building process was the same, namely, gathering information, building consensus, and using those elements in the effort to construct legal norms.

It is the mode of the work that is critical to understanding how norms emerge. In this case, the NGOs provided resources, expertise, contacts, and, finally, application of the standards. The smaller Lawyers Committee was very important in the first three: resources, expertise, and contacts. On the other hand, AI's experience, clout, and name recognition stemming from its other campaign work could make it more effective in the norm application phase.

This case also suggests that a less politicized atmosphere and perhaps a less politicized agent of normative development (e.g., the then-unknown Minnesota Lawyers Committee, and experts associated with scientific investigations) are conducive to the origination of norms, while political clout is more important for implementation. Further, norms of technical assistance may also be initially more acceptable to states—a possibility implicitly acknowledged by the AI medical coordinator who commented that the inclusion of "extra-legal, summary, and arbitrary" killings in the title of the manual seems unnecessarily inflammatory in some instances.

Not waiting for a comprehensive international instrument, AI has adopted its own program of prevention of EJEs. In December 1992, after a second conference on EJEs and disappearances also hosted by the Dutch section, Amnesty International adopted a 14-Point Program for the Prevention of Extrajudicial Executions as it initiated a worldwide campaign for an end to extrajudicial executions.[80] The recommendations, aimed at governments, include reference to the principles developed by the Minnesota lawyers. Early in the process of developing such standards, participants recognized that "no one . . . was so naive as to think that the drafting and enacting of death inquiry standards will prevent or eliminate all arbitrary killings in the future. But such standards can provide a working 'inquiry' vocabulary which can be useful in many circumstances."[81] Investigation, although it occurs after the deed is committed, is now linked to prevention efforts since it implies, like a municipal investigation of any suspicious death, detection of the true course of events and punishment for those who committed the crime. NGOs, governments, and IGOs can now refer to international standards of investigation. The idea of a thorough autopsy now has an international reference point rather than a reliance on widely varying national standards of investigation.

The involvement of the Lawyers Committee, a small, new NGO in comparison to AI, shows effective NGO involvement that replicates AI's norm-building cycle. AI's resources and experience helped to identify the need for the services that the Lawyers Committee could provide, but the Lawyers Committee's involvement shows that the role of NGOs in norm emergence is not unique to AI or the larger human rights NGOs.

Chapter Six

NGOs AND NORMS IN INTERNATIONAL POLITICS

WHEN QUESTIONS pertaining to human rights norms are considered at the United Nations, Amnesty can be found in the workroom if NGOs are permitted, and outside in the hall if they are not. While NGO activities have been subject to varying constraints over the years, consultative arrangements have permitted NGOs to observe the public business of the UN, distribute reports, submit written statements on UN agenda items, make oral statements or "interventions," receive UN documents, use UN library facilities, and become involved in work on international legal instruments.[1] These opportunities are now exercised routinely, but many result from Amnesty's work to stretch the boundaries on NGOs' participation. The legitimacy and care that AI exhibited over decades prepared the way for more frequent and more significant opportunities for many more NGOs to advocate their own goals at the United Nations.

AI is not the only organization to pursue stronger normative restraints on states, but it became a leader by providing both professional expertise and grassroots contacts. AI has influenced and has been influenced by other organizations since its founding. In its early years, Amnesty learned a great deal from both the International Committee of the Red Cross and the International Commission of Jurists (ICJ). The ICJ and its regional affiliates were prominent partners with AI on some norm-building projects over the years. Another large NGO, the U.S.-based Human Rights Watch, has collaborated more recently with AI and the ICJ in work on global norms. However, AI was unique in that it was the *first* organization to work from a popular base to address human rights, both behaviorally and normatively, at both grassroots and intergovernmental levels. AI was also the first human rights NGO explicitly to build and to tout its objectivity and independence, with the realization that both must be strenuously cultivated to avoid charges of political bias.[2] Its independence put AI in a position to be a legitimate critic of any and all governments participating in human rights violations.[3]

In the introduction to each case study, I presented an account of human rights norms before the advent of AI. Before AI was founded, the "standards of achievement" set down in the Universal Declaration of

Human Rights were seen as compelling goals that the founding states of the UN articulated as a response to behavior of the states that had been vanquished in World War II. Those declaratory provisions received the perfunctory verbal adherence of UN members, but despite the universal scope of the Universal Declaration, states were protected in Article 2(7) of UN Charter from any encroachment upon their domestic jurisdiction by the United Nations or by other states, a feature of the international normative structure that limited scrutiny on human rights issues.

Until the 1970s, human rights concerns as outlined in the International Covenants on human rights did not progress very far from the conceptualization presented in the Universal Declaration of Human Rights, either in terms of definitive formulation of specific violations or obligations laid upon states. This was true with regard to the prohibition of torture;[4] but especially so with regard to disappearances and extrajudicial executions, which had hardly even been conceptualized in international law, even as late as 1973. Before AI came along, ideas about human rights existed, but the related legal and practical concepts were undeveloped conceptually, and monitoring techniques were weak or nonexistent.

The case studies, therefore, demonstrated AI's leadership in the emergence of specific international norms concerning torture, disappearances, and extrajudicial executions. It is impossible to discern what the course of events would have been in the absence of Amnesty's work, but one can speculate that the status and effect of present-day human rights norms would have been very different, and probably later in coming, without AI. The independent impact of AI's participation in the overall mobilization of public opinion on human rights is difficult to calculate, but AI's international, public campaigning projects are recalled by many participants and observers as defining events and, in some cases, are mentioned in UN materials. For torture, disappearances, and political killings, information from all over the world, collected by AI, spurred a generalized concern about human rights in the public realm. At the same time, Amnesty's low-profile participation in standard-setting efforts carried out by intergovernmental working groups fostered the creation of formal norms by the UN. To excise Amnesty's initiatives from the historical record would tear holes in the existing web of measures that have emerged to deal with the treatment of political prisoners, torture disappearances, and political killings.

Any effort to understand and theorize about the emergence of international human rights norms must pay attention to the historical prominence of Amnesty International and like-minded NGOs as international actors. Overall, this study has focused in detail on how norms have emerged with regard to these problems in the human rights arena. Before proceeding, however, a summary of the general theoretical significance of NGOs in the emergence of principled international norms and how AI created its own niche within this framework is in order.

I have argued that the attributes of nongovernmental organizations that keep them independent of state interests also place NGOs in a position to act as legitimate advocates of principled norms in the international system. But those attributes alone do not explain how AI and other NGOs eventually became integral to what the human rights scholar R. J. Vincent called "the gradual accumulation of standards of right conduct" in international politics.[5] I have sought to make two theoretical points in this regard. First, I have argued that the practical techniques pioneered by Amnesty have changed the system in fundamental ways and cannot be accounted for in state-centric models of norm emergence. Second, I have identified a process of principled norm emergence that has been enhanced, and often engendered, by nonstate actors. Nonstate actors have strongly influenced the construction of the rules of international politics in the human rights area, where rules based on principles often conflict with the material and power interests of states. Amnesty International's repertoire of techniques evolved in response to and in tandem with institutional limitations placed on NGOs (and on human rights monitoring and enforcement) in the United Nations, which has become the primary venue for the international contest over human rights issues. Principled norms in the human rights realm have emerged through a practical, discursive process rooted in the tension between facts and ideals.

Undeniably, current human rights abuses provide evidence of further lawless application of force by governments. However, the existence of principled norms challenges the realist picture of the international politics as, at best, arbitrarily ordered. If principled norms emerge in a system such as this, we have to allow for the possibility of systemic change through the construction of new mechanisms of practical accountability based on principles rather than power.

In defiance of power considerations, Amnesty International sought both long-term development of international human rights norms and short-term relief for individual prisoners of state repression. Those two goals dictated very different time frames and very different techniques, but both were rooted in the same loyalty to principle. From an advocacy perspective, AI's activities were, and are, ultimately aimed at exposing objectionable governmental practices from the past, monitoring current practices, and preventing future human rights violations, through both direct efforts to influence government policy and promotion of international law governing states' treatment of individuals. From an analytical perspective, NGO actors have forged a way to elicit new rules based on shared principles within an international social and institutional context ruled by states. I have identified the process as a set of phases leading to the emergence of international norms.

THE UNIQUE CONTRIBUTION OF AMNESTY INTERNATIONAL TO THE EMERGENCE OF HUMAN RIGHTS NORMS

In a discussion of the relationship among law, international morality, and international relations, Terry Nardin posited that shared procedures, rather than agreement over goals, are necessary for a lasting peaceful association of states at the international level.[6] His insight explains why, to secure human rights for all, international norms must protect human dignity and autonomy in all its forms rather than prescribe a particular way of life.

However, to become part of international practice, human rights have to be accepted by states both verbally and behaviorally. Human rights norms limit state actions that threaten respect for persons. Thus, Amnesty's ability to read government interests and strategize about the real implications of various ways to apply law to human rights problems has been informed by maintaining a focus on the humane purposes of direct human rights advocacy. Public awareness of human rights issues strengthens the nongovernmental organization's hand as it works for stronger norms.

Amnesty International pioneered the links between governments, experts, and an international human rights constituency by coordinating members' pressure on governments with expert support for legal norms in international organizations. This contribution has been widely recognized, as observers have credited changes in public opinion with stimulating broader changes in the United Nations climate with relation to human rights matters. According to one observer, by 1979, "Amnesty International and others had created a far better informed public opinion and governments were beginning to be subjected to domestic pressure to do something about human rights."[7] The concrete impact of public involvement on UN mechanisms was described by Theo van Boven, former head of the UN administrative branch responsible for human rights, who noted that such interest changed the whole climate of human rights work in the United Nations: "Broadening political and public concern with human rights created a climate favourable to the establishment of new sub-organs and the development of new fact-finding techniques[,] . . . a broader stream of [human rights] complaints and other expressions of concern, and increasing demands from representatives of governments, non-governmental organizations, and individuals for advice, guidance, and information."[8]

Membership support has enabled Amnesty to undertake independent policy initiatives at the UN. Members in democratic countries are often asked to use the domestic political process to press for their governments' support of human rights treaties, for example, or to stop export of tools that could be used for torture. "You can't move the UN on serious issues unless you've got [national] sections working on the issue" to provide lobbying pressure at home, observed Margo Picken, Amnesty's former UN representative.[9]

Even if norms are not yet strongly enforced, Amnesty has worked with the attitude that norm emergence, and the move toward more detailed monitoring, "must be seen as part of a process. Campaigning for respect for human rights is essentially a technique of step-by-step application of the pressure of international public opinion. The more steps that can be brought in to play, however modestly, the greater are the chances of some kind of success."[10]

Marshaling public opinion is correctly seen as a major role of NGOs, and Amnesty International has uniquely been able to do so over time. However, the genesis of norms owes much to other techniques developed and employed by NGOs in the effort to further norms. Meetings of experts often help to advance common understanding of the issues and build consensus about the best path for the advancement of normative goals; Amnesty International uniquely linked those expert meetings with the development of new techniques in support of human rights that could also draw in nonexperts.

In this vein, the effects of expert meetings as a way to enhance norm emergence differs from that posited by studies of expert involvement in policymaking. According to the theory of epistemic communities, transnational communities of experts gain in influence in times of government uncertainty, and thus they provide the mechanism for the transnational dissemination of ideas.[11] The role of expertise in the dynamic of principled norm emergence is different. Amnesty is situated at the center of actors who formed the erstwhile equivalent of an epistemic community on the human rights issue. Yet, those actors often find themselves in an adversarial or protest position vis-à-vis governments, so that their advice is not always wanted by governments. Further, the conceptual province of principled norms is by no means exclusive to a community of experts. Human rights principles are quite understandable to the ordinary public and to government officials. Expertise is important, but not the most critical problem for human rights advocates. The problem for the emergence of norms is the difficulty of creating an international sense of obligation. A unique and important part of AI activity has involved the moral component. It enabled the organization to enlist public support for upholding standards of treatment of citizens that anyone can understand and identify, and to educate the public on technical issues in the process.

Where expert knowledge is applicable is in thinking about how to develop the existing structure of international legal norms, Amnesty's knowledge of the problems of victims of human rights in various countries provides an important basis for judgment and evaluation of the international normative structure. Amnesty gathers information from personal and organizational contacts, observation missions, and media, academic, and other secondary sources. Its studies of human rights violations and its deep and direct knowledge of the experiences of human rights victims and their families have produced a huge information bank about the situations in various countries, along with intimate knowledge of specific conditions for individual human beings who were the victims of abuses.

Command of the facts informs a number of activities in support of human rights, including the mobilization of individuals in many countries on behalf of individual human rights victims, professional representation in international governmental arenas and provision of standard setting expertise, and collaboration with diverse groups, both governmental and nongovernmental, to resolve technical questions bearing on human rights in the areas of medical issues, legal procedures, and law enforcement.

Amnesty has also contributed directly to the substance of international legal norms. In this area, its contribution has come via participation in norm drafting, and through strategizing about how particular kinds of legal procedures can help to fix and maintain government accountability. Nigel Rodley was a major influence on AI's early strategy for the pursuit of legal matters pertaining to human rights at the UN during his tenure at AI from 1973 to 1990.[12] Rodley and his associates within and outside of Amnesty International were able to identify the "gaps" in human rights law and bridge them with short-term and long-term strategies for new normative projects. Both Rodley and Margo Picken averred that with regard to UN standard setting, just as in public campaigning, they saw AI's role as focusing attention on the human rights principles to which Amnesty International dedicated itself rather than trading positions based on political stakes.[13] As a matter of policy, Amnesty representatives have usually refused to claim credit for contributions to the language of specific drafts.[14] However, personal and written accounts, many of which I have cited in earlier chapters, attest to Amnesty's long-standing influence in this area. Rodley's successor at AI, Helena Cook, acknowledged that AI has both "encouraged and participated in" norm drafting at the UN.[15]

Below, I generalize about how international norms develop in light of the demonstrated importance of NGO involvement in these cases, and speculate about the applicability of the hypotheses generated by this study to general theories of international relations.

THE ROLE OF THE NONGOVERNMENTAL ACTOR IN NORM EMERGENCE

Amnesty International has had important independent effects on state behavior at the systemic level. I have argued that its success has resulted not from direct or indirect embodiment of state interests but from its independent advocacy of principles. Table 1 generalizes on the case studies, summarizing the role nongovernmental actors play as third parties in each phase of the emergence of principled international norms. As I explain more fully the roles NGOs play in each phase of norm emergence, I offer examples of how the norm emergence process may be diverted in each phase if the conditions specified in the table are left unfulfilled.

In the fact-finding phase, NGOs generally take on an observing and reporting role in which their primary activity is comprised of independently initiated reporting on the breach of generally accepted principles of right and wrong. While governments might be motivated to cover up or ignore such breaches, either out of embarrassment or fear of liability, principled NGOs, by definition, are motivated to defend and support principles of right and wrong by bringing breaches to light, asking for state acknowledgment, international recognition, and public scrutiny. Fact finding is an activity that an NGO or any third party may undertake simply by taking steps to investigate and publish reports on such departures from principles. As a phase in the emergence of norms, the fact-finding project is indeed an interpretive one: the NGO is not simply a medium for the transmittal of information. It must verify accuracy, supply context, and strategize about how best to use the facts to attain principled goals. Thus, the impetus for this phase rests on the idea that secrets should not be kept and that objective facts must be preserved and analyzed. That makes objectivity and independence in fact finding integral to NGO activities in this period. The NGO can thereby highlight the gaps between words and deeds effectively and legitimately in light of principles. This phase must be done right—accurately and independently—or none of the other phases will be successful.

TABLE 1
The Nongovernmental Actor in Norm Emergence

Phase of Norm Emergence	Substance or Content of Activity	Goals of Activity	Norm-Generating Role of Nongovernmental Actor
Fact finding	Investigating and reporting; contacting governments; building popular pressure; contributing resources (research, contacts with primary sources)	Recovery and preservation of facts; principled purpose; publicity	Observer/reporter
Consensus building	Facilitating exchange of information and viewpoints; continuing to build popular pressure; sharing and coordinating resources (expertise, experience, contacts with elites)	Building basis for joint action; getting others to act	Popular advocate
Norm construction	Providing examples and analysis of proposed new norms	Articulating shared standards and ideals; promoting more demanding standards of behavior	Expert advocate
Norm application (mobilization)	Invoking shared standards to governments and public (may employ above activities)	Implementing shared standards	Depends on maturity of norm and its institutionalization (roles may include observer/reporter, continued advocacy, or more institutionalized monitoring/reporting)

If the NGO's alliance with principle is broken, its reputation for objectivity is diminished, which adversely affects credibility and, thus, its ability to be a legitimate critic. For example, the U.S. section of Amnesty International established its Washington office in 1977, soon after Congress and President Jimmy Carter's administration brought human rights analysis into the U.S. State Department apparatus. AI began to be asked to testify before Congress and to comment in less formal contexts on the human rights situations of various countries. Amnesty was very willing to present its analysis of various human rights situations before Congress, but deliberately avoided becoming mixed up in the partisan calculus of national security that was part of Washington's policy.[16] It was necessary to maintain AI's independence because, although Congress began to base foreign aid decisions in part on the prospective recipients' human rights records, there was also a loophole to permit any aid that was deemed essential to the United States' national interest.

As long ago as 1966, when AI published its first country reports, AI observed that governments react to the criticisms directed at friends with chagrin and denial, but receive the criticisms of enemies with great interest and publicity. If an NGO's alliance with the facts is broken, its credibility is diminished, especially because governments tend to use such reports for their own purposes. Indeed, as the United States Congress was holding hearings on Iraq's 1990 invasion of Kuwait, an AI report critical of Iraq became part of the debate. AI's report had passed on, as true, reports of an incident in which Iraqi soldiers supposedly massacred Kuwaiti babies lying in their hospital incubators. The story turned out to be false, but it became fodder for a rallying cry for swift action against Iraq. Some of the reports coming out of Kuwait were fabricated by Kuwait in a bid to influence world opinion as congressional decisions were being made.[17] The rare error in AI reporting redounded to the organization's embarrassment when it was revealed that the incident never happened and that AI and Congress were misled. Amnesty quickly disavowed the errors in the report, but on the five-year anniversary of the invasion, former president George Bush continued to invoke Amnesty International's report to justify the decision to pursue war against Iraq. Such use of AI reports is not desirable from the point of view of maintaining a reputation for objectivity and independence, although it may be an unavoidable consequence of attaining a high public profile and a high level of legitimacy. The incident exhibits the difficulty of remaining independent of government interests: facts seem to speak for themselves, and whether or not the "facts" are correct, once in the public domain they will be employed by interested parties for their own purposes.

In the consensus-building phase of norm emergence, the NGO's role is primarily that of popular advocate. The NGO continues to articulate the principles by which it operates and to advertise the gap between facts and principle that has been and continues to be documented. Now, as a popular advocate, the NGO is also in a position to facilitate public and elite consensus about the need for norms. In this phase, the NGO must develop a basis for joint action. The NGO advocate needs to get others— both governments and the public—to act. In this phase, the NGO can develop and share the expertise and knowledge it has gathered through fact finding and previous experience. Elite contacts with experts and governmental policymakers are helpful in this phase as the NGO tries to foster agreement among them on the need for norms. These contacts can increase the expertise of the NGO and make the case for new norms stronger in the international arena, especially when combined with popular pressure to support the articulation of new standards of government behavior.

In this phase, NGOs sometimes face major obstacles to agreement on their chosen issues. Amnesty International's efforts to abolish the death penalty can be seen as an example of troubled consensus building. Amnesty International has achieved some success in campaigning for a global end to the death penalty, but it has had difficulty accomplishing a firm, principled consensus against it. This problem is especially evident in the United States. At the elite and activist levels, Amnesty has facilitated conferences on the death penalty since 1977. But the failure of the public at large to support a consensus against the death penalty has inhibited global norm emergence in the application phase, even though an optional protocol to the International Covenant on Civil and Political Rights already exists, which calls for an end to the death penalty. Part of the difficulty may be due to the complexity involved in achieving a social consensus that distinguishes between the strong opprobrium directed at violent crime and ideas about acceptable forms of legalized punishment in societies that adhere to the rule of law.

Of all the phases of norm development, the norm construction phase is the most technical, and the concomitant NGO role reflects that. International standards are being articulated in legal terms that situate such standards with respect to existing legal norms. During the period of norm construction, the principled NGO can play the role of expert advocate. From expertise gained through long-term study of and involvement with a particular issue, the NGO can often offer cogent analysis of the potential effects of proposed norms.

The principled NGO's purpose at this stage is to foster the articulation of shared standards or ideals in ways that will serve as legal guides to behavior. Expertise combined with principle is extremely important during norm construction. Even when all participants are loyal to the same principles, difficulties can arise. Consider an example from the debate over how to construct stronger norms against disappearances. As mentioned in the chapter on disappearances, some advocates of norms against disappearances pressed for the strongest possible penalties against the crime. Anyone familiar with the devastating effects that the terror of unresolved disappearances wreak on families and on societies would find it hard to argue for moderation. However, experienced human rights lawyers suggested that, from the viewpoint of protecting the lives of victims and potential victims of disappearances, norms on disappearances must not work at cross-purposes with other norms on human rights and crimes against humanity. If sanctions for disappearances matched or exceeded those for other crimes involving killing, for example, perpetrators of disappearances might have added incentive to do away with their victims. With the victim gone, culpability might never be determined. Such arguments are sensitive for all concerned, but the clearer the NGO's attributes of independence, expertise, and loyalty to principle, the more its analysis of such matters can help to form opinion, and the more able it is to develop the climate of objective discourse, relatively undistorted by interest, that is necessary for such discussions to take place among experts.

Even if the NGO is overruled by state actors, who alone have the official standing to adopt newly constructed international law, the NGO as an expert advocate can provide principled criticism and interpretation from its standpoint as a third party in the international system. At the final stages of norm construction, Amnesty has sometimes taken an outsider's stance in order to point out where political compromises have dulled the potential application of the formal norm, as with the Convention against Torture. As a practical matter, NGOs as expert advocates, and their allies among governments, have sometimes through their criticism and interpretation been able to mold governments' half-hearted, UN-based administrative creations into useful tools for monitoring human rights violations. The creation of the UN Working Group on Enforced or Involuntary Disappearances is a good example.

In the final phase of norm emergence, norm application, the NGO's role may vary. As I have suggested earlier, the process of norm emergence is rather cyclical, in that new norms often build on earlier, more established principles and norms. Thus, the NGO role in the norm-application phase depends to some extent on the level of institutionalization of principles, as well as on how the norm itself has been constructed. For example, is there an official role for NGOs in reporting mechanisms? If legal mechanisms allow a place for NGO testimony and input, or for standing in official discussions, then NGOs may derive a practical observing and reporting role through institutionalized intergovernmental norms. Although NGOs are rarely fully and irrevocably vested participants in international processes, they have increasingly been recognized as important contributors to the application of norms. For example, in 1998 when former Chilean president Augusto Pinochet's extradition hearings related to alleged human rights abuses began in Britain, Amnesty International, Human Rights Watch, and other nongovernmental human rights groups were invited to submit written briefs. The NGOs continued to use official and unofficial opportunities to be involved in the case as it unfolded.

NGOs make choices about the topics they address and their level of participation in governmental processes. Some may welcome opportunities for increased input in the process of applying new norms, while remaining wary of compromising principles. In Amnesty's case, a strong internal mandate has helped it maintain independence, while perhaps keeping it from being as flexible in cooperation with other NGOs or with governments as might sometimes have seemed optimal in the short term. AI's independent loyalty to principle, rather than a friendly search for expedient compromises, has had beneficial long-term effects on the reinforcement and application of the principles behind emergent human rights norms in the areas of prisoner treatment, torture, disappearances, and extrajudicial killings. There is no doubt, however, that NGOs vary in the degree to which they are willing to work with one another and with governments. AI's stalwart position taking has not always been well received. It has been criticized at times for narrowness and lack of flexibility, both by outsiders and by its own members.

From the theory and case studies presented above, it is now possible to draw some general theoretical conclusions. An NGO seems best able to bring about norm emergence when its purpose is independent from any one state or group's point of view; when it has resources in the form of information or expertise that states could not or would not gather on their own; and when it can convey a sense that its independence is a result of representing generally accepted principles or broad public opinion, preferably both. In advocating the emergence of new norms, the NGO may find a source of strength in prior principles—existing social standards of right and wrong—that explicitly refer to concrete behavior and demonstrate applicability to real or new cases. If prior principles are weakly accepted or nonexistent, part of the principled NGO's activity may include building a discourse that draws connections between facts and principles in real cases, and in so doing, leads to a strengthened interpretation of principles as they relate to standards of behavior.

For leverage among states, NGOs have often attained a respected third-party status through apolitical, disinterested support for principles. But the case studies have also presented instances where, when AI did not have institutional standing, its typical third-party role could be performed in certain circumstances by particular *states* in the advocacy of human rights norms. For example, the Scandinavian states and the Netherlands, who as states have greater access to intergovernmental arenas than do NGOs, have performed this sort of normative advocacy in intergovernmental circles. If the third-party normative advocate is not an NGO, it must have an analogous identity with regard to the issue area; that is, it must be materially disinterested but committed to principles of right and wrong. Few states, however, are able to maintain such a stance with regard to principled norms over long periods because their histories, their constituencies, and their ties to other issues and actors are more complex than those of a more narrowly focused nongovernmental actor.

THE CONUNDRUM OF NORM EMERGENCE

For new norms of international practice to emerge, changes must occur in collective definitions of acceptable state behavior. New norms are not necessarily based on brand new principles or ideals: human rights ideals, for example, have existed for much longer than associated norms as standards for state behavior. The *ideals* associated with international human rights are much older than the UN's institutionalization of the *idea* that state action must be guided by international standards of human rights. The internationally shared definitions of "good" behavior—these ideals—have not changed as dramatically as the less constrictive standards of acceptable behavior—norms—which, over the last thirty years or so, have risen closer to the ideal. Still, it hardly needs to be pointed out that actual human rights behavior frequently diverges from that prescribed by norms. As new norms emerge, we should expect that the principles upon which they are based will be violated and tested.

The case studies bear this out. The contrast between states' verbal support for norms and actual state behavior is sometimes a source of cynicism about whether legal norms have real meaning in the international system. Yet, if one recognizes that norms emerge in cyclical phases characterized by differing forms of activity, interaction, and communicative claims, one can see how state violations of principles can, and often do, become focal points for the articulation of changes in behavioral standards. If my conclusions are correct, the success of principled NGOs is determined by their ability to articulate and apply their principles with reference to states' behavior, thereby vesting international events with normative meaning.

The fact that principled norms prescribe a mode of action for states that often contradicts action ruled by immediate self-interest is a feature of the normative dynamic that led Barkun to call international law a "third party" in the international system.[18] Kratochwil added that norms represent a third-party point of view that implicitly or explicitly sets up standards of behavior as communicative reference points.[19] I have shown the ways in which NGOs like AI have adopted that third-party point of view and actively promoted it with reference to state action, even when norms themselves were not fully institutionalized. This dynamic has been a key element in the emergence of human rights norms, and I would expect it to be present in studies of the emergence of other kinds of principled norms in the international system.

Still, we cannot assume that principled claims always lead to untrammeled behavioral improvement. The historical emergence of the body of human rights norms has led to some undesired changes in state behavior, because some states have tried to evade increased accountability rather than submit to it. This is a logical possible outcome of increased accountability. On the one hand, norms proscribe certain behavior on the basis of shared principles. On the other hand, by increasing potential penalties for outlawed behavior, normative proscription may stop one form of behavior but, instead of diminishing violations, give states an incentive to develop innovations in techniques of human rights abuse. For example, even as Amnesty International's advocacy for political prisoners through prisoner adoption showed results, it became harder for AI to employ the strategy as its main form of activity. States began to use other forms of repression that in many cases were faster and more secret and, therefore, harder to detect or reverse, such as short-term detention and torture, disappearances, and political killings. To remain effective advocates, then, Amnesty International and other human rights NGOs had to come to terms with such innovations by developing innovative techniques of their own.

In the phenomenon of evasion, we can observe a shift in the prescriptive status of norms on human rights from words that hardly mattered to more potent forms of human rights promotion and monitoring from which violators now feel compelled to hide. Rather than being a cause for pessimism, the dynamic I have described makes a strengthened, comprehensive web of norms on human rights—and the broad perspective of global organizations like Amnesty International, the ICJ, and Human Rights Watch—more pressing. Recent calls to rationalize UN human rights mechanisms, now that many different and overlapping kinds of norms are in place, acknowledge progress and change. Further, human rights NGOs have been able to achieve further normative goals by working together on projects like the campaign for a UN High Commissioner on Human Rights, an idea revived by AI and pressed by a coalition of NGOs at the 1993 UN World Conference on Human Rights, as well as the campaign for an International Criminal Court, achieved in 1998.

Also in 1998, the UN adopted a declaration commonly referred to as the Declaration on Human Rights Defenders,[20] the first norm that explicitly protects those who seek to advance human rights. All three projects were the result of years of work by Amnesty International and its fellow NGOs. Pressing for more meaningful, thorough implementation of the web of existing human rights norms will remain a challenging task for such organizations.

HUMAN RIGHTS NORMS AND INTERNATIONAL RELATIONS

Through the case studies I have presented an account of how international human rights norms have emerged through the work of Amnesty International and other nongovernmental organizations that employed their moral credibility, expertise, and popular representativeness to advocate the establishment of new norms. This study builds upon and advances the broader literature on norms in international relations. As I noted at the beginning of this study, a number of theoretical and empirical efforts have already established a working consensus that "norms matter" in international politics. The theoretical basis for a belief that social meanings attached to patterns of behavior make a difference in international politics has long existed as an alternative to power politics models of international relations; the ways in which norms matter have more recently been developed and advanced through theoretical and empirical research. Such work has demanded new theories to deal with the evidence of norms' impact on international politics.

Although in the introduction I argued against assuming that the international system was a hostile anarchy, it is fair to assume that in the present international system states will sometimes find their interests constructed (and constricted) in ways that coincide with normative prescriptions, and sometimes not. Norms help states to define their interests.[21] In previous chapters, we have seen how NGOs, through deliberate social action, build and shape norms, especially principled ones, that would be unlikely to emerge naturally out of state considerations of self-interest.

The theoretical assertion that norms are important may seem simple or self-evident to an outside observer. However, it has been a necessary first step because realist assumptions have become so embedded in our theories of international politics. By attaching meaning to action, a social context of shared beliefs—whether it is couched in any of the sometimes widely diverging assumptions and terminology of studies of global civil society, constructivism, an international society perspective, sociological institutionalism, neoliberal institutionalist theories about cooperation, or studies of the influence of ideas—accounts for behavior in ways that more parsimonious assumptions about power and strategic interest as the primary motivations of states do not.

Theories about norms now need to be developed further. Studies of norms have led to much productive theorizing, sometimes in unison, sometimes at cross purposes. But methodological pluralism in studies of norms can be beneficial to the process of learning how social elements affect behavior in international politics, a question that has previously been understudied.

Case studies make up a crucial part of theory building about empirical phenomena, and my study is aimed at making a contribution in this vein. My case studies suffer from the limitations of scope that are inherent in any case study research, in that they focus just on human rights. At a broader level, by asking how new norms emerge, this study contributes to our understanding of change in prevailing international political practices. In researching the emergence of new norms based on principled beliefs I have sought to demonstrate a process and a causal mechanism. In the language of empirical theory, the successive phases I have described characterize the *process* of principled norm emergence, while the work of NGOs in invoking principle by way of expert knowledge and public pressure represents the *causal mechanism* for the norms' establishment. Although the cases focus on the emergence of human rights norms, they are aimed at investigating the general impact and operation of moral principles on international action, and could apply to other topical domains where principles and interest meet.

In a departure from much international theorizing, this study also sketches the intersection of the international legal structure and less formal norms in international politics, which has been identified as a topic needing more thorough treatment in international theory.[22] In the empirical section of this study I have taken international law seriously as a marker for points of international consensus while noting the socially reinforced nature of obligation that much international law, including human rights law, relies on for effect.

What is the next stage, then, for the study of international norms? To understand norms as standards of behavior implies that there is a dynamic relationship, a tension, between standards as they are expressed communicatively in the international social context and the observation and interpretation of behavior. There is much still to understand about the role such tension plays in influencing behavior internationally. The gap between words and deeds that is so often evident with regard to contemporary human rights standards has life and death effects. State hypocrisy on human rights means violent death, torture, and injustice for citizens.

The fact that norms are supposed to apply disinterestedly allows them to gain widespread verbal acceptance when there is agreement on the underlying principle. But international legal norms may be manipulated. For example, a state may become an advocate of norm application when it is convenient, or it may try to cloak its own purposes in principled rhetoric. In such cases, the need for a third-party advocate for norms increases, since social pressure and consistent criticism may be the most effective way to reinforce the principles behind the norms.

In the choice to work in intergovernmental channels, AI consciously took on and continues to take on the conscious role of a third party. That role requires continuous legitimation, however, which AI and NGOs like it build from a constituent base and the cultivation of principled objectivity with regard to reporting and analysis. AI characterizes its own role as representing membership, and it is a membership-governed organization. But its ability to do important legal work in its interactions with states has been as significant. Its interpretive clout has required knowledge of the diplomatic language of states, although its campaigns have been built on concern over the concrete practices of governments.

The case studies suggest that when principled bystanders (in these cases, NGOs) problematize the gap between words and deeds, they are taking the first step toward clarifying shared standards and, thus, an initial step toward the emergence of stronger norms. It does not suggest that hypocrites melt when challenged or that all bystanders have unstained values at heart; far from it. Every day in politics we witness organizations' and individuals' unwillingness to engage in communication separately from their own interest. However, the fact that human rights NGOs and NGOs in other issue areas have repeatedly been able to tap into the invocation of principle to encourage changed behavior and changing definitions of acceptable behavior suggests that social actors (in these case studies, states or state leaders), if they breach norms or their foundational principles, must tolerate a certain amount of cognitive and political tension in order to *remain* hypocrites or *refrain* from further conversation with their adversaries about mutually understood standards of behavior.

For the scholar of social phenomena, then, the nature of hypocrisy as a social dynamic becomes a compelling question. When is hypocrisy a stage on the way to or from another state of affairs? Is hypocrisy a reason for hope, or despair?[23]

The case studies presented here are intended as steps toward deeper and more general theory building on the role of principle in international politics, and on the dynamics of compliance with international norms once they are established. The case studies suggest that it is not any magical power of words that causes change, but the "weak force" of social pressure to conform with principled standards. It has been difficult to study international phenomena as social phenomena before, and perhaps it was not as important before the late twentieth century's explosive increase in the level of transnational contacts. Now, however, that very increased interaction calls for more attention to the nature of international discourse on many topics and its effect on how international politics is conducted.

AI and other NGOs have pressed states to create binding norms for themselves. NGOs take advantage of the cognitive effects of norms when they highlight the difference between words and action. By invoking public opinion, they implicitly appeal to a wider audience. By offering information and expertise pertaining to departures from principle, NGOs highlight the contrast between ideals and practice. They also forge productive links with sympathetic states that are committed to fostering new norms' emergence and enhancing the impact of existing norms.

All of these functions of NGOs suggest that a less state-centric conception of international relations is essential to understanding the creation and maintenance of international norms. The importance of third parties lies not in the contention that realist issues are passé or that states can no longer be understood as self-interested actors. It is that, when normative issues are represented by NGOs or other third-party actors, largely through communicative mechanisms, they change the environment in which states must act. By advocating changing international human rights norms, NGOs have helped to mold expectations of international behavior and to demand that states conform.

APPENDIX

INTERVIEWS

(Conducted by the author unless otherwise noted)

Anonymous, Boulder, Colorado, 25 July 1993.
Peter Benenson, Oxford, U.K., 27 November 1996.
Andrew Blane, New York, New York,14 May 1996.
Ann Blyberg, Washington, D.C., 27 September 1995.
Reed Brody, New York, New York, 13 May 1996.
Jan Herman Burgers, The Hague, The Netherlands, 13 November 1993. (Conducted by Kathryn Sikkink.)
Patricia Feeney, Oxford, U.K., 27 October 1993.
Barbara Frey, Minneapolis, Minnesota,17 May 1993.
Roberto Garretón, Santiago, Chile, 4 November 1992. (Conducted by Kathryn Sikkink and the author.)
Stefanie Grant, New York, New York, 14 May 1996.
Menno Kamminga, Rotterdam, The Netherlands, 11 November 1993. (Conducted by Kathryn Sikkink.)
Edy Kaufman, College Park, Maryland, 10 September 1993.
Nélida Navajas, Buenos Aires, Argentina, 280 October 1992. (Conducted by Kathryn Sikkink and the author.)
Dick Oosting and Marzel Zwanborn, Utrecht, The Netherlands, 12 November 1993. (Conducted by Kathryn Sikkink.)
Margo Picken (telephone), London, U.K.,11 December 1996.
Eric Prokosch, London, U.K., 9 November 1993.
Slavomir Redo (telephone), Vienna, Austria, 4 November 1993.
Michael Reed-Hurtado (telephone), Minneapolis, Minnesota, 29 November 1994.
Nigel Rodley, Colchester, U.K., 14 October 1993.
Elsa (Coca) Rudolfi, Santiago, Chile, 20 November 1992.
Lindsey Thomas, Minneapolis, Minnesota,13 May 1993.
Theo van Boven, Maastricht, The Netherlands, 8 November 1993. (Conducted by Kathryn Sikkink.)
David Weissbrodt, Minneapolis, Minnesota, 20 September 1994.
James Welsh, London, U.K., 11 October 1993.
José Federico Westerkamp and Angela Westerkamp, Buenos Aires, Argentina, 7 October 1992.
Clayton Yeo (telephone), London, U.K., 4 November 1993.
José Zalaquett, Santiago, Chile, 19 November 1992.
Marzel Zwanborn. See Dick Oosting.

NOTES

CHAPTER ONE
AMNESTY INTERNATIONAL IN INTERNATIONAL POLITICS

1. Thomas Buergenthal, *International Human Rights in a Nutshell* (St. Paul: West, 1995), 87–88.

2. Nigel Rodley, author's interview, Colchester, U.K., 14 October 1993.

3. The story of Amnesty International's founding has been widely recounted. See Lionel Elvin, "Chairman's Report," *Amnesty International Movement for Freedom of Opinion and Religion: First Annual Report, 1961–62,* in *Amnesty International: A Major Collection of Published and Unpublished Research Material* (Zug, Switzerland: Inter Documentation Company, 1991 [microfiche], 2–3; Martin Ennals, "Amnesty International and Human Rights," in Peter Willetts, ed., *Pressure Groups in the Global System* (New York: St. Martin's, 1982), 63–65; William Korey, " 'To Light a Candle': Amnesty International and the 'Prisoners of Conscience,' " in Korey, *NGOs and the Universal Declaration of Human Rights: 'A Curious Grapevine'* (New York: St. Martin's, 1998), 159–80; Egon Larsen, *A Flame in Barbed Wire: The Story of Amnesty International* (New York: W. W. Norton, 1979), 10–18; Jonathan Power, *Amnesty International: The Human Rights Story* (New York: McGraw-Hill, 1981), 10–11; Marie Staunton and Sally Fenn, eds., with Amnesty International USA, *The Amnesty International Handbook* (Claremont, Calif.: Hunter House, 1991), 5; Thomas Claudius and Franz Stepan, *Amnesty International: Portrait einer Organisation* (Munich: R. Oldenbourg Verlag, 1978), 15–24; and David Winner, *Peter Benenson* (Milwaukee: Gareth Stevens, 1991), 1–2, 11–14.

4. Peter Benenson, "The Forgotten Prisoners," *The Observer* (London), 28 May 1961, 20.

5. Claudius and Stepan, *Amnesty International,* 17.

6. Ennals, "Amnesty International," 82 n.1.

7. Amnesty International [AI], *Annual Report 1961–62* (London: International Secretariat, 1962), 5–6. The early annual reports cited in this chapter have been published on microfiche in AI, *Amnesty International: A Major Collection of Published and Unpublished Research Material* (Zug, Switzerland: Inter Documentation Company, 1991).

By comparison, in 1998 the organization tallied one million members in over 140 countries and territories, including more than 4,200 registered local groups. (AI, "Selected Statistics," Appendix IX, *Amnesty International Report 1999* [London: AI Publications, 1999], 404.)

8. Power, *Amnesty International,* 13.

9. Amnesty International, *Annual Report 1961–62,* 6.

10. Peter Benenson, author's interview, Oxford, U.K., 27 November 1996.

11. AI, "Amnesty in Human Rights Year," *Annual Report 1967–68* (London: International Secretariat, 1968), 4.

12. Howard Tolley, Jr., *International Commission of Jurists: Global Advocates for Human Rights* (Philadelphia: University of Pennsylvania Press, 1994), 108.

13. The representative was Niels Groth. (See AI, *Annual Report 1963–64* [London: International Secretariat, 1964], 9; and AI, *Annual Report 1964–65* [London: International Secretariat, 1965], 11.)

14. Andrew Blane, author's interview, New York, 14 May 1996.

15. Margo Picken, author's interview, telephone, London, 11 December 1996.

16. Jody Williams, "Address to the National Press Club," Washington, D.C., 19 November 1997, http://npc.press.org/archive /williams.htm (20 November 1997). Williams coordinated the International Campaign to Ban Landmines and won the 1997 Nobel Peace Prize for her efforts.

17. See William Korey, "The NGO 'Prototype': The Anti-Slavery Society," in Korey, *NGOs and the Universal Declaration*, 117–37.

18. David P. Forsythe, "Human Rights and the International Committee of the Red Cross," *Human Rights Quarterly* 12 (1990): 273, 281–82.

19. On principled beliefs, see Judith Goldstein and Robert O. Keohane, eds., *Ideas and Foreign Policy* (Ithaca, N.Y.: Cornell University Press, 1993), 9; Kathryn Sikkink's chapter on human rights in that volume, "The Power of Principled Beliefs," 139–70; and Sikkink, "Human Rights, Principled Issue-Networks, and Sovereignty in Latin America," *International Organization* 47 (1993): 411–41.

20. Benenson, "Forgotten Prisoners."

21. Ann Marie Clark and James A. McCann, "Enforcing International Standards of Justice: Amnesty International's Constructive Conflict Expansion," *Peace and Change* 16 (1991): 379–99.

22. Benenson, "Forgotten Prisoners."

23. "Universal Declaration of Human Rights," UN General Assembly Resolution 217 A (III), UN Doc. A/810, 12 December 1948.

24. Stephanie Grant, author's interview, New York, 14 May 1996.

25. Benenson, interview.

26. "The Annual Report of the Anti-Slavery Society for the Year ended March 31, 1968," UN Doc. E/C.2/664 (1968), 4, quoted in John Carey, *UN Protection of Civil and Political Rights* (Syracuse, N.Y.: Syracuse University Press, 1970), 157.

27. Ibid.

28. On Amnesty's mandate, see Peter R. Baehr, "Amnesty International and Its Self-Imposed Limited Mandate," *Netherlands Quarterly of Human Rights* 12 (1994): 5–21.

29. See Edy Kaufman, "Prisoners of Conscience: The Shaping of a New Human Rights Concept," *Human Rights Quarterly* 13 (1991): 354.

30. AI, "Amnesty International and the Use of Violence," first drafted in 1973; revised and reprinted in AI, *Amnesty International Policy Manual 1992* (New York: Amnesty International USA, April 1992), 8.

31. AI, *Annual Report 1962–63*, 9. The 1963 report is the only place in which the possibility of confidential communication is mentioned in Amnesty's public records.

32. The account of events in the following paragraph draws upon Power, *Amnesty International*, 17–20; Tolley, *International Commission of Jurists*, 126; and Larsen, *Flame in Barbed Wire*, 32–35.

33. Tolley, *International Commission of Jurists*, 127.

34. MacBride denied knowledge of the CIA links, and argued that in any case there were no strings attached to any funds the ICJ received. (Tolley, *International Commission of Jurists*, 125–27). He remained on Amnesty's International Executive Committee until 1974. MacBride won the Nobel Peace Prize in 1974 for his human rights work.

35. Power, *Amnesty International*, 16; and Benenson, interview. Author's interview did not touch directly on the matters mentioned above.

36. See Amnesty International, "Revised Guidelines for the Acceptance of Funds and Fund-Raising by Amnesty International (Adopted by the 1987 International Council)," in AI, *Policy Manual 1992*, 43–46.

37. Power, *Amnesty International*, 31.

38. Funding for the International Secretariat has been provided primarily by AI's national sections. The global AI headquarters' 1998–99 budget was based on receiving an estimated 25 percent of the income raised by national sections. (See AI, "Selected Statistics," *Annual Report 1999*, 404.) The largest single source of support for the International Secretariat, amounting to over 20 percent of the total in 1998–99, is the contribution from the large, relatively wealthy U.S. national section. (AIUSA, "Where Does the Money Go?" online at http://www.amnestyusa.org/join/funding.html.)

39. H.L.A. Hart, *The Concept of Law* (Oxford: Clarendon Press, 1961), 56.

40. Michael O'Flaherty, *Human Rights and the UN: Practice before the Treaty Bodies* (London: Sweet and Maxwell, 1996), 4.

41. Ibid., 12.

42. AI, *Annual Report 1964–65*, 7.

43. AI, *Annual Report 1965–66* (London: International Secretariat, 1966), 7.

44. Grant, interview.

45. AI, *Annual Report 1965–66*, 8.

46. Benenson, interview.

47. AI reorganized its International Secretariat in the mid-1990s, consolidating some departments and renaming them. For most of the period covered by this study, the headquarters included the following departments in addition to its financial and administrative offices: Campaign and Membership; the Documentation Centre; the Legal Office; Press and Publications; and Research. (Staunton and Fenn, *Amnesty International Handbook*, 106.)

48. Grant, interview.

CHAPTER TWO
HOW NORMS GROW

1. Kenneth N. Waltz, *Theory of International Politics* (Reading, Mass.: Addison-Wesley, 1979), 88.

2. Ibid.

3. Thucydides, *The Pelopponesian War* (New York: Modern Library, 1951), 331.

4. James Boyd White, "The Dissolution of Meaning: Thucydides' History of His World," in *When Words Lose Their Meaning* (Chicago: University of Chicago Press, 1986), 59–92.

5. Robert Axelrod, *The Evolution of Cooperation* (New York: Basic Books, 1984).

6. Friedrich V. Kratochwil, *Rules, Norms, and Decisions* (Cambridge, U.K.: Cambridge University Press, 1989), 74–75.

7. Alexander Wendt, "Anarchy Is What States Make of It," *International Organization* 46 (1992): 391–425.

8. Lea Brilmayer, *American Hegemony: Political Morality in a One-Superpower World* (New Haven: Yale University Press, 1994).

9. Hedley Bull, *The Anarchical Society* (New York: Columbia University Press, 1977), 74.

10. See especially Martha Finnemore, *National Interests and International Society* (Ithaca, N.Y.: Cornell University Press, 1996), Margaret E. Keck and Kathryn Sikkink, *Activists beyond Borders* (Ithaca, N.Y.: Cornell University Press, 1998); Audie Klotz, *Norms in International Relations* (Ithaca, N.Y.: Cornell University Press, 1995); David Halloran Lumsdaine, *Moral Vision in International Politics* (Princeton, N.J.: Princeton University Press, 1993); Sikkink, "Human Rights, Principled Issue-Networks, and Sovereignty."

11. Stephen D. Krasner, "Sovereignty, Regimes, and Human Rights," in *Regime Theory and International Relations*, ed. Volker Rittberger (Oxford: Clarendon, 1993), 167.

12. Menno Kamminga, *Inter-State Accountability for Violations of Human Rights* (Philadelphia: University of Pennsylvania Press, 1992).

13. See Stephen D. Krasner, "Structural Causes and Regime Consequences," in *International Regimes*, ed. Krasner (Ithaca, N.Y.: Cornell University Press, 1983), 1–21; Krasner, "Sovereignty, Regimes, and Human Rights"; and Jack Donnelly, "International Human Rights: A Regime Analysis," *International Organization* 40 (1986): 599–642.

14. Donnelly, "International Human Rights," 615–16.

15. Egon Schwelb, *Human Rights and the International Community: The Roots and Growth of the Universal Declaration of Human Rights, 1948–1963* (Chicago: Quadrangle Books, 1964), 37.

16. Theo van Boven, "The Role of Non-Governmental Organizations in International Human Rights Standard-Setting: A Prerequisite of Democracy," *California Western International Law Journal* 20 (1990): 210.

17. David Forsythe, *The Internationalization of Human Rights* (Lexington, Mass.: Lexington Books, 1991), 121–27; Kathryn Sikkink, "The Power of Principled Ideas: Human Rights Policies in the United States and Western Europe," in *Ideas and Foreign Policy: Beliefs, Institutions, and Political Change*, ed. Judith Goldstein and Robert O. Keohane (Ithaca, N.Y.: Cornell University Press, 1993), 144–45.

18. Jack Donnelly, *Universal Human Rights in Theory and Practice* (Ithaca, N.Y.: Cornell University Press, 1989), 226, n.17.

19. Albert S. Yee, "Thick Rationality and the Missing 'Brute Fact': The Limits of Rationalist Incorporation of Norms and Ideas," *Journal of Politics* 59, no. 4 (1997): 1001–39.

20. Volker Rittberger, ed., *Regime Theory and International Relations* (Oxford: Clarendon, 1993), especially Andrew Hurrell, "International Society and the Study of Regimes: A Reflective Approach," in that volume, 49–72.

21. Bull, *Anarchical Society*, 13.

22. Terry Nardin, *Law, Morality, and the Relations of States* (Princeton, N.J.: Princeton University Press, 1983).

23. Kratochwil, *Rules, Norms, and Decisions*.

24. Buergenthal, *International Human Rights in a Nutshell*, 23–30. The quoted phrase comes from Article 55 of the UN Charter.

25. Michael Gunter, "Toward a Consultative Relationship between the United Nations and Non-Governmental Organizations?" *Vanderbilt Journal of Transnational Law* 10 (1977): 557–58.

26. Ann Marie Clark, Elisabeth J. Friedman, and Kathryn Hochstetler, "The Sovereign Limits of Global Civil Society: A Comparison of NGO Participation in UN World Conferences on the Environment, Human Rights, and Women," *World Politics* 51 (1998): 10.

27. For the concept of the UN as a framework, see David P. Forsythe, *The Internationalization of Human Rights* (Lexington, Mass.: Lexington Books, 1991), 55; and the general discussion in Thomas G. Weiss, David P. Forsythe, and Roger A. Coate, *The United Nations and Changing World Politics*, 2nd ed. (Boulder: Westview, 1997), 12–14.

28. Klotz, *Norms in International Relations*, 74.

29. Recent book-length studies include Keck and Sikkink, *Activists beyond Borders*; Jackie Smith, Charles Chatfield, and Ron Pagnucco, eds., *Transnational Social Movements and Global Politics: Solidarity beyond the State* (Syracuse, N.Y.: Syracuse University Press, 1997); Tolley, *International Commission of Jurists*; and Peter Willetts, ed., *"Conscience of the World": The Influence of Non-Governmental Organisations in the UN System* (Washington, D.C.: Brookings, 1996); a notable earlier work is Willetts, *Pressure Groups in the Global System*.

30. Henry C. Steiner and Philip Alston, *International Human Rights in Context* (Oxford: Clarendon, 1995), 380.

31. See Alexander Wendt and Raymond Duvall, "Institutions and International Order," in *Global Changes and Theoretical Challenges*, ed. Ernst-Otto Czempiel and James N. Rosenau (Lexington, Mass.: Lexington Books, 1989), 55, and, more recently, Finnemore, *National Interests in International Society*.

32. Krasner, "Structural Causes," 2.

33. See Thomas Risse-Kappen and Hans-Peter Schmitz, "Principled Ideas, International Institutions, and Domestic Change: Human Rights and the Idea of European Unity—Conceptual Considerations," paper prepared for presentation at the American Political Science Association annual meeting, New York, N.Y., 31 August–4 September 1994, 2.

34. Friedrich Kratochwil and John Gerard Ruggie, "International Organization: A State of the Art on an Art of the State," *International Organization* 40 (1986): 743–75.

35. Kratochwil, *Rules, Norms, and Decisions*, 10.

36. Rittberger, "Research on International Regimes in Germany: The Adaptive Internationalization of an American Social Science Concept," in *Regime Theory and International Relations*, ed. Rittberger, 3–22. See also Jürgen Habermas, *Theory of Communicative Action* (Boston: Beacon, 1984); and Yee's comments on interpretive rationality in Yee, "Thick Rationality," 1028–32.

37. Klotz, *Norms in International Relations*, 14.

38. See Hart, *The Concept of Law.*

39. Bull, *The Anarchical Society,* 13. (Emphasis added.)

40. Michael Walzer, *Just and Unjust Wars* (New York: Penguin, 1977), 54.

41. Schwelb, *Human Rights and the International Community,* 65.

42. P. H. Kooijmans, "Human Rights—Universal Panacea?" *Netherlands International Law Review* 37 (1990): 317.

43. E. W. Vierdag, "Some Remarks about Special Features of Human Rights Treaties," *Netherlands Journal of International Law* (1994): 128.

44. For example, the Code of Conduct for Law Enforcement Officials, described in Nigel Rodley, *The Treatment of Prisoners under International Law,* 2nd ed. (Oxford: Clarendon, 1999), 355–68; and the UN's *Manual on the Effective Prevention and Investigation of Extra-Legal, Arbitrary, and Summary Executions* (New York: UN Publications, 1991), discussed in chapter 5.

45. Jürgen Habermas, *Between Facts and Norms* (Cambridge, Mass.: MIT Press, 1996), 370.

46. Rodley, interview.

47. Picken, interview.

48. For a "spiral model" of the impact of human rights norms on individual countries, see Thomas Risse, Stephen C. Ropp, and Kathryn Sikkink, eds., *The Power of Human Rights* (Cambridge, U.K.: Cambridge University Press, 1999).

49. For example, see the conflict between NGO "networkers" and "lobbyists" described in Clark, Friedman, and Hochstetler, "Sovereign Limits of Global Civil Society."

CHAPTER THREE
TORTURE

1. Rittberger, "Research on Regimes in Germany," 10–11.

2. Nigel Rodley, "The Development of United Nations Activities in the Field of Human Rights and the Role of Non-Governmental Organizations," in *The US, the UN, and the Management of Global Change,* ed. Toby Trister Gati (New York: New York University Press, 1983), 264.

3. Buergenthal, *International Human Rights in a Nutshell,* 87–88.

4. See Rodley, *Treatment of Prisoners,* 18–19. This and subsequent references are to the 2nd (1999) edition, unless otherwise noted.

5. Barry M. Klayman, "The Definition of Torture in International Law," *Temple Law Quarterly* 51 (1978): 452; Nehemiah Robinson, *The Universal Declaration of Human Rights: Its Origin, Significance and Interpretation* (New York: Institute of Jewish Affairs, 1950), 42–43.

6. See Donnelly, *Universal Human Rights,* 224–25.

7. AI, *Annual Report 1966–67,* 5.

8. AI, *Annual Report 1967–68,* 2.

9. Van Coufoudakis, "Greek Foreign Policy, 1945–1985, Seeking Independence in an Interdependent World," in *Political Change in Greece before and after the Colonels,* ed. Kevin Featherstone and Dimitrious K. Katsoudas (New York: St. Martin's, 1987), 233.

10. Peter Schwab and George D. Frangos, *Greece under the Junta* (New York: Facts on File, 1973), 15.

11. Henry Kamm, "Leader Uncertain If 'the New Greece' Needs a Parliament," *New York Times*, 4 May 1967, 1.

12. Schwab and Frangos, *Greece*, 20–21.

13. Ibid., 14–15.

14. Kamm, "Leader Uncertain."

15. AI, *Torture in Greece: The First Torturers' Trial, 1975* (London: AI Publications, 1977), 11.

16. Grant, interview.

17. Excerpted in AI, *Torture in Greece*, 79–82.

18. Grant, interview; AI, "The Greek Mission," in *Amnesty International Annual Report 1967–68* (London: International Secretariat, 1968), 6.

19. Council of Europe, European Court of Human Rights, *The Greek Case, Yearbook of the European Convention of Human Rights 1969* (The Hague: Martinus Nijhoff, 1972), 21, para. 43.

20. Council of Europe, "Documentary Evidence Relating to Article 3: Documentary Evidence Submitted by the Applicant Governments," Annex I.B.1, 11, in Council of Europe, European Commission of Human Rights, *The Greek Case, Report of the Commission* (Strasbourg, bound typescript, n.d.). See also J. D. Armstrong, "The International Committee of the Red Cross and Political Prisoners," *International Organization* 39 (1985): 638–39.

21. See "Decision of the Commission as to the admissibility of certain new allegations made by the governments of Denmark, Norway, and Sweden in the proceedings concerning: Application no. 3321/67 by the government of Denmark against the government of Greece; Application no. 3322/67 by the government of Norway against the government of Greece; Application no. 3323/67 by the government of Sweden against the government of Greece; Application no. 3344/67 by the government of the Netherlands against the government of Greece: Decision of the European Commission of Human Rights (31 May 1968)," in Council of Europe, European Commission of Human Rights and European Court of Human Rights, *Yearbook of the European Convention on Human Rights 1968* (The Hague: Martinus Nijhoff, 1970), 748.

22. Ibid.

23. Ibid., 750.

24. Council of Europe, "Introductory Report on the Situation in Greece by Mr. van der Stoel," Council of Europe Doc. 2384, 23 September 1968.

25. "Annex III: List of Witnesses Heard by the Sub-Commission under Article 3 of the Convention," in Council of Europe, *The Greek Case* (Strasbourg, n.d.).

26. In 1999, the UN Economic and Social Council changed the name of the Sub-Commission on the Prevention of Discrimination and the Protection of Minorities to the Sub-Commission on the Promotion and Protection of Human Rights. Below, the Sub-Commission is referred to by its name at the time of the events being discussed.

27. UN ECOSOC Res 1235 (XLII), 6 June 1967. Emphasis added.

28. Nigel Rodley, "UN Non-Treaty Procedures for Dealing with Human Rights Violations," in *Guide to Human Rights Practice*, 2nd ed., ed. Hurst Hannum (Philadelphia: University of Pennsylvania Press, 1992), 64.

29. Ibid.

30. Sam Pope Brewer, "Greece Accused in U.N. of Terror," *New York Times*, 21 February 1968, 16, col. 4.

31. See discussion of the circumstances surrounding the creation of the confidential "1503 procedure," UN ECOSOC Res. 1503 (XLVIII) of 27 May 1970, in Rodley, "The Development of UN Activities," 273–74, and William Korey, *NGOs and the Universal Declaration*, 127–30. The confidentiality restrictions lasted for several years, but were loosened after a little less than a decade. The review procedure instituted by Resolution 1503 has evolved into one that is now used frequently by NGOs.

32. Kathleen Teltsch, "UN Unit Said to Report Greeks Violate Human Rights," *New York Times*, 21 September 1972, 18.

33. William Korey, *NGOs and the Universal Declaration*, 129.

34. Kamminga, *Inter-State Accountability*, 84.

35. Duncan Forrest, Bernard Knight, and Morris Tidball-Binz, "The Documentation of Torture," in *A Glimpse of Hell: Reports on Torture Worldwide*, ed. Duncan Forrest (New York: New York University Press and Amnesty International, 1996), 169. A discussion of the ICRC's style with regard to publicity and other matters appears in Forsythe, "Human Rights and the International Committee of the Red Cross," 278–84.

36. "Two Groups Accuse Greece on Torture," *New York Times*, 18 October 1972, 12, col. 4.

37. MacBride's influence in NGO coalition building at the UN is documented and discussed in Howard Tolley, "Popular Sovereignty and International Law: ICJ Strategies for Human Rights Standard Setting," *Human Rights Quarterly* 11 (1989): 562–65.

38. Sean MacBride, "Introduction" to AI, *Annual Report 1970–71* (London: International Secretariat, 1971), 4.

39. "Campaign for the Abolition of Torture," *Amnesty International Newsletter* 3, no. 2 (February 1973): 1.

40. AI, *Report on Torture*, 2nd ed. (New York: Farrar, Straus and Giroux, 1975).

41. Stefanie Grant, Foreword, in AI, *Annual Report 1973–74* (London: International Secretariat, 1974), 24.

42. AI, *Report on Torture*, 114.

43. Niall MacDermot, "Law and the Prevention of Torture," *Review of the International Commission of Jurists*, no. 11 (December 1973): 23–27. The article is "based upon a report given by the secretary-general of the International Commission of Jurists, to a Conference on Torture convened by the British Section of Amnesty International in London on October 20, 1973."

44. AI, *Conference for the Abolition of Torture, Paris, 10–11 December 1973, Final Report*, AI Index no. PUB 29/00/74 (London: International Secretariat, 1974), 29–30.

45. "Continuing Action against Torture," *Amnesty International Newsletter* 3, no. 10 (October 1973): 2.

46. AI, *Annual Report 1973–74*, 15.

47. "Conference Secretary Appointed," *Amnesty International Newsletter* 3, no. 5 (May 1973): 3.

48. "Anti-Torture Petition 'Wired' to UN," *Amnesty International Newsletter* 4, no. 1 (January 1974): 1. A facsimile of the document appears in AI, *Conference for the Abolition of Torture*, 4.

49. "Appeal Passes One Million Signature Goal," *Amnesty International Newsletter*, vol. 3, no. 12 (December 1973): 2.

50. AI, *Annual Report 1973–74*, 13.

51. Rodley, interview.

52. For example, "Allegations of Torture in Brazil," cited in *Amnesty International Newsletter* 2, no. 10 (October 1972): 2.

53. "Ten Torture Cases in PoC Week," *Amnesty International Newsletter* 3, no. 11 (November 1973): 3.

54. "New Amnesty Techniques Explored and Far-Reaching Growth Plan Endorsed," *Amnesty International Newsletter* 3, no. 10 (October 1973): 2.

55. Edy Kaufman, interview, College Park, Maryland, 10 September 1993.

56. Amnesty International, *Torture in the Eighties* (London: AI Publications, 1984), 2.

57. AI, *Annual Report 1977*, 32.

58. Van Boven, "Role of Non-Governmental Organizations," 213.

59. Thomas E. Skidmore and Peter H. Smith, *Modern Latin America* (New York: Oxford University Press, 1989), 130–35.

60. Van Boven, "Role of Non-Governmental Organizations," 213.

61. Elsa (Coca) Rudolfi, interview, Santiago, Chile, 20 November 1992.

62. "Amnesty International News in Brief," *Amnesty International Newsletter* 4, no. 10 (October 1974): 4. In addition to Rudolfi, prisoners of conscience from Bulgaria, Cuba, Indonesia, Morocco, Rhodesia, Saudi Arabia, South Vietnam, the Soviet Union, Spain, Uruguay, and the U.S.A. were featured.

63. Kaufman, "Prisoners of Conscience," 366. A similar newsletter feature, now called "Worldwide Appeals," still exists.

64. Rudolfi, interview.

65. Kit Kennedy, "Women Political Prisoners Tortured," *Majority Report*, 22 February 1975, 4.

66. See Organization of American States, Inter-American Commission on Human Rights, *Report on the Situation of Human Rights in Chile 1985*. OAS Doc. OAS/Ser.L/V/II.66, Doc. 17, 27 September 1985, chap. 6, paras. 22–26.

67. See Caroline Moorehead, "The Power of Shame as a Weapon," *The Times* (London), 16.

68. AI, *Annual Report 1973–74*, 39.

69. Roberto Garretón, interview conducted by Kathryn Sikkink and the author, Santiago, Chile, 4 November 1992.

70. José Zalaquett, author's interview, Santiago, Chile, 19 November 1992.

71. J. Herman Burgers and Hans Danelius, *The United Nations Convention against Torture* (Dordrecht: Martinus Nijhoff, 1988), 13.

72. UN, General Assembly Resolution 3059 (XXVIII), 2 November 1973.

73. Rodley, *Treatment of Prisoners*, 21.

74. Ibid., 19.

75. UN discussion over the question of torture in 1973, quoted in Burgers and Danelius, *UN Convention,* 13–14.

76. AI, *Annual Report 1973–74,* 14.

77. Ibid., 10.

78. "UNESCO Ban Fails to Halt Conference," *Amnesty International Newsletter* 4, no. 1 (January 1974): 1.

79. Sean MacBride, "Preface," in *Conference for the Abolition of Torture, Final Report,* 7.

80. Van Boven, "Role of Non-Governmental Organizations," 213. See also Burgers and Danelius, *UN Convention,* 13.

81. AI, "Quadrennial Report, 1973–77, Submitted by Amnesty International," in UN, ECOSOC, *Quadrennial Reports on the Activities of Non-Governmental Organizations Granted Consultative Status to Categories I and II by the Economic and Social Council,* UN Doc. E/C.2/R.49/Add.101, 2 December 1977, 4.

82. Ibid.

83. "Staff," *Amnesty International Newsletter* 3, no. 2 (February 1973): 1.

84. Dick Oosting (with Marzel Zwanborn), interview conducted by Kathryn Sikkink, Utrecht, The Netherlands, 12 November 1993. Oosting, a lawyer by training, had been active in the Dutch section of AI, and had translated AI's *Report on Torture* into Dutch. In December 1977, Oosting became deputy secretary-general of AI, and served in that capacity until 1982. ("IEC Names Dick Oosting to Fill First Post in New Anti-Torture Department," *Amnesty International Newsletter* 4, no. 3 [March 1974]: 4; "AI's Executive Plans Activities for 1979," *Amnesty International Newsletter* 8, no. 1 [January 1978]: 2.)

85. AI, *Annual Report 1974–75,* 18.

86. UN General Assembly Resolution 3218 (XXIX). Quoted in Burgers and Danelius, *UN Convention,* 14.

87. Burgers and Danelius, *UN Convention,* 14.

88. Virginia Leary, "A New Role for Non-Governmental Organizations in Human Rights: A Case Study of Non-Governmental Participation in the Development of International Norms against Torture," *UN Law/Fundamental Rights,* ed. Antonio Cassese (Aalphen aan den Rijn, Sijthoff and Noordhoof, 1979), 202.

89. Burgers and Danelius, *UN Convention,* 19.

90. Leary, "A New Role," 202.

91. Rodley, *Treatment of Prisoners,* 356.

92. "Code of Ethics for Lawyers, Relevant to Torture and Other Cruel, Inhuman or Degrading Treatment or Punishment," also in 1975. (Burgers and Danelius, *UN Convention,* 19.)

93. "AI Urges UN Body to Recommend Machinery for Stopping Torture and Protecting Prisoners against Ill Treatment," *Amnesty International Newsletter* 5, no. 9 (September 1975): 1.

94. Leary, "A New Role," 203.

95. Ibid.

96. Rodley, *Treatment of Prisoners,* 357.

97. Ibid., 358.

98. UN General Assembly Res. 34/169, 17 December 1979.

99. Claudius and Stepan, *Amnesty International*, 292.

100. For an account comparing the wording and content of the Code of Conduct with regard to the Declaration of The Hague, see Rodley, *Treatment of Prisoners*, 355–62.

101. UN General Assembly Res. 37/194. (Burgers and Danelius, *UN Convention*, 21–22; see also Rodley, *Treatment of Prisoners*, 371–72.)

102. Leary, "A New Role," 204; Burgers and Danelius, *UN Convention*, 15.

103. Burgers and Danelius, *UN Convention*, 15.

104. Jan Herman Burgers, interview conducted by Kathryn Sikkink, The Hague, The Netherlands, 13 November 1993. Burgers, coauthor with Danelius of *UN Convention* (cited above), served as a member of the Netherlands' delegation to the UN Commission on Human Rights.

105. Oosting, interview.

106. Leary, "A New Role," 204.

107. "AI Secretary General Visits United Nations," *Campaign for the Abolition of Torture Monthly Bulletin* 2, no. 11 (November 1975): 4.

108. UN General Assembly Res. 3542 (XXX), 9 December 1975.

109. Leary, "A New Role," 204–5.

110. See Burgers and Danelius, *UN Convention*, xi, 34–36.

111. Ibid., 26.

112. Ibid., 37–38.

113. François de Vargas, "History of a Campaign," in *Torture: How to Make the International Convention Effective*, ed. by International Commission of Jurists and Swiss Committee Against Torture (Geneva: International Commission of Jurists and Swiss Committee Against Torture, 1980), 44.

114. Burgers and Danelius, *UN Convention*, 27.

115. Ibid., 105.

116. Ibid., 32.

117. UN Doc. E/CN.4/1427, reprinted in Burgers and Danelius, *UN Convention*, 218.

118. The wording was proposed by the representative from Argentina, representing a new government after the fall of the Argentine military government in 1982. (Burgers and Danelius, *UN Convention*, 84.) The Argentine diplomatic delegation had been a major antagonist in the Commission only a few years earlier, when the issue of disappearances under the military government of Argentina had come to the fore. (See chapter 4, below.) In fact, Burgers and Danelius note that the "radical change" in the Argentine position at the Commission greatly facilitated final agreement on the draft of the convention in the 1984 session (*UN Convention*, 92).

119. Burgers and Danelius, *UN Convention*, 39.

120. Ibid., 80.

121. Intervention of Mr. N. Rodley, Amnesty International, "Interventions Relating to the Report on 'Responsibilities for the Organs of the European Convention, Including the Committee of Ministers,' " in Council of Europe, *Proceedings of the Sixth International Colloquy about the European Convention on Human Rights, 13–16 November 1985* (Dordrecht: Martinus Nijhoff, 1988), 1058.

122. Niall MacDermot, "How to Enforce the Torture Convention," in International Commission of Jurists and Swiss Committee Against Torture, *Torture*, 19.

123. "Introduction," International Commission of Jurists and Swiss Committee Against Torture, *Torture*, 5. See also Burgers and Danelius, *UN Convention*, 28.

124. Burgers and Danelius, *UN Convention*, 91.

125. Ibid., 104–6. See UN General Assembly, "Torture and Other Cruel, Inhuman or Degrading Treatment or Punishment, Report of the Third Committee," UN Doc. A/39/708, 7 December 1984, paras. 12 and 13.

126. International Commission of Jurists, "Draft Convention on Torture, Intervention by Niall MacDermot, Secretary General of the International Commission of Jurists," typescript, Geneva, 29 February 1984, 1–2.

127. Amnesty International, "Oral Statement by Amnesty International, Convention Against Torture," delivered by Secretary-General Thomas Hammarberg to the 40th session of the U.N. Commission on Human Rights, typescript, 28 February 1984.

128. AI, *Torture in the Eighties* (London: Amnesty International Publications, 1984), 3.

129. The final convention does establish extensive jurisdiction, although conditions for extradition may be subject to interpretation, depending on a state's own domestic law.

130. "Twelve-Point Program for the Prevention of Torture," adopted by Amnesty International in October 1983, in AI, *Torture in the Eighties*, 249–51.

131. Burgers and Danelius, *UN Convention*, 102–3.

132. Bolivia, Colombia, Costa Rica, Denmark, the Dominican Republic, Finland, Gambia, Greece, Norway, Samoa, and Spain, followed by Australia, Austria, Belgium, France, Iceland, Panama, Portugal, Singapore, and the United Kingdom. (Ibid., 103.)

133. Amnesty International, "Ratification of Human Rights Instruments: Oral Statement by Amnesty International," mimeo, AI Index no. IOR 41/08/85, 1985, 2.

134. The Working Group on Enforced or Involuntary Disappearances was created in 1980 (see below, chapter 4), and the Special Rapporteur on Summary or Arbitrary Executions was created in 1982 (see below, chapter 5).

135. As of September 1998, twenty thematic mechanisms were in effect.

136. Peter H. Kooijmans, "The Role and Action of the UN Special Rapporteur on Torture," in *The International Fight against Torture*, ed. Antonio Cassese (Baden-Baden, Germany: Nomos, 1991), 58.

137. Ibid.

138. Ibid.

139. Helena Cook, "The Role of Amnesty International in the Fight against Torture," in *The International Fight against Torture*, ed. Cassese, 181–82.

140. UN Commission on Human Rights Resolution 1985/33.

141. Nigel Rodley, "United Nations Action Procedures against 'Disappearances,' Summary or Arbitrary Executions, and Torture," in *Human Rights*, ed. Peter Davies (London: Routledge, 1988), 95.

142. Menno Kamminga, "The Thematic Procedures of the U.N. Commission on Human Rights," *Netherlands International Law Review* 34 (1987): 311.

143. Ibid., 301.

144. Chapter 4 below offers a more detailed discussion of the genesis of the first thematic mechanism's reporting procedures (those of the Working Group on Enforced or Involuntary Disappearances) and the adoption of existing NGO techniques.

145. Burgers and Danelius, *UN Convention*, 29.

146. Ibid., 30.

147. MacDermot, "How to Enforce the Convention," 35.

148. Amnesty International, "New International Instruments: The Draft Declaration on the Protection of All Persons from Enforced Disappearance; The Draft Optional Protocol to the Convention Against Torture and Other Cruel, Inhuman or Degrading Treatment or Punishment, Oral Intervention by Amnesty International," UN Commission on Human Rights, 48th Session, Delivered February 1992, typescript, AI Index IOR 41/02/92, 1992, 3.

149. UN Commission on Human Rights Res. 1992/43, 3 March 1992.

150. Burgers, interview.

151. In addition, Burgers claimed that Jean-Jacques Gautier, whom he referred to as "the father of the European Convention [for the Prevention of Torture and Inhuman or Degrading Treatment or Punishment]," was also motivated by the AI campaign. (Burgers, interview.)

CHAPTER FOUR
DISAPPEARANCES

1. Amnesty International, *"Disappearances": A Workbook* (New York: Amnesty International USA, 1981), 2.

2. Geneva Convention Relative to the Protection of Civilian Persons in Time of War of 12 August 1949, article 147, quoted in Rodley, *Treatment of Prisoners*, 243.

3. David Pion-Berlin and George A. Lopez, "Of Victims and Executioners: Argentine State Terror, 1975–1979," *International Studies Quarterly* 35 (1991): 64; T. David Mason and Dale A. Crane, "The Political Economy of Death Squads: Toward a Theory of the Impact of State-Sanctioned Terror," *International Studies Quarterly* 33 (1989): 178.

4. Amnesty International, *Guatemala: Amnesty International Briefing Paper No. 8* (London: Amnesty International Publications, December 1976), 1.

5. See aid data from U.S. Department of Defense, *Military Assistance Facts, 15 February 1967*, cited in Richard Newbold Adams, *Crucifixion by Power* (Austin: University of Texas, 1970), 264.

6. AI, *Annual Report 1970–71* (London: AI Publications, 1971), 64.

7. AI, *Briefing Paper No. 8.*

8. Picken, interview.

9. AI, *Annual Report 1968–69*, no page numbers.

10. Ann Marie Clark, " 'A Calendar of Abuses': Amnesty International's Guatemala Campaigning," in *NGOs and Human Rights*, ed. Claude E. Welch, Jr. (Philadelphia: University of Pennsylvania Press, forthcoming).

11. AI, *Amnesty International Report 1977* (London: AI Publications, 1977), 32.

12. Comisión Nacional de Verdad y Reconcilación, *Informe Rettig* (Santiago: La Nación & Las Ediciones del Ornitorrínco, 1991) vol. 2, 881, 883.

13. AI, *Annual Report 1973–74*, 40.

14. Comisión Nacional, *Informe Rettig*, vol. 1, 448.

15. Amnesty International, "Legal Aspects of Disappearances," 1981 mimeo, AI Doc. Index ACT 03/12/81, 4.

16. OAS, Inter-American Commission on Human Rights, *Report of the Situation of Human Rights in Chile*, OAS Doc. OAS/Ser.L/V/II.66, Doc. 17, 27 September 1985, 72–73.

17. Cecilia Medina Quiroga, *The Battle of Human Rights* (Dordrecht: Martinus Nijhoff, 1988), 263ff.

18. UN General Assembly Res. 3219, 6 November 1974.

19. UN Commission on Human Rights Res. 8, 27 February 1975.

20. AI, *Annual Report 1975–76* (London: AI Publications, 1976), 92–93. See also Brody and González, *"Nunca Más*: An Analysis," 366, n. 2.

21. Patricia Feeney, author's interview, Oxford, U.K., 27 October 1993.

22. Eduardo Crawley, *A House Divided* (New York: St. Martin's Press, 1984), 421, 424. See also Pion-Berlin and Lopez, "Of Victims and Executioners."

23. Comisión Nacional sobre la Desaparición de Personas, *Nunca Más: Informe de la Comisión Nacional sobre la Desaparición de Personas* (Buenos Aires: Editorial Universitaria de Buenos Aires, 1992), 293, 298.

24. Guest, *Behind the Disappearances*, 37.

25. Crawley, *A House Divided*, 430–1.

26. Feeney, interview.

27. Ibid.

28. Marysa Navarro, "The Personal Is Political: Las Madres de Plaza de Mayo," in *Power and Popular Protest*, ed. Susan Eckstein (Berkeley: University of California Press, 1989): 248–49.

29. AI, *Report of an Amnesty International Mission to Argentina, 6–15 November 1976* (London: Amnesty International Publications, 1977), 16. The figure is also cited in AI, *Annual Report 1975–76*, 120.

30. Brysk, *Politics of Human Rights in Argentina*, 52.

31. AI, "The 1978 World Cup and Human Rights: What Sportspeople Think," mimeo, 17 May 1978, AI Index AMR 13/34/78.

32. AI, *Disappeared Prisoners in Chile* (London: Amnesty International Publications, March 1977).

33. AI, *Annual Report 1979* (London: Amnesty International Publications), 55. The UN dissolved the Ad Hoc Working Group on Chile in 1979 and appointed Felix Ermacora as its official Expert on the Question of the Fate of Missing and Disappeared Persons in Chile, to continue looking into the problem there. AI praised Ermacora's first report for placing its discussion of disappearances in Chile in the context of the occurrence of disappearances elsewhere.

34. On the rise of the human rights network, see Sikkink, "Human Rights, Principled Issue-Networks, and Sovereignty," and Keck and Sikkink, *Activists beyond Borders*; for a discussion of international attention to Argentina, see Brysk, *Politics of Human Rights in Argentina*, 51–62.

35. Nélida Navajas, interviewed by Kathryn Sikkink and the author, Buenos Aires, 28 October 1992.

36. Brysk, *Politics of Human Rights in Argentina*, 53–54.

37. UN General Assembly Res. 33/173, 20 December 1978.

38. Guest, *Behind the Disappearances*, 135.

39. Kramer and Weissbrodt, "The 1980 UN Commission," 18.

40. See Brysk, *Politics of Human Rights in Argentina*, 45–51.

41. Navarro, "Personal Is Political," 249.

42. Kramer and Weissbrodt, "The 1980 UN Commission," 18.

43. AI, "The Problem of Disappearances in Argentina," mimeo, 10 April 1979, AI Index AMR 13/25/79, 2.

44. Ibid., 1–2.

45. AI, "The 'Disappeared' of Argentina: List of Cases Reported to Amnesty International, March 1976–February 1979," mimeo, AI Index AMR 13/35/79, May 1979.

46. AI, "The Missing People of Argentina," *Amnesty International Newsletter* 9, no. 7 (July 1979): 4.

47. OAS, Inter-American Commission on Human Rights, *Report on the Situation of Human Rights in Argentina* (Washington, D.C.: Organization of American States, 1980).

48. AI, "The Problem of Disappeared Persons," oral statement by the representative of Amnesty International under item 8 of the 32nd session of the UN Sub-Commission on Prevention of Discrimination and Protection of Minorities, Geneva, 29 August 1979, mimeo, AI Index POL 35/01/79, 2.

49. AI, *Amnesty International Report 1980* (London: Amnesty International Publications, 1980), 107.

50. Rodley, interview.

51. Guest, *Behind the Disappearances*, 124.

52. Theo van Boven, interview conducted by Kathryn Sikkink, Maastricht, The Netherlands, 8 November 1993.

53. Menno Kamminga, interview conducted by Kathryn Sikkink, Rotterdam, The Netherlands, 11 November 1993.

54. UN Doc. E/CN.4/1435, 26 January 1981, paras. 10, 30.

55. Ibid., para. 190.

56. Rodley, "United Nations Action Procedures," 74.

57. Kamminga, "Thematic Procedures," 317.

58. Rodley, interview.

59. Rodley, *Treatment of Prisoners*, 192.

60. See Amnesty International, "Declaration of Stockholm," 11 December 1977, reproduced in Amnesty International, *When the State Kills* (London: Amnesty International Publications, 1989), Appendix 12, 155–56.

61. Clayton Yeo, author's interview (telephone), London, 4 November 1993.

62. Zalaquett, interview.

63. Ibid.

64. Ann Blyberg, author's interview, Washington, D.C., 27 September 1995.

65. Ibid.

66. Ibid.

67. Ibid.

68. Ibid.

69. Zalaquett, interview. The papers, edited by Rebecca Babcock-Martos, were published as AI-USA, *Disappearances: A Workbook*.

70. Blyberg, interview.

71. AI-USA, *Disappearances: A Workbook*, 88.

72. For example, see Amnesty International, *Getting Away with Murder* (London: Amnesty International Publications, October 1993), 9.

73. Amnesty International, "Statement on 'Disappearances,' " delivered to the 33rd session of the UN Sub-Commission on the Prevention of Discrimination and Protection of Minorities, Geneva, 28 August 1980, mimeo.

74. Ibid.

75. Amnesty International, "Disappearances," Oral statement by Amnesty International to the United Nations Commission on Human Rights (37th Session), 17 February 1981, mimeo.

76. The WGEID has been renewed regularly, even after Argentina returned to a democratically elected civilian government in 1983.

77. Emilio F. Mignone, *Derechos Humanos y Sociedad* (Buenos Aires: Centro de Estudios Legales y Sociales and Ediciones del Pensamiento Nacional, 1991), 54–55.

78. Michael T. Kaufman, "Emilio F. Mignone, 76, Dies; Argentine Human Rights Campaigner," *New York Times*, 25 December 1998, B11.

79. Mignone, *Derechos Humanos y Sociedad*, 58 (author's translation).

80. AI, "Legal Concern, Argentina: Dr. Emilio Fermín Mignone, Dr. José Federico Westerkamp, Boris Pasik, Dr. Augusto Conte MacDonell, Carmen Aguiar de Lapacó, Marcelo Parrilli," Urgent Action 49/81, AI Index AMR 13/03/81, 3 March 1981.

81. José Federico and Angela Westerkamp, author's interview, 7 October 1992, Buenos Aires.

82. Anonymous, author's interview, Boulder, Colorado, 25 July 1993.

83. AI, "Legal Concern," and AI, "Human Rights Activists Detained," press release, AI Index NWS 01/04/81, 4 March 1981.

84. Amnesty International, press release, AI Index NWS 01/05/81, 11 March 1981.

85. Navarro, "Personal Is Political," 249.

86. Mignone, *Derechos Humanos*, 57–58 n. 31.

87. Ibid., 56.

88. Quotes drawn by AI from Report of the UN Working Group on Enforced or Involuntary Disappearances, UN Doc. E/CN.4/1435, 26 January 1981; in AI, "Legal Aspects of 'Disappearances,' " mimeo, AI Index ACT 03/12/81, 7.

89. For example, see Grupo Iniciativa para una Convención contra la Desaparición Forzada de Personas, *La Desaparición Forzada como Crimen de Lesa Humanidad* (Buenos Aires: Grupo de Iniciativa, 1989).

90. Brody and González, "*Nunca Más*: An Analysis," 372; Reed Brody, author's interview, New York, New York, 13 May 1996; and David Weissbrodt, author's interview, Minneapolis, 20 September 1994.

91. Tolley, *International Commission of Jurists*, 171.

92. Reed Brody, "Commentary on the Draft UN 'Declaration on the Protection of All Persons from Enforced or Involuntary Disappearances,' " *Netherlands Quarterly of Human Rights* 4 (1990): 382.

93. Rodley, quoted in Brody, "Commentary," 386.

94. Brody, interview; Brody, "Commentary."

95. Brody and González, "*Nunca Más*: An Analysis," 372.

96. Rodolfo Matarollo, "Informe Introductorio del Grupo de Iniciativa," in Grupo de Iniciativa, *La Desaparición Forzada*, 135–36.

97. Brody and González, "*Nunca Más*: An Analysis," 371.

98. UN Working Group on Enforced or Involuntary Disappearances, "Report of the Working Group on Enforced or Involuntary Disappearances," Item E, "Draft Declaration on the Protection of All Persons from Enforced or Involuntary Disappearances Prepared by the Working Group on Detention of the Sub-Commission on Prevention of Discrimination and Protection of Minorities," UN Doc. E/CN.4/1990/13, 24 January 1990, 8, paras. 30 and 31.

99. Ibid. On the definitional problems that remain, see Rodley, *Treatment of Prisoners*, 245–48.

100. Ibid., 8–9, para. 32.

101. Brody, "Commentary," 383.

102. Tolley, *International Commission of Jurists*, 171.

103. International Commission of Jurists, "UN Group Condemns Disappearances," press release, Geneva, Switzerland, 11 November 1991.

104. UN ECOSOC Res. 1992/5, 20 July 1992; "Declaration on the Protection of All Persons from Enforced Disappearances," UN General Assembly Res. 46/133, UN Doc. A/47/49 (1992).

105. UN, Commission on Human Rights, *Report of the Working Group on Enforced or Involuntary Disappearances*, UN Doc. E/CN.4/1990/13 (1990), 10, para. 37.

106. Brody and González, "*Nunca Más*: An Analysis," 374–75, 402; Michael Reed-Hurtado, author's interview, telephone, Minneapolis, 29 November 1994. (Reed-Hurtado, then a law student, observed drafting meetings of the convention concurrent with the 1994 session of the UN Sub-Commission on the Prevention of Discrimination and Protection of Minorities and interned with the Andean Commission of Jurists in 1994.)

107. The 1982 conference, also sponsored by the Dutch section and held in Noordwijkerhout, focused mainly on political killings and is described in more detail in the next chapter.

108. Amnesty International, "International Conference on Extrajudicial Executions and Disappearances," mimeo, translation of Dutch section news release, AI Index NWS 11/35/92, 3 September 1992, 6.

109. Amnesty International, *"Disappearances" and Political Killings, Human Rights Crisis of the 1990s* (Amsterdam: Amnesty International, 1994), 4 (title page, reverse).

110. Revised versions of some of the papers were published in AI, *"Disappearances" and Political Killings*.

111. AI, *"Disappearances" and Political Killings*, 105–6.

112. Rodley, "United Nations Action Procedures," 85.

113. UN General Assembly Res. 47/132, on the "Question of Enforced or Involuntary Disappearances," 18 December 1992.

114. AI, "Amnesty International 14-Point Program for the Prevention of 'Disappearances'," Appendix 8 of AI, *"Disappearances" and Political Killings,* 289,–91; and AI, "Amnesty International 14-Point Program for the Prevention of Extrajudicial Executions," Appendix 9, ibid., 292–94.

115. UN General Assembly Res. 43/173, 9 December 1988.

116. UN General Assembly Res. 40/34, 29 November 1985.

117. Adopted by the First UN Congress on the Prevention of Crime and the Treatment of Offenders, 1955.

118. Brody and González, *"Nunca Más: An Analysis,"* 371.

119. Ibid., 405 n. 216.

120. UN, Commission on Human Rights, *Report of the Working Group on Enforced or Involuntary Disappearances,* UN Doc. E/CN.4/1998/43, 12 January 1998.

121. Bauer, Jan, "Report on United Nations Commission on Human Rights, 55th Session, 22 March–30 April 1999" (Prepared for International Centre for Human Rights and Democratic Development, 23 July 1999), accessed online at http://www.hri.ca/uninfo/unchr99/.

122. Human Rights Internet, "Disappearances," in *For the Record 1998: The UN Human Rights System,* vol. 1 (Ottawa: Human Rights Internet and Canadian Department of Foreign Affairs and International Trade, 1998), accessed on-line at http://www.hri.ca/fortherecord1998/vol1/disappearances.htm.

123. See Bauer, "Report on the UN Commission on Human Rights."

124. Amnesty International, "Background Briefing: 55th UN Commission on Human Rights," AI Index IOR 41/05/99, March 1999.

125. Amnesty International, "International Organizations: Rhetoric and Reality," in *Amnesty International Report 1999* (London: Amnesty International Publications, 1998), 57.

126. UN, Commission on Human Rights, Sub-Commission on the Promotion and Protection of Human Rights, "Draft International Convention on the Protection of All Persons from Enforced Disappearance," Res. 1999/24, 26 August 1999.

CHAPTER FIVE
EXTRAJUDICIAL EXECUTIONS

1. Edy Kaufman and Patricia Weiss Fagen, "Extrajudicial Executions: An Insight into the Global Dimension of a Human Rights Violation," *Human Rights Quarterly* 3, 4 (Fall 1981): 86.

2. Anders Uhlin, *Indonesia and the "Third Wave of Democratization"* (New York: St. Martin's Press, 1997), 40.

3. Convention on the Prevention and Punishment of the Crime of Genocide, UN General Assembly Res. 260A (III), 9 December 1948.

4. Zalaquett, interview.

5. AI, *Amnesty International Report 1978* (London: Amnesty International Publications, 1978), 123.

6. "Human Rights Watch Looks Within," interview with Kenneth Roth in *New Yorker* ("Talk of the Town"), 13 December 1993, 53.

7. AI, *Amnesty International Report, 1975–76* (London: Amnesty International Publications, 1976), 83–84.

8. At the same time, the program was also expanded to cover disappearances, threats to health, and fair-trial issues. (AI, *Amnesty International Report 1976–77* [London: Amnesty International Publications, 1977], 32.)

9. AI, *Amnesty International Report 1978*, 95.

10. AI, *Amnesty International Report 1979*, 64.

11. Amnesty International, "Declaration of Stockholm." AI has since revised its understanding of EJEs, and sees them as distinct from the death penalty.

12. Eric Prokosch, author's interview, London, 9 November 1993. Prokosch joined the International Secretariat staff as campaign coordinator in 1979.

13. Yeo, interview.

14. Ibid.

15. Oosting, interview.

16. Marzel Zwanborn (with Dick Oosting), interview conducted by Kathryn Sikkink, 12 November 1993, Utrecht, The Netherlands. Zwanborn joined the staff of the Dutch AI section in 1980.

17. "Abolition of the Death Penalty," joint statement by forty-two international nongovernmental organizations concerned with human rights in consultative status with the UN Economic and Social Council, submitted to the Sixth United Nations Congress on the Prevention of Crime and the Treatment of Offenders (Caracas, Venezuela, 25 August–5 September 1980), reprinted in AI, *When the State Kills*, 257–58.

18. Prokosch, interview. On the events regarding the death penalty at the Crime Congress, see also Rodley, *Treatment of Prisoners*, 208–9.

19. Resolution 5, Sixth UN Congress on the Prevention of Crime and the Treatment of Offenders, Report at Ch. 1, UN Doc. A/CONF.87/14/Rev.1 (1981). Rodley discusses this resolution in some detail in *Treatment of Prisoners*, 179–80.

20. See Kamminga, "Thematic Procedures." Summary killings are sometimes called "extralegal executions."

21. UN General Assembly Res. 35/172, 15 December 1980.

22. UN Doc. E/AC.57/1982/4, 22 January 1982, items 62 and 63, pp. 11–12.

23. Amnesty International, "Murder by Governments," oral statement by Amnesty International to the UN Commission on Human Rights, typescript, 10 March 1981.

24. UN General Assembly Res. 36/22, 9 November 1981.

25. Soon after, van Boven's contract with the UN was not renewed; observers traced his firing to his willingness to name names of human rights violators. (See Guest, *Behind the Disappearances*, 353–57.)

26. See also Rodley, "UN Action Procedures," 86. On the operation of the special rapporteur, see Kamminga, "Thematic Procedures."

27. UN, Commission on Human Rights Res. 1982/29, 11 March 1982; ECOSOC formally established the position in UN ECOSOC Res. 1982/35, 7 May 1982.

28. The creation of the Special Rapporteur on Torture was the second, in 1985, and others have been created since then.

29. David Weissbrodt, personal conversation with the author, 5 November 1994, Minneapolis.

30. As Weissbrodt notes, there was a difference from the WGEID mandate, which asked the Working Group to "respond effectively" to reports. The Special Rapporteur's mandate did no such thing. (David Weissbrodt, "The Three 'Theme' Special Rapporteurs of the UN Commission on Human Rights," *American Journal of International Law* 80 [1986]: 685–99.)

31. Ibid.

32. Rodley, *Treatment of Prisoners*, 1st ed., 160.

33. Weissbrodt notes that the Special Rapporteur on Torture later benefited from the experiences of the Special Rapporteur on Summary or Arbitrary Executions and the WGEID (Weissbrodt, "Three 'Theme' Special Rapporteurs").

34. See "The International Conference on Extrajudicial Executions," in Amnesty International, *Political Killings by Governments* (London: Amnesty International Publications, 1983), 100–17.

35. Prokosch, interview.

36. "Final Statement of the International Conference on Extrajudicial Executions, Amsterdam, 2 May 1982," reprinted in AI, *Political Killings by Governments*, Appendix 2, 120–21.

37. Amnesty International, "Extrajudicial Executions," mimeo, 25 August 1982.

38. United Nations High Commissioner for Human Rights, "Extrajudicial, Summary or Arbitrary Executions," Fact Sheet No. 11 (Rev. 1) (Geneva: Office of the UN High Commissioner for Human Rights, 1997).

39. Frank Newman and David Weissbrodt, "Special Rapporteur on Extrajudicial, Summary or Arbitrary Executions," in *International Human Rights*, ed. Newman and Weissbrodt (Cincinnati: Anderson, 1996), 196–97.

40. UN Doc. E/CN.4/1992/30, para. 647.

41. On the topic of norms, for example, see "Extrajudicial Executions: International Legal Standards and Remedies," Circular No. 6, AI Index ACT/03/21/ 82 (external), 23 March 1982, which was distributed during the campaign.

42. "The Minnesota Protocol," in *Corporate Columns* (Minneapolis: Blue Cross Blue Shield of Minnesota, March–June 1987), 4.

43. Fraser was a former U.S. representative who had helped develop U.S. foreign policy on human rights during the Carter administration.

44. The Minnesota Lawyers International Human Rights Committee, formed in 1983, changed its name to Minnesota Advocates for Human Rights in October 1992. Below, the group is referred to as the Minnesota Lawyers Committee, as it was known during the early work on the Protocol.

45. David Weissbrodt, author's interview, 20 September 1993, Minneapolis.

46. Ibid.

47. Barbara Frey, author's interview, Minneapolis, 17 May 1993.

48. Lindsey Thomas, author's interview, Minneapolis, 13 May 1993. At the time of the interview, Thomas was assistant medical examiner for Hennepin County, Minnesota.

49. Ibid.

50. Jorgen L. Thomsen, Karin Helweg-Larsen, and Ole Vedel Rasmussen, "Amnesty International and the Forensic Sciences," *American Journal of Forensic Medicine and Pathology* 5, no. 4 (December 1984): 305.

51. Thomsen et al., "Sudden and Suspicious Deaths outside the Deceased's Own Country—Time for an International Protocol," *Forensic Science International* 20 (1982): 70–75.

52. Thomsen et al., "AI and the Forensic Sciences," 309.

53. Two of the people affiliated with AAAS were Eric Stover, then staff officer of the Commission on Scientific Freedom and Responsibility, and Kari Hannibal, who coauthored *The Breaking of Bodies and Minds*.

54. Frey, interview. The final document, Minnesota Lawyers International Human Rights Committee, "The Minnesota Protocol: Preventing Arbitrary Killing through an Adequate Death Investigation and Autopsy" (Minneapolis: Minnesota Lawyers International Human Rights Committee, Subcommittee on Inquiry Procedures, June 1987), is published in the microfiche collection, Inter Documentation Company, *Human Rights Documents* (Leiden, The Netherlands: Inter Documentation Company, 1991), Doc. 17 (3001).

55. Frey, interview.

56. Weissbrodt, interview. The conference was cosponsored by the Spring Hill conference center in Minnesota. Other contributors for the conference included Space Center, Inc., Minnesota Blue Cross and Blue Shield, Hennepin County Medical Foundation, the Stichting Human Rights Foundation, and the Minnesota Physicians Foundation of the Minnesota Medical Association. (Penny Parker and Karen Curtis, "Report of the Minnesota Conference: Promoting Human Rights through Adequate Inquiry Procedures" [Minneapolis: Spring Hill Center, Minn., report on conference proceedings, held at Minnesota Lawyers International Human Rights Committee, 21–23 October, 1987], 1. On microfiche in *Human Rights Documents*, Doc. 19, 3601.)

57. Frey, interview.

58. Parker and Curtis, "Report of the Minnesota Conference," Appendix C: Draft Principles on the Effective Prevention and Investigation of Extra-Legal, Arbitrary and Summary Executions.

59. Ibid.

60. David Weissbrodt and Terri Rosen, "Principles against Executions," *Hamline Law Review* 13 (1990): 584.

61. David Weissbrodt, letter to Christian Hoppe, Counsellor, Permanent Mission of Denmark, to the United Nations, 9 June 1988, written in Weissbrodt's capacity as legal counsel to the Minnesota Lawyers International Human Rights Committee.

62. Weissbrodt, interview.

63. Lindsey Thomas, address to the American Academy of Forensic Sciences, typescript, February 1986.

64. Weissbrodt, interview.

65. Ibid.

66. Ibid.

67. Slawomir Redo, author's interview, telephone, Vienna, Austria, 4 November 1993.

68. The Centre for Human Rights became the Office of the UN High Commissioner for Human Rights after the High Commissioner post was established in 1993.

69. The Crime Commission later became more politicized, after the decision was made to hold the 1990 meeting of the Congress on Crime Prevention and Control (Crime Congress) in Havana in 1990, which was unacceptable to the United States. The U.S., supported by the British government and some others, then refused to attend. The Committee on Crime Prevention and Control was reorganized into the Commission on Crime Prevention and Control, peopled by representatives with diplomatic portfolios rather than legal or technical experts. Although some of the same people continued to serve on the commission, the creation of new standards was no longer politically feasible in the committee. (Weissbrodt, interview.)

70. UN ECOSOC Res. 1984/48.

71. Redo, interview.

72. Ibid.

73. Ibid.

74. James Welsh, author's interview, London, 11 October 1993.

75. Redo, interview.

76. Ibid.

77. Frey, interview.

78. Welsh, interview.

79. David Kausman, Amnesty International, letter to Barbara Frey, executive director of the Minnesota Advocates, 13 September 1994.

80. For text, see "Amnesty International 14-Point Program for the Prevention of Extrajudicial Executions," in Amnesty International, *"Disappearances" and Political Killings*, Appendix 9, 292.

81. Parker and Curtis, "Report of the Minnesota Conference," 1.

CHAPTER SIX
NGOs AND NORMS IN INTERNATIONAL POLITICS

1. Rodley, "UN Non-Treaty Procedures," 81.

2. Guest, *Behind the Disappearances*, 78.

3. In practice, AI has been targeted for criticism from all ideological camps; for example, see Amnesty International, *AI in Quotes* (London: Amnesty International Publications, 1985), pamphlet, no page numbers.

4. Klayman, "The Definition of Torture," 467.

5. R. J. Vincent, *Human Rights and International Relations* (Cambridge, U.K.: Cambridge University Press, 1986), 108.

6. Nardin, *Law, Morality, and the Relations of States.*

7. Philip Alston, "The Commission on Human Rights," in *The United Nations and Human Rights*, ed. Alston (Oxford: Oxford University Press, 1992), 159.

8. Theo van Boven, "The Role of the United Nations Secretariat," in *The United Nations and Human Rights*, 552.

9. Picken, interview.

10. Rodley, "The Development of United Nations Activities," 268.

11. Peter Haas, "Do Regimes Matter? Epistemic Communities and Mediterranean Pollution Control," in *International Organization* 43, 3 (1989): 380.

12. Helena Cook, "Amnesty International at the United Nations," in *'Conscience of the World': The Influence of Non-Governmental Organisations in the UN System*, ed. Peter Willetts (Washington, D.C.: Brookings, 1996), 210 n.2.

13. Rodley, interview; Picken, interview.

14. For example, see Margo Picken, "The Role of the NGO in the Implementation of Human Rights within the Framework of the UN," paper delivered to an international colloquium on human rights at the University of Montreal (mimeo, AI Index IOR 41/07/85, 28 February 1985), para. 13.

15. Cook, "Amnesty International at the UN," 189.

16. Grant, interview.

17. See *Counterfeit Coverage*, video recording, NDP, 1992.

18. Michael Barkun, *Law without Sanctions* (New Haven: Yale University Press, 1968).

19. Kratochwil, *Rules, Norms, and Decisions*.

20. UN Doc. A/RES/53/144, Declaration on the Right and Responsibility of Individuals, Groups and Organs of Society to Promote and Protect Universally Recognized Human Rights and Fundamental Freedoms, UN General Assembly Res. 53/144, 8 March 1999.

21. Finnemore, *National Interests in International Society*.

22. Martha Finnemore and Kathryn Sikkink, "International Norm Dynamics and Political Change," *International Organization* 52, no. 4 (1998): 916.

23. Tom J. Farer and Felice Gaer, "The UN and Human Rights: At the End of the Beginning," in *United Nations, Divided World*, ed. Adam Roberts and Benedict Kingsbury (Oxford: Clarendon, 1993), 295.

BIBLIOGRAPHY

Adams, Richard Newbold. 1970. *Crucifixion by Power: Essays on Guatemalan National Social Structure, 1944–1966*. Austin: University of Texas Press.

Alston, Philip. 1992. "The Commission on Human Rights." In *The United Nations and Human Rights: A Critical Appraisal*, ed. Philip Alston, 126–210. Oxford: Oxford University Press.

Amnesty International. 1991. *Amnesty International: A Major Collection of Published and Unpublished Research Material*. Microfiche. Zug, Switzerland: Inter Documentation Company.

Amnesty International. 1962. *Amnesty International Movement for Freedom of Opinion and Religion: First Annual Report, 1961–62*. London: Amnesty International Publications. (On microfiche in Amnesty International: A Major Collection of Published and Unpublished Research Material [Zug, Switzerland: Inter Documentation Company, 1991].)

Amnesty International. 1992. *Amnesty International Policy Manual 1992*. New York: Amnesty International Publications.

Amnesty International. 1999. *Amnesty International Report 1999*. London: Amnesty International Publications.

Amnesty International. 1997. *Amnesty International Report 1997*. London: Amnesty International Publications.

Amnesty International. 1980. *Amnesty International Report 1980*. London: Amnesty International.

Amnesty International. 1979. *Amnesty International Report 1979*. London: Amnesty International Publications.

Amnesty International. 1978. *Amnesty International Report 1978*. London: Amnesty International Publications.

Amnesty International. 1974. *Annual Report 1973–74*. London: Amnesty International Publications.

Amnesty International. 1971. *Annual Report 1970–71*. London: Amnesty International Publications.

Amnesty International. 1965. *Annual Report 1964–65*. London: Amnesty International Publications.

Amnesty International. 1969. *Annual Report 1968–69*. London: Amnesty International Publications.

Amnesty International. 1968. *Annual Report 1967–68*. London: International Secretariat.

Amnesty International. 1966. *Annual Report 1965–66*. London: International Secretariat.

Amnesty International. 1964. *Annual Report 1963–64*. London: International Secretariat.

Amnesty International. 1963. *Annual Report 1962–63*. London: International Secretariat.

Amnesty International. 1974. *Conference for the Abolition of Torture, Paris, 10–11 December 1973, Final Report*. London: Amnesty International Publications.

Amnesty International. 1977a. "Declaration of Stockholm," 11 December 1977, reproduced in Amnesty International, *When the State Kills . . . The Death Penalty: A Human Rights Issue* (London: Amnesty International Publications, 1989), Appendix 12, 155–56.

Amnesty International. 1981. *"Disappearances": A Workbook.* New York: Amnesty International USA.

Amnesty International. 1994. *"Disappearances" and Political Killings, Human Rights Crises of the 1990s: A Manual for Action.* Amsterdam: Amnesty International.

Amnesty International. 1977. *Disappeared Prisoners in Chile: Report on Prisoners Held in Secret Detention Camps.* London: Amnesty International Publications.

Amnesty International. 1993. *Getting Away with Murder: Political Killings and Disappearances in the 1990s.* London: Amnesty International Publications.

Amnesty International. 1976. *Guatemala: Amnesty International Briefing Paper No. 8.* London: Amnesty International Publications.

Amnesty International. 1983. *Political Killings by Governments.* London: Amnesty International Publications.

Amnesty International. 1977. *Report of an Amnesty International Mission to Argentina, 6–15 November 1976.* London: Amnesty International Publications.

Amnesty International. 1984. *Torture in the Eighties.* London: Amnesty International Publications.

Amnesty International. 1977. *Torture in Greece: The First Torturers' Trial, 1975.* London: Amnesty International Publications.

Amnesty International. 1989. *When the State Kills . . . The Death Penalty: A Human Rights Issue.* London: Amnesty International Publications.

Amnesty International. 1988. Intervention of Mr. N. Rodley, in "Interventions Relating to the Report on 'Responsibilities for the Organs of the European Convention, Including the Committee of Ministers.' " In Council of Europe, *Proceedings of the Sixth International Colloquy about the European Convention on Human Rights, 13–16 November 1985*, 1056–60. Dordrecht: Martinus Nijhoff.

Arendt, Hannah. 1968. "Truth and Politics." In *Between Past and Future*, 227–64. New York: Viking.

Armstrong, J. D. 1985. "The International Committee of the Red Cross and Political Prisoners." *International Organization* 39, no. 4: 615–42.

Axelrod, Robert. 1984. *The Evolution of Cooperation.* New York: Basic Books.

Baehr, Peter R. 1994. "Amnesty International and Its Self-Imposed Limited Mandate." *Netherlands Quarterly of Human Rights* 12, no. 1: 5–21.

Barkun, Michael. 1968. *Law without Sanctions.* New Haven: Yale University Press.

Brilmayer, Lea. 1994. *American Hegemony: Political Morality in a One-Superpower World.* New Haven: Yale University Press.

Brody, Reed. 1990. "Commentary on the Draft U.N. 'Declaration on Enforced or Involuntary Disappearances.' " *Netherlands Quarterly of Human Rights* 4: 381–94.

Brody, Reed, and Felipe González. 1997. "*Nunca más*: An Analysis of International Instruments on 'Disappearances.' " *Human Rights Quarterly* 19: 365–408.

Brysk, Alison. 1994. *The Politics of Human Rights in Argentina.* Stanford, Calif.: Stanford University Press.

Buergenthal, Thomas. 1995. *International Human Rights in a Nutshell.* 2nd ed. St. Paul, Minn.: West.

Bull, Hedley. 1977. *The Anarchical Society: A Study of Order in World Politics.* New York: Columbia University Press.

Burgers, J. Herman, and Hans Danelius. 1988. *The United Nations Convention against Torture: A Handbook on the Convention against Torture and Other Cruel, Inhuman and Degrading Treatment or Punishment.* Dordrecht: Martinus Nijhoff.

Carey, John. 1970. *UN Protection of Civil and Political Rights.* Syracuse, N.Y.: Syracuse University Press.

Clark, Ann Marie. Forthcoming. " 'A Calendar of Abuses': Amnesty International's Guatemala Campaigning." In *NGOs and Human Rights: Promise and Performance,* ed. Claude E. Welch, Jr. Philadelphia: University of Pennsylvania Press.

Clark, Ann Marie, and James A. McCann. 1991. "Enforcing International Standards of Justice: Amnesty International's Constructive Conflict Expansion." *Peace and Change: A Journal of Peace Research* 16, no. 4: 379–99.

Clark, Ann Marie, Elisabeth J. Friedman, and Kathryn Hochstetler. 1998. "The Sovereign Limits of Global Civil Society: A Comparison of NGO Participation in UN World Conferences on the Environment, Human Rights, and Women." *World Politics* 51, no. 1: 1–35.

Claudius, Thomas, and Franz Stepan. 1978. *Amnesty International: Portrait einer Organisation.* Munich: R. Oldenbourg Verlag.

Comisión Nacional sobre la Desaparición de Personas. 1992. *Nunca más: Informe de la Comisión Nacional sobre la Desaparición de Personas.* 17th ed. Buenos Aires: Editorial Universitaria de Buenos Aires.

Comisión Nacional de Verdad y Reconciliación. 1991. *Informe Rettig: Informe de la Comisión Nacional de Verdad y Reconciliación.* La Nación & Las Ediciones del Ornitorrínco.

Cook, Helena. 1996. "Amnesty International at the United Nations." In *'Conscience of the World': The Influence of Non-governmental Organisations in the UN System,* ed. Peter Willetts, 181–213. Washington, D.C.: Brookings.

Cook, Helena. 1991. "The Role of Amnesty International in the Fight against Torture." In *The International Fight against Torture,* ed. Antonio Cassese, 172–86. Baden-Baden, Germany: Nomos.

Coufoudakis, Von. 1987. "Greek Foreign Policy, 1945–1985: Seeking Independence in an Interdependent World." *Political Change in Greece before and after the Colonels,* ed. Kevin Featherstone and Dimitrous K. Katsoudas, 230–52. New York: St. Martins Press.

Council of Europe, European Court of Human Rights. N.d. Bound typescript. *The Greek Case, Report of the Commission.* Strasbourg: Council of Europe.

Council of Europe, European Court of Human Rights. 1972. *The Greek Case, Yearbook of the European Convention on Human Rights 1969.* The Hague: Martinus Nijhoff.

Council of Europe, European Commission of Human Rights and European Court of Human Rights. 1970. *Yearbook of the European Convention on Human Rights 1968.* The Hague: Martinus Nijhoff.

Crawley, Eduardo. 1984. *A House Divided: Argentina, 1880–1980.* New York: St. Martin's Press.

Donnelly, Jack. 1986. "International Human Rights: A Regime Analysis." *International Organization* 40, no. 3: 599–642.

Donnelly, Jack. 1989. *Universal Human Rights in Theory and Practice.* Ithaca, N.Y.: Cornell University Press.

Ennals, Martin. 1982. "Amnesty International and Human Rights." In *Pressure Groups in the Global System,* ed. Peter Willetts, 63–83. New York: St. Martin's Press.

Farer, Tom J., and Felice Gaer. 1993. "The UN and Human Rights: At the End of the Beginning." In *United Nations, Divided World: The UN's Roles in International Relations,* ed. Adam Roberts and Benedict Kingsbury, 240–96. Oxford: Clarendon Press.

Finnemore, Martha. 1996. *National Interests in International Society.* Ithaca, N.Y.: Cornell University Press.

Finnemore, Martha, and Kathryn Sikkink. 1998. "International Norm Dynamics and Political Change." *International Organization* 52, no. 4: 887–917.

Forrest, Duncan, Bernard Knight, and Morris Tidball-Binz. 1996. "The Documentation of Torture." In *A Glimpse of Hell: Reports on Torture Worldwide,* ed. Duncan Forrest, 167–86. New York: New York University Press and Amnesty International.

Forsythe, David P. 1991. *The Internationalization of Human Rights.* Lexington, Mass.: Lexington Books.

Forsythe, David P. 1990. "Human Rights and the International Committee of the Red Cross." *Human Rights Quarterly* 12: 265–89.

Goldstein, Judith, and Robert O. Keohane, eds. 1993. *Ideas and Foreign Policy: Beliefs, Institutions, and Political Change.* Ithaca, N.Y.: Cornell University Press.

Grupo Iniciativa para una Convención contra la Desaparición Forzada de Personas. 1989. *La desaparición Forzada como crimen de lesa humanidad: El Nunca Más y la comunidad internacional.* Buenos Aires: Grupo de Iniciativa.

Guest, Iain. 1990. *Behind the Disappearances: Argentina's Dirty War against Human Rights and the United Nations.* Philadelphia: University of Pennsylvania Press.

Gunter, Michael. 1977. "Toward a Consultative Relationship between the United Nations and Non-Governmental Organizations?" *Vanderbilt Journal of Transnational Law* 10: 557–87.

Haas, Peter. 1989. "Do Regimes Matter? Epistemic Communities and Mediterranean Pollution Control." *International Organization* 43, no. 3: 377–403.

Habermas, Jürgen. 1996. *Between Facts and Norms.* Cambridge, Mass.: MIT Press.

Habermas, Jürgen. 1984. *Theory of Communicative Action.* Boston: Beacon Press.

Hart, H.L.A. 1961. *The Concept of Law.* Oxford: Clarendon Press.

Hurrell, Andrew. 1993. "International Society and the Study of Regimes: A Reflective Approach." In *Regime Theory and International Relations,* ed. Volker Rittberger, 49–72. Oxford: Clarendon Press.

Kamminga, Menno T. 1992. *Inter-State Accountability for Violations of Human Rights.* Philadelphia: University of Pennsylvania Press.

Kamminga, Menno T. 1987. "The Thematic Procedures of the UN Commission on Human Rights." *Netherlands International Law Review* 34: 299–323.

Kaufman, Edy. 1991. "Prisoners of Conscience: The Shaping of a New Human Rights Concept." *Human Rights Quarterly* 13: 339–67.

Keck, Margaret E., and Kathryn Sikkink. 1998. *Activists beyond Borders*. Ithaca, N.Y.: Cornell University Press.

Klayman, Barry M. 1978. "The Definition of Torture in International Law." *Temple Law Quarterly* 51: 449–517.

Klotz, Audie. 1995. *Norms in International Relations*. Ithaca, N.Y.: Cornell University Press.

Kooijmans, Peter H. 1991. "The Role and Action of the UN Special Rapporteur on Torture." In *The International Fight against Torture*, ed. Antonio Cassese, 56–70. Baden-Baden, Germany: Nomos.

Kooijmans, Peter H. 1990. "Human Rights—Universal Panacea? Some Reflections on the So-Called Human Rights of the Third Generation." *Netherlands International Law Review* 37: 315–29.

Korey, William. 1998. *NGOs and the Universal Declaration of Human Rights: "A Curious Grapevine."* New York: St. Martin's Press.

Kramer, David, and David Weissbrodt. 1981. "The 1980 U.N. Commission on Human Rights and the Disappeared." *Human Rights Quarterly* 3, no. 1: 18–33.

Krasner, Stephen D. 1993. "Sovereignty, Regimes, and Human Rights." In *Regime Theory and International Relations*, ed. Volker Rittberger, 139–67. Oxford: Clarendon Press.

Krasner, Stephen D. 1983. "Structural Causes and Regime Consequences." In *International Regimes*, ed. Stephen Krasner, 1–21. Ithaca, N.Y.: Cornell University Press.

Kratochwil, Friedrich V. 1989. *Rules, Norms, and Decisions: On the Conditions of Practical and Legal Reasoning in International Relations*. Cambridge, U.K.: Cambridge University Press.

Kratochwil, Friedrich V., and John Gerard Ruggie. 1986. "International Organization: A State of the Art on an Art of the State." *International Organization* 40, no. 4: 743–75.

Larsen, Egon. 1979. *A Flame in Barbed Wire: The Story of Amnesty International*. New York: W. W. Norton.

Leary, Virginia. 1979. "A New Role for Non-Governmental Organizations in Human Rights: A Case Study of Non-Governmental Participation in the Development of International Norms against Torture." In *UN Law/Fundamental Rights: Two Topics in International Law*, ed. Antonio Cassese, 197–210. Aalphen aan den Rijn, The Netherlands: Sijthoff and Noordhoff.

Lumsdaine, David Halloran. 1993. *Moral Vision in International Politics: The Foreign Aid Regime, 1949–1989*. Princeton, N.J.: Princeton University Press.

MacDermot, Niall. 1973. "Law and the Prevention of Torture." *Review (of the International Commission of Jurists)* 11: 23–27.

Mason, David, and Dale A. Crane. 1989. "The Political Economy of Death Squads: Toward a Theory of the Impact of State-Sanctioned Terror." *International Studies Quarterly* 33: 175–98.

Medina Quiroga, Cecilia. 1988. *The Battle of Human Rights: Gross, Systematic Violations and the Inter-American System*. Dordrecht: Martinus Nijhoff.

Mignone, Emilio. 1991. *Derechos humanos y sociedad: El caso Argentino*. Buenos Aires: Ediciones de Pensamiento Nacional.

Nardin, Terry. 1983. *Law, Morality, and the Relations of States.* Princeton, N.J.: Princeton University Press.

Navarro, Marysa. 1989. "The Personal Is Political: Las Madres de Plaza de Mayo." In *Power and Popular Protest: Latin American Social Movements,* ed. Susan Eckstein, 241–58. Berkeley: University of California Press.

Newman, Frank, and David Weissbrodt. 1996. "Special Rapporteur on Extrajudicial, Summary or Arbitrary Executions." In *International Human Rights,* 2nd ed., ed. Frank Newman and David Weissbrodt, 196–97. Cincinnati: Anderson.

O'Flaherty, Michael. *Human Rights and the UN: Practice before the Treaty Bodies.* London: Sweet and Maxwell.

Organization of American States (OAS). 1980. *Report on the Situation of Human Rights in Argentina.* Washington, D.C.: Organization of American States.

Pion-Berlin, David, and George A. Lopez. 1991. "Of Victims and Executioners: Argentine State Terror, 1975–79." *International Studies Quarterly* 35: 63–86.

Power, Jonathan. 1981. *Amnesty International: The Human Rights Story.* New York: McGraw-Hill.

Risse, Thomas, Stephen C. Rapp, and Kathryn Sikkink, eds. 1999. *The Power of Human Rights: International Norms and Domestic Change.* Cambridge, U.K.: Cambridge University Press.

Risse-Kappen, Thomas, and Hans-Peter Schmitz. 1994. "Principled Ideas, International Institutions, and Domestic Change." Paper prepared for the annual meeting of the American Political Science Association, New York, N.Y., 31 August–4 September 1994. Mimeo.

Rittberger, Volker, ed. 1993. *Regime Theory and International Relations.* Oxford: Clarendon Press.

Rittberger, Volker. 1993. "Research on International Regimes in Germany." In *Regime Theory and International Relations,* ed. Volker Rittberger, 3–22. Oxford: Clarendon Press.

Robinson, Nehemiah. 1950. *The Universal Declaration of Human Rights: Its Origin, Significance and Interpretation.* New York: Institute of Jewish Affairs.

Rodley, Nigel. 1983. "The Development of United Nations Activities in the Field of Human Rights and the Role of Non-Governmental Organizations." In *The US, the UN, and the Management of Global Change,* ed. Toby Trister Gati, 263–82. New York: New York University Press.

Rodley, Nigel. 1987. *The Treatment of Prisoners under International Law.* 1st ed. Oxford: Clarendon Press.

Rodley, Nigel. 1999. *The Treatment of Prisoners under International Law.* 2nd ed. Oxford: Clarendon Press.

Rodley, Nigel. 1992. "UN Non-Treaty Procedures for Dealing with Human Rights Violations." In *Guide to International Human Rights Practices.* 2nd ed., ed. Hurst Hannum, 60–85. Philadelphia: University of Pennsylvania Press.

Rodley, Nigel. 1988. "United Nations Action Procedures against 'Disappearances,' Summary or Arbitrary Executions, and Torture." In *Human Rights,* ed. Peter Davies, 74–98. London: Routledge.

Schwab, Peter, and George Frangos. 1973. *Greece under the Junta.* New York: Facts on File.

Schwelb, Egon. 1964. *Human Rights and the International Community: The Roots and Growth of the Universal Declaration of Human Rights, 1948–1963.* Chicago: Quadrangle Books.

Sikkink, Kathryn. 1993a. "Human Rights, Principled Issue-Networks, and Sovereignty in Latin America." *International Organization* 47, no. 3: 411–41.

Sikkink, Kathryn. 1993b. "The Power of Principled Ideas: Human Rights Policies in the United States and Western Europe." In *Ideas and Foreign Policy: Beliefs, Institutions, and Political Change,* ed. Judith Goldstein and Robert O. Keohane, 139–70. Ithaca, N.Y.: Cornell University Press.

Skidmore, Thomas E., and Peter H. Smith. 1989. *Modern Latin America.* New York: Oxford University Press.

Smith, Jackie, Charles Chatfield, and Ron Pagnucco, eds. 1997. *Transnational Social Movements and Global Politics: Solidarity beyond the State.* Syracuse, N.Y.: Syracuse University Press.

Staunton, Marie, and Sally Fenn, eds., with Amnesty International USA. 1991. *The Amnesty International Handbook.* Claremont, Calif.: Hunter House.

Steiner, Henry C., and Philip Alston, eds. 1996. *International Human Rights in Context.* Oxford: Clarendon Press.

Thomsen, Jorgen L., Karin Helweg-Larsen, and Ole Vedel Rasmussen. 1984. "Amnesty International and the Forensic Sciences." *American Journal of Forensic Medicine and Pathology* 5, 4: 305–11.

Thomsen, Jorgen L., Karin Helweg-Larsen, and Ole Vedel Rasmussen. 1982. "Sudden and Suspicious Deaths outside the Deceased's Own Country—Time for an International Protocol." *Forensic Science International* 20: 70–75.

Thucydides. 1951. *The Pelopponesian War.* New York: Modern Library.

Tolley, Howard B., Jr. 1994. *The International Commission of Jurists: Global Advocates for Human Rights.* Philadelphia: University of Pennsylvania Press.

Tolley, Howard B., Jr. 1989. "Popular Sovereignty and International Law: ICJ Strategies for Human Rights Standard Setting." *Human Rights Quarterly* 11: 561–85.

Uhlin, Anders. 1997. *Indonesia and the Third Wave of Democratization.* New York: St. Martin's Press.

United Nations Office at Vienna, and Centre for Social Development and Humanitarian Affairs. 1991. *Manual on the Effective Prevention of Extra-Legal, Arbitrary and Summary Executions.* New York: United Nations Publications.

van Boven, Theo. 1990. "The Role of Non-Governmental Organizations in International Human Rights Standard-Setting: A Prerequisite of Democracy." *California Western International Law Journal* 20: 207–25.

van Boven, Theo. 1991. "The Role of the United Nations Secretariat." In *The United Nations and Human Rights: A Critical Appraisal,* ed. Philip Alston, 549–79. Oxford: Oxford University Press.

de Vargas, Francois. 1980. "History of a Campaign." In *Torture: How to Make the International Convention Effective,* ed. International Commission of Jurists and Swiss Committee Against Torture, 41–46. Geneva: International Commission of Jurists and Swiss Committee Against Torture.

Vierdag, E. W. 1994. "Some Remarks about Special Features of Human Rights Treaties." *Netherlands Journal of International Law* 25: 119–42.

Vincent, R. J. 1986. *Human Rights and International Relations.* Cambridge, U.K.: Cambridge University Press.

Waltz, Kenneth N. 1979. *Theory of International Politics.* Reading, Mass.: Addison-Wesley.

Walzer, Michael. 1977. *Just and Unjust Wars.* New York: Penguin.

Weiss, Thomas G., David P. Forsythe, and Roger A. Coate. 1997. *The United Nations and Changing World Politics.* 2nd ed. Boulder: Westview.

Weissbrodt, David. 1986. "The Three 'Theme' Special Rapporteurs of the UN Commission on Human Rights." *American Journal of International Law* 80: 685–99.

Weissbrodt, David, and Terry Rosen. 1990. "Principles against Executions." *Hamline Law Review* 13: 579–621.

Wendt, Alexander. 1992. "Anarchy Is What States Make of It." *International Organization* 46: 391–425.

Wendt, Alexander, and Raymond Duvall. 1989. "Institutions and International Order." In *Global Changes and Theoretical Challenges,* ed. Ernst-Otto Czempiel and James N. Rosenau, 51–74. Lexington, Mass.: Lexington Books.

White, James Boyd. 1986. "The Dissolution of Meaning: Thucydides' History of His World." In *When Words Lose Their Meaning,* by James Boyd White, 59–92. Chicago: University of Chicago Press.

Willetts, Peter. 1996. "The Impact of Promotional Pressure Groups on Global Politics." In *'Conscience of the World': The Influence of Non-Governmental Organisations in the UN System,* ed. Peter Willetts, 114–29. Washington, D.C.: Brookings.

Willetts, Peter, ed. 1982. *Pressure Groups in the Global System: The Transnational Relations of Issue-Orientated Non-Governmental Organizations.* New York: St. Martin's Press.

Winner, David. 1991. *Peter Benenson.* Milwaukee: Gareth Stevens.

Yee, Albert S. 1997. "Thick Rationality and the Missing 'Brute Fact': The Limits of Rationalist Incorporation of Norms and Ideas." *Journal of Politics* 59, no. 4: 1001–39.

INDEX

CPSIA information can be obtained
at www.ICGtesting.com
Printed in the USA
LVHW031549201220
674690LV00003B/503